Urlaubsparadiese Europas

Peter Reisberg

Urlaubsparadiese Europas

Bildquellenverzeichnis:
Ernst Baumann 11, Willi P. Burkhardt 27, 30, 32, 35, Ciganowich 59,
FISA Industrias Graficas 56, Hans Huber 12, I.C.P. Pedone 43, Pressebild Jeiter 5,
7, Robert Löbl 6, 8, 9, 10, 13, 14, 15, 16, 17, 18, 19, 20, 21, 22, 23, 24, 25, 26, 28,
29, 31, 33, 34, 36, 37, 38, 39, 40, 41, 42, 46, 47, 48, 49, 50, 51, 54, 55, 57, 58,
60, 61, 62, 63 sowie Photos des Schutzumschlags, Marzari 65, 66, Gerhard
Rauchwetter 70, Klaus Rohmeyer 1, 2, 3, 4, S.E.F. 68, Tortoli 52, 64,
Trimboli 44, 45, 53, 67, 69, 71.

Inhalt

Bilderverzeichnis

Deutschland

Schleswig-Holstein

Dem Süddeutschen fällt es schwer, das Land zwischen Nord- und Ostsee ohne weiteres schön zu finden. Hüben Meer und drüben Meer, dazwischen flaches Land; keine Berge und viel Wind. Dazu Menschen, die offenbar kaum den Mund aufbringen, und wenn, dann versteht man sie nicht – so oder ähnlich lauten die pauschalen Vorurteile.

Mit Erklärungen ist wenig auszurichten. Will man das Wesen dieses Landes, seinen herben Charme kennenlernen und erfassen, muß man einfach dort gewesen sein. Nein, nicht auf Westerlands Jahrmarkt der Eitelkeit – das wäre dasselbe wie Frankreich in Nizza zu suchen –, sondern an irgendeinem Frühlings- oder Herbsttag, wandernd in der Stille der flachen Hügel zwischen Plön und Eutin, an waldumstandenen Bächen entlang; oder auf einem Dünensaum der Halligen, wo Meer und Weite zur Vision des Unendlichen verschmelzen. Da tritt alles wichtige, sehenswerte, beachtungsheischende der Landschaft zurück, überläßt dem Himmel und den Wolken das Spiel mit Farbe und Form, gibt dem Menschen Zeit und Anstoß, zu sich selbst zu finden. Die gelöste Poesie der Natur besänftigt den unsteten Geist, der frische Wind bläst alle Unrast fort, beruhigt und entspannt das Gemüt. Man erkennt, daß einst Matthias Claudius nur in einer ausgewogenen Welt wie dieser die Worte zu seinem Abendlied geschrieben haben konnte: Der Mond ist aufgegangen, / Die goldnen Sternlein prangen / Am Himmel hell und klar; / Der Wald steht schwarz und schweiget, / Und aus den Wiesen steiget / Der weiße Nebel wunderbar ...

Schleswig-Holstein ist der Entstehung nach die jüngste der deutschen Landschaften. Vor etwa 10 000 Jahren hinterließen die abtauenden Gletscher den hügeligen Geestrücken in der Mitte des Landes; weite Teile waren bis ins 10. nachchristliche Jahrhundert Sumpfgebiet, wurden erst durch Eindeichung und Entwässerung nutzbares Land. Die Spuren der Besiedelung reichen bis in die Bronzezeit um 1800 v. Chr. zurück. Funde aus dieser Zeit zeugen vom Handel mit Schweden und Irland. In die Geschichte tritt das Land um 700: Die Friesen bilden ein Großreich unter König Radbold, erschlagen 719 den heiligen Bonifatius. 785 bis 804 erobert Karl der Große das Friesenreich und Holstein. Um 1203 wird das Land dänisch, seither dauern 750 Jahre die deutsch-dänischen Streitigkeiten an. Die Schaumburger vereinigen 1386 Schleswig und Holstein und bringen es als dänisches Lehen an sich. Als ihr Stamm erlischt, wählen die Stände 1460 den Dänenkönig Christian I. zum Herrn. Im 16. und 17. Jahrhundert wird das Land wiederholt von den rivalisierenden Dänen, Holländern, Braunschweigern, Oldenburgern und Schweden zerteilt und zersplittert. 1713 erobert es Friedrich IV. im Nordischen Krieg für Dänemark, ab 1773 sind beide Herzogtümer – bei Wahrung ihrer Selbständigkeit – unter dänischer Krone vereint. Der Wiener Kongreß erklärt 1815 Holstein zum Glied des Deutschen Bundes, nicht aber Schleswig und Lauenburg. Darüber bricht eine jahrzehntelange, teilweise kriegerische Auseinandersetzung aus, die mit den Kriegen der Preußen und Österreicher gegen die Dänen in den Jahren 1864 und 1866 endet; sie bringen Schleswig-Holstein endgültig an Preußen. Die Grenzstreitigkeiten dauern aber im kleineren Rahmen noch bis 1946 an.

Am Rand der in groben Zügen skizzierten Geschichte gibt es noch andere Ereignisse, wie die Entwicklung Hamburgs und Lübecks zu freien Reichs- und Hansestädten und wichtigen Handelszentren, die aber als selbständige Gebilde die ethnologische Struktur Schleswig-Holsteins nur am Rand berühren. Daraus erklärt sich die noch heute spürbare geringe völkische Verbundenheit der Landbevölkerung mit diesen Großstädten. Einschneidender war für sie ein anderes Geschehnis: Im 17. Jahrhundert brach eine gewaltige Sturmflut in die Nordseeküste ein, riß weite Landstriche mit sich, wodurch sich die Uferlinie um 50 Kilometer nach Osten verschob. Die Reste des ehemaligen Landes sind die heutigen nordfriesischen Inseln und die Halligen.

Dem Unkundigen mag Schleswig-Holstein als eine gleichförmige Landschaft erscheinen, doch bei näherer Betrachtung zeigt sie vielerlei unterschiedliche Gesichter. Schon emotionell trennt man zunächst die Bereiche von Nordsee- und Ostseeküste. Die Ostsee – gebändigter, ruhiger und verklärter als die rauhe Nordsee – hat zumeist weich geformte, leicht überhöhte Ufer, die nicht von den »Tiden«, den Gezeiten mit Ebbe und Flut, behelligt werden. Es konnten sich reiche, kraftvolle Stadtwesen entwickeln: *Lübeck,* im Mittelalter einer der größten Handelsplätze Europas, mit dem imposanten Holstentor, der prachtvollen, aus dem Jahr 1350 stammenden Marienkirche, dem gotischen Dom und dem berühmten Renaissance-Rathaus; *Kiel,* Schleswig-Holsteins Landeshauptstadt, im letzten Krieg weitgehend zerstört und modern wieder aufgebaut, mit der Howaldtswerft, einem der größten Schiffsbaubetriebe der Welt, und dem lebhaft-bunten Hafen, der bis ins Zentrum reicht; *Schleswig,* das Haithabu der Wikinger, schon im 10. Jahrhundert Bischofssitz; *Flensburg,* mit der 600 Jahre alten Marienkirche, dem berühmten Nordertor und dem stimmungsvollen Hafen.
Die 400 Kilometer lange Küstenlinie der Ostsee von Lübeck bis Flensburg,

vielgewunden und mit den Förden, den buchtartigen Einschnitten, tief ins Land greifend, ist eine komplexe Urlaubsregion mit meilenlangen, feinsandigen Strandabschnitten, wegen ihrer sanft abfallenden Wassertiefen vor allem ein Paradies für Kinder. Außer dem luxuriösen Weltbad Travemünde säumen Dutzende von familenfreundlichen Ferienorten die Ufer– wie *Timmendorfer Strand, Sierksdorf, Kellenhusen, Heiligenhafen, Hohwacht, Marina Wendtorf, Damp* und viele andere. Nicht minder urlaubsfreundlich ist das Hinterland. Vor Schleswig zieht sich die Schlei, Deutschlands einziger Fjord, fünfzig Kilometer weit ins Binnenland. Über das sanfthügelige Terrain sind 120 Seen verstreut, die sich um *Plön, Malente* und *Eutin* zur verträumten Heide- und Wasserlandschaft der Holsteinischen Schweiz gruppieren. Dazwischen bezaubern behäbige Bauernhäuser aus Klinker und Backstein, verschlafene Dörfer und Kleinstädtchen aus Andersens Märchenwelt. Nicht nur die Seefahrt hat hier Tradition – in Travemünde liegt die stolze »Passat« lebenslänglich vor Anker –, sondern auch die Pferdezucht und der Reitsport; in Kiel hat man Meteor, dem »Dicken«, Deutschlands erfolgreichstem Turnierpferd, sogar ein Denkmal gesetzt.

Von anderem Charakter ist das Land an der Westseite vor der Nordsee. Hier liegen die brettebenen, dem Meer in Jahrhunderten abgerungenen Marschlandschaften mit Rinder-, Pferde- und Schafherden. Dithmarschen, das Land, wo »Milch und Öl fließt«, Eiderstedt, Nordfriesland. Davor das Wattenmeer mit dem großartigen Naturschauspiel von Ebbe und Flut, den einsamen Halligen und den turbulenten Ferieninseln: *Sylt*, Zentrum der Lebensgenüsse; *Föhr*, Insel der Bauern und Windmühlen; *Amrum*, Eiland der großen Sandbänke. Weit draußen in der Deutschen Bucht stemmen sich die roten Felsklippen von *Helgoland* seit Jahrtausenden dem »Blanken Hans« mit trutziger Gestik entgegen; ein paar Meilen ostwärts hat Trischen gegen Meer und Sturm die Waffen gestreckt: es versinkt langsam, aber stetig im Meer, dem bestimmenden Element dieses Gebietes.

⑤ Burg Eltz bei Moselkern, Inbegriff romantischer deutscher Burgenherrlichkeit. Seit 1157 unversehrt, türmten die einstigen Besitzer, im Schutz des Geländes und des rustikalen Gemäuers vor feindlichem Zugriff sicher, Wohnung auf Wohnung. Daß dabei einigen der Burgherren gar nicht so kriegerisch zumute war, bezeugen die aufgesetzten lustigen Fachwerktürmchen.

⑥ Im Moseltal, dem »Land der brüchigen Mauern und gefüllten Humpen«. An sonnigen Herbsttagen wird der Flußlauf in vielen Abschnitten eine anmutige Komposition aus Gold und Blau. Über der Ellersberger Moselschlinge stehen die Ruinen der einstigen Metternich'schen Burg; gegenüber schmiegt sich das Weindorf Bruttig ans Ufer. Auf den Hängen reift der edle Tropfen des »Bruttiger Rathausberg«.

Rhein und Mosel

Eines ist gewiß: Puritanische Abstinenzler haben dieses Land nicht erfunden. Wahrscheinlich verlor der liebe Gott bei der Welterschaffung den Winkel ein wenig aus dem Blickfeld, wofür ihm sein heidnischer Kollege Bacchus kräftig ins Handwerk pfuschte. Er muß aber dann doch ein Auge zugedrückt haben, sonst hätte er kaum die »Weinkirche« in Ehrenthal bei St. Goarshausen zugelassen, die Gotteshaus, Schänke und Weinkeller in einem Bau vereinte und für die man den Kirchenschlüssel beim Wirt holen mußte. Daß sich Christentum und Lebensfreude auch sonst hier gut vertragen, davon zeugt der alte Winzerspruch, wonach der beste Wein dort wächst, wo die Kirchenglocken am schönsten klingen.

»Der Rheingau hat mich hervorgebracht, jener begünstigte Landstrich, welcher wohl zu den lieblichsten der bewohnten Erde gehört. Hier blühen, vom Rheingaugebirge vor rauhen Winden bewahrt und der Mittagssonne glücklich hingebreitet, jene berühmten Siedlungen, bei deren Namensklang dem Zecher das Herz lacht, hier Rauenthal, Johannisberg, Rüdesheim ...«, so läßt Thomas Mann seiner champagnerhaften Frohnatur Felix Krull ihren Lebensbericht beginnen. Der holsteinische Dichter ist nur einer von Hunderten großer Geister, die dem Rhein ihre Reverenz erwiesen, sich an seinen Ufern für kurze Zeit oder auf Dauer niedergelassen haben. Man kann kaum mit dem Aufzählen anfangen, denn eigentlich waren sie alle da; Cäsar und Napoleon, Goethe und Beethoven, Gutenberg und Heinrich Heine.

Die Landschaft um Rhein und Mosel ist eine der schönsten und romantischsten Gegenden Deutschlands. Daran ändert auch nichts, daß der Strom inzwischen zur Großwasserstraße mit pausenlosem Schiffsverkehr in beiden Richtungen wurde, daß man im Wasser längst nicht mehr baden kann und daß er das Symbolkleid übersteigerten Nationalbewußtseins schon lange abgestreift hat. Denn nach wie vor ist das Land ein zauberhafter Paradiesgarten, im Frühling vom Brautschleier eines Blütenmeeres bedeckt, im späten Jahr von süßer, goldgelber Reife durchströmt, allzeit und überall voll köstlicher, verschwenderischer Schönheit und Fülle. Nach wie vor kuscheln sich die pittoresken, oft nur aus einer Häuserzeile bestehenden Fachwerkdörfer an die Ufer, stehen die stolzen Burgen auf den Hängen; Burgen mit wehrhaften Mauern und Türmen, prunkvolle und dürftige, verfallene und nachgemauerte,

klassische und kitschige, doch alle malerisch ins große Panorama eingefügt, das auch Stilsünden gnädig verzeiht.

Das Land um Rhein und Mosel ist erklärtes Ziel von Urlaubern und Reisenden aus aller Welt. Das war schon immer so, wenn auch zumeist in viel rauherer Art als heute. Als erste »Touristen« kamen um das Jahr 55 v. Chr. die Römer. Weil es ihnen so gut gefiel, blieben sie gleich vierhundert Jahre da, gründeten die Städte Trier, Köln, Koblenz, Mainz und Bonn, verbreiteten das Christentum und die spätantike Kultur. Dann kamen Alemannen und Franken an den Strom, gingen schließlich im Frankenreich Karls des Großen auf, das von Dänemark bis Spanien reichte. Vom Jahr 1000 bis 1945 waren die Rheinlande fortgesetzt Zankapfel zwischen Deutschen und Franzosen, mußten viele Kriege erdulden. Im Verlauf des Dreißigjährigen Krieges wurde allein Bacharach am Rhein achtmal geplündert. Spektakuläres geschichtliches Datum ist die Neujahrsnacht 1813/14, als Marschall Blücher bei Kaub über das Eis des Rheins stürmte und die Truppen Napoleons verfolgte. Heute ist der Rhein vom heißumkämpften Schicksalsstrom zur völkerverbindenden Wasserader Europas geworden. Die Raubritterburgen haben ihre Schrecken verloren, Festungen wie Ehrenbreitstein sind verstaubtes Geschichtsrelikt und das monströse Niederwalddenkmal interessiert nur noch Amerikaner, die bei Vergleichen der riesenhüftigen, vollbusigen Germania mit dem zierlichen deutschen »Fräuleinwunder« ungläubig die Köpfe schütteln.

Trotz vieler Uferstraßen an Rhein und Mosel sind Schiffahrten immer noch die schönste Art, die Landschaft kennenzulernen. Der Rhein zeigt seine eindrucksvollsten Bilder auf dem Abschnitt zwischen Mainz und Koblenz. Nach der flachen oberrheinischen Tiefebene erheben sich bei Eltville die ersten sanften Uferhänge, bedeckt mit einem unabsehbaren Heer von Rebstöcken. Von der grünsilbrigen Riesenfolie hebt sich am Nordufer Schloß Johannisberg ab, das 1816, nach Napoleons Hinauswurf, Fürst Metternich von den Habsburgern als Lehen erhielt. Als Gegenleistung hatte der Fürst regelmäßig eine Auswahl von Spitzenweinen nach Wien zu senden. Diese Vertragsregel wird noch heute befolgt, auch wenn der Adressat sich geändert hat. Rüdesheim taucht auf, Inbegriff des weinseligen Rheindorfes, immer noch einladend und liebenswürdig, obzwar pseudoromantisch verkitscht. Aufregend wird es im »Binger Loch«; da treten die Felsen hart und frech an die Ufer, zwingen den Rhein zu Engstellen und Stromschnellen, deren Durchfahrt auch heute noch Lotsen erfordert. Nach Bingen entfaltet der Strom seine klassischen Panoramen: Wasser, Felsberge, bald von dichtem Blattwald verhüllt, bald von den vielstufigen Terrassen der Rebstöcke erstürmt, lauschige Ortschaften von lächelnder Würde; Burgen und Ruinen, kühn hochgereckt oder listig versteckt, an die zwei Dutzend insgesamt. Jede von ihnen wüßte eine Sage, eine Geschichte aus alter Zeit zu erzählen. Dann das melodramatische Ereignis der Loreley. Eigentlich ein schütter begrünter Felsblock wie viele andere, doch von Heinrich Heines und Friedrich Silchers Lied mit sehnsuchtsvoller Schwermut beladen, die tief ins deutsche Gemüt träufelt. Nach St. Goarshausen wird die Kulisse sanfter, die Landschaft zärtlicher, die Hänge dehnen und strecken sich. Weit grüßt die dottergelbe Burg Stolzenfels ins Land, an Kühen, Pappeln und Kohlenhalden vo bei erreichen wir Koblenz.

Nicht minder reizvoll ist eine Fahrt auf der Mosel. Auf ihrem umständlichen Weg durch das rheinische Schiefergebirge zieht sie soviele Schleifen wie kein anderer Fluß in Europa. Die weich geformten Uferhänge sind übersät mit unabsehbaren Weingärten; das matte Graublau des Schiefers und der Dörfer mischt einen Hauch von Melancholie in die weinselige Fröhlichkeit. Ehe sie deutschen Boden erreicht, hat sie schon eine lange Reise hinter sich, war in Epinal, Toul und Metz. Wo sie Saar und Sauer aufnimmt, steht Trier, die älteste Stadt nördlich der Alpen. Die Römer haben es 15 v. Chr. gegründet, Renaissance, Barock und Rokoko bereicherten es mit Kirchen und Abteien, Adelshöfen und Palästen. Ältestes Baudenkmal ist die Porta Nigra, eine imposante Torburg der Römer aus dem 4. Jahrhundert. Auf der Fahrt am Fluß entlang lesen sich die Ortsschilder der heimeligen Dörfer wie Flascheneti- ketten eines feudalen Weinkellers: Klüsserath, Trittenheim, Piesport, Bern- kastel, Zeltingen, Ürzig, Kröv, Traben-Trarbach, Zell. Von den Hügeln und Hängen grüßen alte Burgen; deren Prototyp ist Burg Eltz bei Moselkern: Seit 1157 setzten die Burgherren bei jeder Familienvergrößerung eine Wohnein- heit mehr auf das Fundament, ganz zuoberst mit lustigen Fachwerktürmchen – schufen gleichsam das Urmodell einer Hochhaussiedlung. Dafür darf die Traumburg der Ritterromantik auch unsere Fünfhundertmarkscheine zieren.

Schwarzwald und Bodensee

Eine ganze Weile war es recht still um den südwestlichsten Winkel des bundesdeutschen Landes. Die Welt unserer Zeit, zusammengeschrumpft auf ein paar Flugstunden, verlockte mit gleißenderen Urlaubszielen – mit Korsika und Kreta, mit Teneriffa und Tahiti, mit Tunesien und Thailand. Nun ist man dabei, das Land um Schwarzwald und Bodensee wiederzuentdecken. Mag sein, daß dabei derselbe nostalgische Gemütsanflug mitspielt, der uns Großmutters Kohlebügeleisen als etwas ungeheuer Reizvolles erscheinen läßt. Vielleicht auch die überraschend erlebte Offenbarung, daß ein aufbrechender Frühlingsmorgen im Schwarzwald – wenn das frische Grün der Birken und Buchen die dunkle Folie der Tannenwälder umzaubert, wenn das ganze Tal in Weiß und Rosa jubiliert mit den Blüten der Kirschen und Pflaumen, der Äpfel und Birnen, der Pfirsich- und Mandelbüsche – daß ein solcher Frühlingsmorgen den täglich mit monotoner Routine wiederkehrenden Sonnenuntergang auf den Seychellen mühelos in den Schatten stellt. Wohl auch deshalb, weil diese Landschaft unserem Wesen näher liegt, weil wir ein Teilchen ihrer selbst sind.

Die Geschichte von Schwarzwald und Bodensee ist nicht identisch. Wohl besetzten die Römer den ganzen Bereich, wurden aber vom 3. bis 6. Jahrhundert von den Alemannen vertrieben. In der Folgezeit ist jedoch der Bodenseeraum viel mehr Brennpunkt geschichtlicher Ereignisse und kultureller Entwicklung als der damals noch schwer zugängliche Schwarzwald: Während der Bereich um den Bodensee mit den Städten Konstanz, St. Gallen, Ravensburg, Lindau und Überlingen vom 12. bis 15. Jahrhundert zu einem Zentrum europäischer Wirtschaft und Kultur aufblüht, wird der Schwarzwald zur gleichen Zeit erst zaghaft besiedelt. 1499 besiegen die Eidgenossen im »Schwabenkrieg« die Habsburger, teilen den gemeinsamen Wirtschaftsraum, Bodensee und Rhein werden zur Grenze; die kulturelle Einheit jedoch blieb bis heute erhalten. Nach 1500 verlor diese Handelsmacht an Bedeutung, mußte ihre Position im Welthandel an die Seestädte Venedig und Genua, London und Amsterdam abtreten. Nun, da an den Ufern des »Schwäbischen Meers« Ruhe, aber auch Armut einkehrte, entbrannten im Norden, in den Tälern vor dem Schwarzwald, wo die Markgrafen von Baden und die Herzöge von Württemberg regierten, die langen kriegerischen Auseinandersetzungen mit Frankreich; gegen Ende des 17. Jahrhunderts verwüstet der Sonnenkönig Ludwig XIV. das Land. Seit dem Ende der Ära Napoleons zählen der Schwarzwald und das Nordufer des Bodensees zum deutschen Reichs- und jetzigen Bundesgebiet.

Von Nordosten, aus dem Württembergischen kommend, weiß man nicht so recht, wo der Schwarzwald anfängt. Da wandelt sich die Feldfluren- und Obstgartenlandschaft der Schwäbischen Alb behutsam zum Schwarzwälder Kolorit. Umso deutlicher präsentiert er sich von der anderen Seite, von Nordwesten. Wer von Karlsruhe rheinaufwärts fährt, kann schwerlich der zauberhaften Verlockung widerstehen, die von der blaugrünen Bergsilhouette auf den gleichförmigen Rheintalboden ausstrahlt: Die Zugänge werden von einem Reigen malerischer Städtchen behütet – wie *Ettlingen, Gaggenau, Rastatt, Bühl* und *Achern.* Glanzvollster Empfangs-»Saal« aber ist das renommierte *Baden-Baden,* das sich im Tal des Oosbaches an die untersten Hänge der Waldkulisse schmiegt. Vor zweitausend Jahren wußten schon die Römer die heilenden Quellen und das schmeichelhafte Klima ihres Aquae Aureliae zu schätzen, und seit dieser Zeit hat eigentlich Baden-Baden nie aufgehört, etwas Besonderes zu sein. Es ist Deutschlands berühmtester Kurort, glanzvolles Auftrittsparkett der Prominenz, aber auch ein verschlafenes alemannisches Kleinstädtchen mit Winkeln und Erkern, Steigen und Brückchen, Treppen und Brunnen. Seine zeitlose, übernationale Noblesse äußert sich nicht im prunkhaften Zurschaustellen, sondern ist seine Gesinnung. Das Ortsbild ist verwachsen mit dem Grün der Umgebung, das sich mit Flieder und Kastanien, Forsythien, Tulpen, Rhododendron, Linden, Akazien und Rotdorn in hunderterlei Spielarten der Farben und Düfte sublimiert.

Ein Netz von Ausflugsstraßen durchzieht den Schwarzwald. Da gibt es die *Schwarzwald-Tälerstraße,* die sich an den romantischen Flußläufen von Murg und Kinzig entlang von Nord nach Süd schlängelt, die *Grüne Straße,* die Frankreich mit dem Bodensee verbindet, die *Badische Weinstraße,* die – parallel zur Rheintalautobahn – an den Westhängen des Schwarzwalds von Weinort zu Weinort torkelt. Die attraktivste von allen ist die *Schwarzwald-Hochstraße,* die über den tausend Meter hohen Kamm des Nordschwarzwalds zwischen Baden-Baden und Freudenstadt eine Brücke schlägt. Sie gewährt großartige Einblicke in das endlose Dunkelgrün der Nadelwälder, in denen einst Wisent, Ur und Elch hausten. Paradoxerweise wurde der um die dominierenden Gipfel von Feldberg und Belchen gelegene Hochschwarzwald viel früher besiedelt als der Nordschwarzwald, der bis ins vorige Jahrhundert als undurchdringlicher Urwald galt; in seinen Talnischen lebten die Holzfäller, Waldbauern, Glasmaler und Köhler. Reizvoll ist es, von der Schwarzwald-Hochstraße mit Abstechern in die Täler hinunterzusteigen, um die köstlichen Kontraste zwischen »schwarzem Tann« und »heiterem Wein« zu erleben – in das lauschige *Murgtal,* ins *Bühler Tal,* das zur Erntezeit im Blau der Zwetsch-

gen ertrinkt, oder nach *Allerheiligen,* wo die Ruinen der vom Blitz zerstörten
Klosterkirche seltsam unwirklich mit den Wipfeln der Bäume um einen Platz
an der Sonne ringen.

Eine eigenartige Charakteristik hat *Freudenstadt,* einer der großen Anziehungspunkte. Herzog Friedrich I. von Württemberg beauftragte seinen Baumeister Heinrich Schickhardt, eine noch nie dagewesene Prunkstadt in Form
eines Mühlebrettspiels anzulegen, in dessen Mitte ein Wasserschloß thronen
sollte. Doch das Silberbergwerk im Christophstal, dessen Erträge das Projekt
finanzieren sollten, wurde plötzlich unrentabel, das Bauvorhaben blieb in den
Anfängen stecken. Ein Brand zerstörte 1632 den Rest. Wiederaufgebaut, ver-
sank die Stadt 1945 unter Bombenangriffen erneut in Schutt und Trümmer.
Beim letzten Wiederaufbau erinnerte man sich der Pläne Schickhardts und
versuchte, dieses Schmuckkästchen wenigstens in seiner ursprünglichen Konzep-
tion wiederherzustellen.

Der mittlere Schwarzwald ist eine Landschaft der beschaulichen Talzüge, in
bewaldete Hügelketten eingebettet, verziert mit schönen alten Walmdachhäu-
sern und romantischen Burgen. Hübsche Flecken wie *Schiltach, Schramberg,
Wolfach, St. Georgen* oder *Triberg* laden zur kurzen oder längeren Bleibe ein.
Im kleinen *Alpirsbach* südlich von Freudenstadt ist die großartige Klosterkirche aus dem 12. Jahrhundert zu bewundern, schönstes Beispiel der Hirsauer
Schule.

Zur großen Mittelgebirgsszenerie entfaltet sich der Hochschwarzwald mit dem
wildromantischen *Höllental,* durch das die Straße von Freiburg zwischen lotrecht hochflutendem Felsgestein hinaufzieht; dem Schauinsland, einer prächtigen Aussichtskuppe über Freiburg, Rheintal und Kaiserstuhl; der zerklüfteten Wutachschlucht und den beiden Wassersportbecken Titisee und Schluchsee.
Wie ein barocker Rahmen zu einem schönen Gemälde, so gehören die Städte
ringsherum zur Schwarzwälder Landschaft. *Offenburg, Freiburg, Donaueschin-
gen, Rastatt, Pforzheim, Villingen* – es sind zuviele, um sie hier aufzuzählen,
geschweige denn zu beschreiben. Alle zeichnen sich aus durch ihre heimelige
Note, ihre sehenswerten Kirchen und Bauten, ihre schwäbisch-alemannische
Atmosphäre und eine vortreffliche Gastlichkeit.

Nur ein kleiner Sprung ist es vom Schwarzwald zum Bodensee, dem mit 540
Quadratkilometer Fläche zweitgrößten See Mitteleuropas. Seine malerischsten
Ufer liegen in der westlichen Hälfte, wo er sich im Überlinger-, Zeller-, Gna-
den- und Untersee buchtenreich verzweigt, während sich der große Obersee zu
meerähnlicher Weite dehnt. Mit mächtiger Kulisse beherrscht *Konstanz* den
Ausfluß des Rheins; seine prächtigen Bauten, das Konzilshaus, das Münster

Unserer Lieben Frau, die Dominikanerkirche und das Renaissance-Rathaus zeugen von der einstigen Bedeutung der Stadt als Zentrum des Bodenseeraums. Unweit von Konstanz – durch schmalen Fahrdamm mit dem Festland verbunden – liegt die *Insel Reichenau,* heute Paradies des Gartenbaues mit mehreren Ernten jährlich, einst eine Keimzelle der europäischen Kultur. Ihre Kirchen – St. Georg in Oberzell, St. Maria und St. Markus, Peter und Paul in Niederzell – zählen zu den ältesten Denkmälern mittelalterlicher Kunst auf dem Kontinent. Auf der kleinen *Insel Mainau* schuf Graf Bernadotte mit dem exotischen Garten von mediterraner Pracht ein vielbesuchtes Touristenziel. *Radolfszell* beeindruckt mit dem spätgotischen Münster, *Überlingen* mit der spätgotischen Sandstein-Basilika, dem gotischen Rathaus und wehrhaften Türmen. Vielumschwärmt ist das pittoreske *Meersburg,* über dem eine der ältesten Burganlagen Deutschlands thront. Meistgeknipstes Fotomodell ist die Raitenmühle mit dem oberschlächtigen Wasserrad von neun Metern Durchmesser. In *Friedrichshafen* ist die stilvolle Schloßkirche ebenso besuchenswert wie das Zeppelinmuseum. Nach den Obstwäldern von Kreßbronn entzückt uns die spielzeughafte Kulisse des idyllischen *Wasserburg.* Schließlich beendet *Lindau,* die einst wehrhafte Inselstadt, mit prächtigem mittelalterlichem Stadtbild und modernen Fremdenverkehrs-Einrichtungen den Reigen der Siedlungen auf dem deutschen Ufer.

Selbstredend ist der Bodensee ein Dorado der Badefreunde und Wassersportler; zwar fehlen Mammutstrände adriatischer Ausmaße, doch selbst das kleinste Dorf hat einen beschaulichen Uferstreifen, an dem man paradiesisch schwimmen, rudern, paddeln und rösten kann.

Bayerisches Alpenland

Bayern, das vielgeliebte, oftgeschmähte Land vor den Bergen, das so gar nicht recht ins bundesdeutsche Einheitskorsett passen will, machte offenbar schon immer den Chronisten seine Deutung schwer. Als vor zweihundert Jahren der Berliner Buchhändler Friedrich Nikolai einen Versuch machte, es zu ergründen, nahm er angesichts unzugänglicher Bergwildnis, disharmonischen Kuhglockengebimmels, vollbärtiger Passionsspieler und gröhlender Wildschützen verstört Reißaus und schrieb in seinen umfangreichen Reisebericht die lakonische Schlußfolgerung: »Bayern – kleines, diebisches Bergvolk«. Noch in unseren Tagen meinte ein namhafter Kolumnist, von bundesdeutscher Warte aus gesehen sei es eine Qual, mit den Bayern leben zu müssen. Andere sehen im Land Bayern einen irdischen Paradieswinkel in Weißblau: Weiße Rahmwolken vor dem tiefblauen Himmel, weiße Segel auf tiefblauem See, weiße Schneehänge mit blaubedreßten Skidirndln – und in jeder Ecke weißblaue Gemütlichkeit.

Bayerische Gemütlichkeit, das ist auch ein Begriff, der vielerlei Auslegungen kennt. Symbolisiert er deftige Kraftausdrücke, bierselige Behäbigkeit, ungezwungenes »Anbandeln« oder Schweinsbraten mit Knödeln? Mag von alldem ein Quäntchen dazugehören – treffend ist keiner dieser Begriffe. Am ehesten könnte man sie als Zusammenklang dessen definieren, was man unter »anheimelnd, leutselig, behaglich« versteht, kurzum, eine Atmosphäre, in der man sich wohlfühlt, mit sich und der Welt im Einklang ist.

Davon sollte man nicht ableiten, daß versöhnliche Eintracht eine besondere Zierde des bayerischen Wesens sei. Oft ist es kantig, derb, eigensinnig, häufig verschanzt es sich auch nur hinter solcher Gebärde, weil ihm die alerte Flexibilität fehlt. Immer aber ist das Denken gradlinig, unkompliziert, nüchtern, allem Abstrakten und Hinterlistigen feind. In einem Münchner Bierlokal bemerkte einst ein Berliner zu Heinrich Heine, gutes Weißbier gäbe es hier schon, aber keine Ironie. »Ironie haben wir nicht«, rief die vorbeieilende Kellnerin, »aber jedes andere Bier können Sie doch haben.«

Einer der legendären bayerischen Könige, der »Märchenkönig« Ludwig II., gab Unsummen für den Bau phantastischer Schlösser aus, heute übrigens Bayerns stolze Touristenmagneten. Sein gläubig-idealistischer Sinn spürte nicht, daß eine Clique am Thron sägte. Diese ließ den König für geistesgestört erklären und bewirkte, im Glauben, der Unterstützung durch das Volk sicher zu sein, seinen Sturz und Tod. Doch das bayerische Gemüt

⑪ Ein Stück unversehrter Natur ist der Königssee im Berchtesgadener Land. Blick über den melancholisch-verträumten Wasserspiegel auf die Kapelle St. Bartholomä. Dahinter die Watzmann-Ostwand, eines der anspruchsvollsten Kletterziele in den Ostalpen.

⑫ Herbstmorgen über dem Talbecken von Garmisch-Partenkirchen, Herzstück des Werdenfelser Landes und Deutschlands ranghöchstes alpines Fremdenverkehrszentrum. Links oben die Front des Wettersteingebirges mit Alpspitze (2620 m) und Zugspitze (2963 m), in der rechten Bildmitte das Olympia-Eisstadion.

reagierte anders. Die Volksseele kochte ob dieser schandbaren Tat, identifizierte sich mit dem Wesen des Königs, erhob ihn zur glorreichen Legendenfigur, umkränzte ihn mit Mythos, dichtete Lieder und Moritaten, von denen ein Vers noch heute lebendig ist:

»Ach, nun ruhst du, stolzer König, / In dem kühlen Erdenschoß, / Von dort oben schaust du nicht mehr / Runter auf dein stolzes Schloß. / Ach, du bautest deine Schlösser / Zu des Volkes Wohlergehn, / Und Neuschwanstein, allerschönstes, / kann man noch in Bayern sehn!«

War es nun soziologische Rückständigkeit oder devoter Untertanengeist, der solches bewirkte? Mag sein, daß etwas davon in damaliger Zeit mit hereinspielte. Doch das charakterliche Grundmotiv war ein ehrliches, nüchternlogisches Empfinden, das einerseits Intrigen verabscheute und andererseits die Meinung ausdrückte, daß man das Geld der Obrigkeit sowieso nicht mehr bekäme und es doch erfreulich sei, dafür ein schönes Schloß zu kriegen – heute könnte es auch ein Olympiastadion sein.

So vieldeutig das bayerische Wesen auch sein mag, überschaubar ist die Geschichte des Landes, vor allem des altbayerischen Bereichs vor den Bergen. Um das Jahr 500, mit dem Zerfall des Römischen Reichs, konsolidierte sich aus dem Gemisch der Völkerwanderung der Stamm der Bajuwaren. Unter dem Stammesherzogtum der Agilolfinger bildeten sich rasch stabile Verhältnisse, die Bayern zum ersten eigentlichen Staat des nachantiken Europa werden ließen. Diese altbayerische Kernzelle blieb durch alle Jahrhunderte erhalten, auch wenn zuweilen die Oberhoheit wechselte. Im 8. Jahrhundert entstanden die Bistümer Salzburg, Passau, Regensburg, Freising und Eichstätt. 1070 kam das Land an die Welfen, die ihren Sitz in Regensburg hatten. Heinrich der Löwe, bedeutendster Fürst des Geschlechts, gründete 1158 München. Nach seinem Sturz wurde 1180 das verkleinerte Altbayern dem Pfalzgrafen Otto von Wittelsbach übertragen. Damit begann die Regierungszeit des Wittelsbacher-Geschlechtes, das bis 1918 anhielt. 1825 bestieg König Ludwig I. den Thron. Seine Devise, er werde München gestalten, »... daß keiner sagen kann, er kenne Teutschland, der München nicht gesehen hat«, leitete die große Blüte Bayerns ein. Er formte München zur Stadt der Künste und Wissenschaften, seine Nachfolger Maximilian II. und Ludwig II. setzten sein Werk fort. Die politische Gestalt des heutigen Freistaates Bayern bildete sich nach dem Sturz Napoleons mit dem bayerischen Königreich, das sich 1870 dem Deutschen Reich anschloß.

Vom großen Alpenmassiv besitzt Bayern nur einen schmalen Streifen am Nordrand; umso intensiver ist dieser erschlossen, umhegt und gepflegt. Im Alpenvorland liegen lauschige Städtchen und blitzsaubere Dörfer, deren Zwiebeltürme wie Kuppelmoscheen und deren Spitzkirchtürme wie Minaretts aussehen. Auf den Hügeln und in den Tälern stehen Bauernhöfe wie Puppen-

häuser, eingehüllt in bunten Blumenflor. Wenn der Himmel sattes Föhnblau
ist, liegt ein volles, goldenes Lachen über der Landschaft, das immer noch ein
Lächeln ist, wenn Wolken über die Berge kommen. Das bäuerliche Leben be-
stimmt noch der alte, natürliche Rhythmus, der »Leib und Seel« zusammen-
hält. Sitte, Brauchtum und Tracht sind noch vielerorts lebendig, und dies
nicht in musealer Erstarrung. Anschauliches Beispiel dafür ist das »Dirndl«,
worunter man in Bayern nicht nur ein gutgewachsenes Weibsbild, sondern
auch dessen appetitliche Verpackung versteht; diese Trachtenkleidung hat sogar die Laufstege mondäner Modenschauen erobert.

Über einer Wirtshaustür in der Ramsau steht ein Spruch des bayerischen
Volksdichters Ludwig Ganghofer: »Herr, wen du lieb hast, den lässest du
fallen in dieses Land.« Er meinte damit das *Berchtesgadener* Land, den prächtigsten Landschaftswinkel Bayerns, wo aus dem dunklen Schwarzgrün der
Tannenwälder der Watzmann in den blauen Himmel pfeilt und unter tonlos
grauem Felsgemäuer Königssee und Obersee in kalter Schönheit und zeitloser
Ruhe glitzern. Ganz in der Nähe schürft man Salz aus dem Berg, ein Mineral,
dessen Wert in alter Zeit dem des Goldes gleichkam. Auf seinem Vorkom-
men gründete sich *Bad Reichenhall*, das Kurheilbad von internationalem
Rang. In den waldreichen Chiemgauer Alpen versteckt sich ein Reigen heime-
liger Ferienorte, angeführt von *Inzell*, dem deutschen Eislaufzentrum, dem
komfortablen *Ruhpolding* und dem malerischen *Reit im Winkl*, wo Deutsch-
lands Skiköniginnen wachsen. Zu Füßen der Bergkulisse dehnt sich der *Chiemsee*, größter der zweihundert Seen des Alpenvorlandes, mit kilometerlangen
Bade- und Wassersportufern. In seiner Mitte liegen zwei bedeutende Eilande:
Die Fraueninsel mit altem Kloster und pittoreskem Fischerdorfkolorit, die
Herreninsel mit dem prunkvollen Schloß Herrenchiemsee, zu dem Versailles
Pate stand. Sieben Jahre lang ließ König Ludwig II. daran bauen; ganze acht
Tage wohnte er in den Prachtgemächern.

Im Westen, jenseits des Inns, schließt sich hinter *Bayrischzell* das weitver-
zweigte Wander- und Skipistengebiet um Wendelstein, Sudelfeld und Spit-
zingsee an. Am *Tegernsee* trifft sich in noblen Hotels die Prominenz von
München und anderwärts. Vor eineinhalb Jahrhunderten haben Künstler bereits
das bezaubernde Fleckchen unter dem Wallberg entdeckt: Wilhelm und Franz
von Kobell, Karl Stieler und Heinrich Noë, dann kamen Ludwig Thoma und
Ludwig Ganghofer, Olaf Gulbransson und Leo Slezak. Im Isarwinkel bietet
das beschauliche Kleinstädtchen *Bad Tölz* vielbesuchte Kuranlagen, flußauf-
wärts erfreut *Lenggries* mit seiner rustikalen Atmosphäre. In nordisch-kühler
Waldumrahmung präsentiert sich der rätselhafte *Walchensee*, von dem die
Sage geht, er sei mit dem Meer verbunden; ein paar Kilometer weiter duckt
sich *Mittenwald*, das malerische Geigenbauerdorf, unter die mächtigen Flanken des Karwendelgebirges.

Bayerns bekannteste Alpenkammer ist das Werdenfelser Land mit dem Touristenzentrum *Garmisch-Partenkirchen*, das sich angestrengt bemüht, dörfliches Image zu bewahren. Es lockt mit Deutschlands höchstem Berg, der knapp dreitausend Meter hohen Zugspitze, mit vierzig Bergbahnen und Liften, mit sublimiertem Gastkomfort und bodenständiger Gemütlichkeit. Seit 350 Jahren führen in *Oberammergau* Laienschauspieler im zehnjährigen Rhythmus das Spiel vom Leben und Leiden Christi auf, als Dank für die Befreiung von der Pest. Die Passionsspiele errangen inzwischen solch weltweiten Ruf und Zuspruch, daß der eigentliche fromme Anlaß in Vergessenheit zu versinken droht.

In *Füssen* werden Stadt, Lech und Forggensee vom Hohen Schloß überragt, einst Sommerresidenz der Augsburger Fürstbischöfe, unverändert seit dem 15. Jahrhundert. Nicht weit davon, im dunklen Waldgrün der Tannheimer Berge, thront Neuschwanstein, König Ludwigs II. unvollendeter Schlössertraum einer bayerischen Wartburg. Der Unterschied zweier künstlerischer Epochen wird auch dem Laien deutlich, wenn er die nahegelegene Wieskirche betritt: In der hügeligen Wald- und Wieseneinsamkeit des Lechrains bauten die Brüder Johann Baptist und Dominikus Zimmermann die schönste Rokokokirche der Welt, eine aus Licht, Weiß und Gold geformte, traumhafte Komposition jubilierender Beschwingtheit. Im Umkreis des Ammertaler Bergvorlandes, wegen der vielen Gotteshäuser »Pfaffenwinkel« genannt, finden sich eine ganze Reihe ähnlich schöner Kirchen, wie in *Steingaden, Ilgen, Rottenbuch, Andechs* und *Ettal*, in denen die berühmte Wessobrunner Schule Triumphe ihres künstlerischen Vermögens feiert.

Westlich davon, wo der Talgrund der Iller weit in die Alpen vorstößt, sonnt sich *Oberstdorf* genießerisch im weiten Geländebecken, umkränzt von einem Reigen stattlicher Ski-, Aussichts- und Wanderberge. Hinter der Walserschanze öffnet sich das Nebenstübli des *Kleinen Walsertals:* Da kuscheln sich liebliche Dörfer in die Falten der Hangmatten, man bezahlt auf österreichischem Boden mit Deutscher Mark und bezieht unverfälschtes Naturerleben aus erster Hand.

Vom großen Bodensee besitzt Bayern nur ein winziges, dafür umso attraktiveres Fleckchen: *Lindau*, die trutzige Inselstadt, in der man schwäbisch spricht und bayerisch denkt. Alte Wehrmauern, finstere Türme, das breitbürgerliche Rathaus und die schöne Peterskirche künden von glanzvoller Zeit, in der Lindau dank des Bodenseehandels zu den reichsten deutschen Städten zählte. Draußen am Hafen späht, in Erz gegossen, seit Jahr und Tag der bayerische Löwe in die Weite des Wasserspiegels, allzeit bereit, die Handelsflotten würdig zu empfangen.

Österreich

Salzburg und Salzkammergut

»Salzburg, Hauptstadt des gleichnamigen österreichischen Bundeslandes, im beckenartig erweiterten Salzachtal, 420 m ü. M., 127 500 Ew. . . .« So steht es im Brockhaus, dann wird es wohl stimmen. Demnach gehört es zu Österreich. Gehört? Salzburg hat nie zu jemandem gehört. Zu allen Zeiten war es ein hybrides, stolzes Wesen, das es nie erduldet hätte, jemandes Untertan zu sein. In der Vergangenheit stritten kaiserliche und kirchliche Fürsten um die Vorherrschaft, wobei diese meist die Oberhand behielten Heute »gehört« es der ganzen Welt, und das fürstliche Szepter schwingt ein begnadeter Dirigent.

Salzburg entstand, lange, bevor es Wien und München gab. Es wurde sozusagen mit Salz gebaut; Holz, Kupfer und Gold aus den Tauern, und die Einnahmen aus dem Handel kamen dazu. So floß unermeßlicher Reichtum zusammen, aus dem die Stadt erwuchs, die wir heute als bedeutendstes mittelalterliches und barockes Freilichtmuseum nördlich der Alpen bewundern. Sieben Fürstbischöfe, jeweils weltliche und kirchliche Herrscher in einer Person, haben daran gebaut. Dies hört sich an wie Stadtgeschichte »aus einem Guß«; doch von Eintracht war keine Rede. Reißen wir aus der Chronik, die sich liest wie ein spannender Roman, ein Blatt heraus:
Im 16. Jahrhundert regierte Fürstbischof Wolf Dietrich von Raitenau, einer der großen Gestalter der Stadt, die Diözese, die sich von Oberbayern bis in die Steiermark erstreckte. Seinen übersteigerten Bauplänen war der alte Dom, 774 von Bischof Virgilius gebaut, im Wege. Als der Dom eines Tages lichterloh brannte, meinte Wolf Dietrich ungerührt: »Brennet es, so lasset es brennen«. Daß er selbst das Feuer gelegt habe, war ihm zuzutrauen, aber nie nachzuweisen. Er beeilte sich, die noch erneuerungsfähigen Kirchenreste abtragen zu lassen. Darauf angesprochen, daß man den Dom doch nicht abreißen dürfe, schließlich habe ihn der große Virgilius gebaut, antwortete er lapidar: »Ach was, Virgilius; die Maurer haben ihn gebaut!« Und er begann sofort mit dem Neubau eines Domes, der an Pracht und Größe alle Kirchen der Welt in den Schatten stellen sollte. Es kam nicht mehr (ganz) dazu. Erzbischof Wolf Dietrich nahm nämlich nicht nur die kirchlichen Würden, sondern als Fürst auch die Freiheiten weltlicher Macht für sich in Anspruch. Er baute für seine Mätresse Salome Alt, mit der er an die zehn Kinder zeugte, das Schloß Mirabell, wurde auch in anderen Dingen selbstherrlich, brachte die Kirche gegen sich auf. Sein Nachfolger, Bischof Markus Sittikus, stürzte ihn und kerkerte

ihn auf Lebenszeit auf der Festung Hohenwerfen ein. Markus Sittikus seinerseits vollendete – in abgeschwächter Form – den Dom in seiner heutigen Gestalt, stand aber an ehrgeizigen Bauplänen seinem Vorgänger wenig nach. Er ließ Schloß Hellbrunn erbauen, das frühbarocke Tusculum am Rand der Stadt, mit seinen auf der Welt einmaligen Wasserspielen, die zum Entzücken der Touristen noch heute funktionieren. Nächst den Wasserbecken steht das kleine Monatsschlößchen, zu dessen Bau ein Freund, Erzherzog Maximilian von Bayern, den Fürstbischof animierte. Daß der Bischof dort seine Freundin, Frau von Marbon, während ihrer Schwangerschaften versteckt haben soll, ist nicht aktenkundig; offenbar hatte Sittikus aus den Fehlern Wolf Dietrichs gelernt.

Ob mit oder ohne sittengeschichtliche Seitenblicke – aus vielen solcher Episoden entstand in zweitausend Jahren Salzburg, wie wir es heute kennen und lieben; mit seiner prächtigen Kulisse zwischen Bergen und Flußufern und seinen einmaligen Bau- und Kunstwerken: Der trutzigen Festung Hohensalzburg, die gleich eine ganze Burgstadt darstellt; dem mächtigen Dom, der 10 500 Menschen Platz gewährt und als größte Kirche im deutschen Sprachraum gilt; dem imposanten Kuppelbau der Kollegienkirche; den filigranen Umrissen der Franziskanerkirche, die Michael Pachers berühmte Madonnenstatue birgt; dem intim-altertümlichen St. Peter mit dem »heimeligen« Friedhof; den Schhössern Mirabell, Leopoldskron, Hellbrunn und Kleßheim und vielen Kirchen, Palästen, Bürgerhäusern und Fassaden, Klöstern und Türmen. Wenn in diesem Zusammenhang das Wort von kunstsinnigen Herrschern gebraucht wird, sollte man daran denken, daß es diesen doch mehr um die Demonstration von Macht und Ruhm ging; den Kunstsinn brachte das Heer der Ausführenden mit, die am Beispiel Salzburg durch die genialen Baumeister Santino Solari und Fischer von Erlach symbolisiert sind.

»Übrigens benachrichtige ich Sie, daß am 27. Januari abends um 8 Uhr die Meinige mit einem Buben glücklich entbunden worden. Der Bub heißt Johannes Chrysostomos Wolfgang Gottlieb.« Der dies meldete, war der Komponist Leopold Mozart, Kapellmeister in Salzburg. Der Bub, kein anderer als Wolfgang Amadeus, gab als Sechsjähriger Konzerte in Wien und München, Paris und London und wurde einer der größten Tonschöpfer der Welt. Auf seinem Namen fußt Salzburgs Rang als Musik- und Theaterstadt. Im imposanten Trakt des Festspielhauses, zu dessen Bau 50 000 Kubikmeter Fels aus dem Nonnberg gesprengt wurden, finden alljährlich die weltweit berühmten Festspiele statt. In jenen Tagen ist Salzburg der Treffpunkt der Welt.

Was sich in Salzburgs Stadtlandschaft andeutet, das harmonische Nebeneinander von Berg und Tal, von Wäldern, Wiesen und Wasser, das steigert sich in seiner Umgebung zur beglückenden Urlaubsregion. Gleich am östlichen Stadt-

rand erhebt sich die gemütliche Silhouette des Gaisbergs. Eine Autostraße
führt bis zum Gipfelplateau, das eine bezaubernde Aussicht auf die Stadt, in
die Zentralalpen und weit ins flache Land bis zum bayerischen Chiemsee
hinaus bietet. Wer höher hinauf will, fährt auf der Alpenstraße südwärts und
erreicht nach acht Kilometer die Kabinenseilbahn zum *Untersberg*. Kaiser
Karl der Große soll der Sage nach in einer Höhle des Massivs schlafen, seinen
Bart um einen Steintisch herumwachsen lassen und erst dann wieder ans Ta-
geslicht treten, wenn alle Völker deutscher Zunge vereinigt sind. Realistische-
rer Berginhalt ist der schöne »Untersberger Marmor«, der in Glanegg gebro-
chen wird und der uns mit seinen roten, weiß geäderten Flächen überall im
Land in Kirchen und Kunstwerken begegnet. In acht Minuten hebt uns die
Seilbahn auf das über 1800 Meter hohe Plateau, das ein umfassendes Panorama gewährt und mit vielen Wanderwegen lockt.

Ein paar Kilometer südlich davon liegt *Hallein*, die uralte Salinenstadt, tra-
ditionelles Zentrum der Salzgewinnung. Sein »weißes Gold« finanzierte im
Mittelalter Salzburgs Prachtbauten, wurde auf Salzach und Donau bis in die
ferne Türkei verschifft. Ein Besuch des Salzbergwerks am Dürrnberg vermittelt
einen interessanten Anschauungsunterricht über den Salzbergbau, den schon
Kelten und Römer hier betrieben. – Von hier weiter salzachaufwärts drängen
sich bald die wuchtigen Felsflanken des Tennen- und Hagengebirges an den
Fluß heran. Bei *Tenneck* und *Werfen* besteht die Gelegenheit, ausnahmsweise
einmal die Berge voninnen zu besichtigen. Die »Eisriesenwelt« ist ein großes
System von Höhlen, Stollen und märchenhaften Eishallen. Neugierige seien
darauf vorbereitet, daß das unterirdische Höhlenreich vierzig Kilometer um-
faßt, Führungen bis zu acht Stunden dauern und es in den Grotten empfindlich
kalt ist.

Warm und lieblich ist es dagegen in Salzburgs östlichem Hinterland, dem seen-
reichen *Salzkammergut*. Man weiß nicht so genau, wo es beginnt und wo es
aufhört; es zieht sich über das Land Salzburg nach Oberösterreich, in die
Steiermark und bis an den Sockel des knapp dreitausend Meter hohen, glet-
schergekrönten Dachstein. Dafür weiß man ganz genau, wo seine schönsten
Fleckchen liegen. Nur eine halbe Autobahnstunde ist es von Salzburg zum
Mondsee, der sich liebenswürdig zwischen die Wiesenhänge im Norden und
die Felskuppen am Südrand schmiegt. Sein schönstes Empfangszimmer ist der
malerische Markt gleichen Namens, von den charakteristischen Türmen der
Pfarrkirche überragt. Kloster Mondsee, 739 vom Bayernherzog Odilo gegründet, war im Mittelalter bedeutendes kulturelles und politisches Zentrum. 1774
brannten Ort und Teile des Klosters nieder. Die Klosterkirche, die nur be-
schädigt wurde, ist seit 1791 Pfarrkirche St. Michael, deren Inneres fünf
prächtige Barockaltäre zieren.

Durch Ralph Benatzki's Singspiel vom »Weißen Rössl« wurde der vielformige *Wolfgangsee* weltbekannt. Das pittoreske *St. Wolfgang*, anheimelnd an die Uferhänge gekuschelt, gilt als Musterplakat des salzburgischen Ferienparadieses. Vor dem Dorf liegt in sommerseliger Bläue der verträumte Seenspiegel, dahinter schnaubt und rattert die asthmatische Zahnradbahn auf den 1783 Meter hohen Riesenbuckel des Schafbergs hinauf. Künstlerisches Juwel des Orts ist der unvergleichliche spätgotische Altar von Michael Pacher in der Pfarrkirche, das reifste Werk des großen Holzbildhauers.

Rund zwei Dutzend Seen, kleine und große, liebliche und elegische, sind über die formenreiche Vorgebirgslandschaft verstreut. Passionierte Wassersportler lieben die Weite des *Attersees*, romantische Naturen den geheimnisvoll düsteren *Hallstätter See*, nostalgische Gemüter zieht es zum malerischen *Traunsee* und Naturliebhaber freuen sich an den unberührten, schilfigen Ufern von *Obertrumer-* und *Mattsee*. Wem dagegen Wasser nur in veredeltem Zustand genießbar erscheint, dem empfiehlt sich ein Besuch in *Bad Ischl,* wo noch die Zunft der »Kaffeesieder« blüht und er anschließend auf den Spuren Franz Lehars und des Kaisers Franz Josef wandeln kann.

Tirol

Erzählt man einem australischen Touristen von Niederösterreich oder Vorarlberg, wird er sich darunter schwerlich etwas vorstellen können. Tirol aber ist (nicht nur für ihn) ein feststehender Begriff. Das sind hohe Berge und liebliche Täler mit niedlichen Almhütten und drallen, rotbackigen Sennerinnen, das sind kernige Burschen voll nie versiegender Manneskraft, die alle aussehen wie Luis Trenker, die Lederhosen und Tirolerhüte tragen, bergkraxeln und fingerhackeln und raufen und skifahren wie die Teufel, allzeit einen juchzenden Jodler in der Kehle und ein lustig' Lied auf den Lippen.

Die Berge und Täler sind nicht anzuzweifeln, doch ansonsten stimmt das Bild nicht so recht. In Tirol trägt man, wie anderwärts, überwiegend Jeans, fährt vorzugsweise mit dem Auto, jodelt allenfalls – gegen mäßige Bezahlung – am Folkloreabend, und die vielen lederbehosten Gestalten sind in der Regel aus Norddeutschland. Daß es schließlich auf der Alm »koa Sünd« gibt, ist nicht einer sublimierten Moral zuzuschreiben, sondern dem Umstand, daß die wenigen, zumeist recht angejahrten Sennerinnen kaum jenem Idealbild der »Alpenvenus« entsprechen, das sich die lüsterne Phantasie zurechtgemalt hat. Allerdings sind die Tiroler nicht ganz unschuldig an diesem verzerrten Bild ihres Landes, kokettieren nicht ungern mit dem weltbekannten Klischee. Es gehört zum Geschäft mit dem Tourismus, und dieses betreiben sie gekonnt. Seit den Freiheitskämpfen gegen Napoleon heißt ihr Motto »Für Gott, Kaiser und Eigenthum«, und da es mittleren nicht mehr gibt, hat sich das Schwergewicht auf den letzten Begriff verlagert. Gelegentlich schießt die Geschäftstüchtigkeit auch einmal übers Ziel hinaus, wie bei dem folgenden, vielbeschmunzelten Vorgang: In den fünfziger Jahren schrieb der Bürgermeister von Kirchbichl, einer kleinen Gemeinde im Unterinntal unweit von Kufstein, an den damaligen britischen Premierminister Winston Churchill: »Mylord! Die Gemeinde Kirchbichl weiß, wie gern Sie an den Gardasee und nach Südtirol reisen. Wir hätten einen Grund, Sie zu bitten, bei Ihrer nächsten Fahrt im nordtirolischen Kirchbichl auszusteigen, um von uns geehrt zu werden. Der Grund liegt in der Namensgleichheit. Denn Kirch-Bichl und Church-Hill sind doch gleichbedeutend mit Gotteshaus-Hügel!« Ob im Touristikgeschäft, ob im Heldentum – der Tiroler neigt zur kleinen Übertreibung, entschärft diese aber zugleich mit verschmitztem Augenzwinkern, das er selbst beim Verkehr mit dem Lieben Gott nicht ganz lassen kann. Man findet es zuweilen in Marterl-

⑱ *Tiroler Skiparadies am Arlberg. Der Start-abschnitt der Abfahrten von der Station Vallugagrat über Ulmer Hütte (rechts), Schindlerkar (Mitte) und Mattunjoch (links) nach St. Christoph und St. Anton. Gegenüber die Ferwallgruppe.*

⑲ *Überall in Tirol schmückt das heimelige Weiß und Braun der Bauernhäuser eine aus Wiese, Wald und Fels gestaltete Landschaft. Charakteristische Details sind die umlaufenden Holzbalkone und die den Dächern aufgesetzten Glockentürmchen. Im Hintergrund reckt sich das Felsmassiv des Kaisergebirges in Wolkenhöhen.*

sprüchen, wie in diesem, von Rudolf Greinz gedichteten: »Der Tod macht net viel Federlesen: / Abikugelt, hingewesen! / Das Leben ist ein großer Mist! / Gelobt sei dennoch Jesus Christ!«

Für Österreich ist Tirol, ähnlich wie Texas für die USA oder Bayern für die deutsche Bundesrepublik, eine eigenwillige, etwas dickschädelige Außenseiter-provinz. Wien und Innsbruck verbindet eine innige Haßliebe; was sich etwa auch darin zeigt, daß die Tiroler aus der gesamtösterreichischen Werbung aus-scheren und eigene Wege gehen, wobei sie streng darauf achten, daß Tirol mit y geschrieben wird.

Österreichisch ist Tirol erst seit 1918; vorher war man habsburgisch, eine ge-fürstete Grafschaft über fünfeinhalb Jahrhunderte. Das soll nicht heißen, Tirol huldige einer separatistischen Strömung; es hat sogar, neben Wien, das be-deutendste historische Profil, war stets eine – wenn auch manchmal unbe-queme – tragende Säule des Habsburger Kaiserhauses. Von den Baiern im 6. Jahrhundert n. Chr. besiedelt, kam es im Mittelalter unter die Herrschaft der Grafen von Tirol, deren Stammburg bei Meran steht. Durch Erbfolgen geriet es an den Grafen von Görz und von diesem 1363 an die Habsburger, die es 1379 zum Fürstentum erhoben. In den folgenden Jahrhunderten kam Tirol zu größter Ausdehnung (bis Brixen und Trient) und kultureller Blüte, besonders unter Kaiser Maximilian I., der Innsbruck zur kaiserlichen Resi-denzstadt erhob. Nach der Niederlage gegen Napoleon mußte Habsburg 1805 Tirol an Bayern abtreten. 1809 kam es zu den Tiroler Freiheitskriegen gegen die bayerisch-französische Herrschaft unter Führung der legendären Volkshel-den Andreas Hofer und Joseph Speckbacher. Der Wiener Kongreß von 1814, der nach Napoleons Sturz die Neuordnung Europas vollzog, gab Tirol dem Habsburger Kaiserreich zurück. Nach dem Ersten Weltkrieg mußte Österreich das Gebiet von Südtirol an Italien abtreten, Osttirol wird durch die neue Grenzziehung geographisch vom Stammland getrennt.

Die Lebensader Tirols ist das tief eingeschnittene Tal des Inn, der das Land, aus dem Engadin kommend, in ganzer Länge durchzieht. An seinen Ufern lie-gen die reizvollen alten Städtchen, wie das von einer mächtigen Burg über-ragte *Kufstein,* dessen ernste Silhouette so gar nicht zu jenem trivialen Jodel-schunkelsong passen will, der zum festen Repertoire aller Almbar-Bands zwi-schen Semmering und Matterhorn zählt; das ländlich-industrielle *Wörgl;* das altersgreise *Rattenberg* und das lebendige *Schwaz* mit prächtigen Kirchen, Klöstern und Schlössern. Solbad *Hall,* einst wichtige Salz- und Handelsstadt, bietet ein unverfälschtes mittelalterliches Stadtbild, *Telfs* ist ein rühriges Ge-werbestädtchen mit historischem Hintergrund, *Landeck,* das westliche Tor, steht auf bronzezeitlichem Siedlungsboden. Weit überragt werden alle Siedlungen von der Landeshauptstadt *Innsbruck,* der Großstadt im Gebirge, Knoten im

Schnittpunkt der großen Verkehrsströme. Das Föhnblau des Himmels, die grüne Patina der Kupferdächer und das Braun und Rot der Häuser geben den Farbakkord, die prachtvollen Kirchen, Türme, Paläste und Fassaden die kaiserliche Atmosphäre. Dazu schauen die Felsköpfe der 2500 Meter hohen Karwendelkette beherrschend in alle Gassen herein. Juwel unter den Sehenswürdigkeiten ist das »Goldene Dachl«, ein mit 3400 vergoldeten Kupfer-»ziegeln« gedeckter Erker. Schade, daß der klassische Umriß der Stadt immer mehr von nüchternen Betonhochbauten erdrückt wird.

Tirols touristisches Aushängeschild ist die großartige Szenerie seiner Täler und Berge, alpine Landschaft schlechthin. Von der Innfurche strahlen Dutzende von Seitentälern aus; nach Norden in die Felsregionen der Kalkalpen mit dem Lechtaler-, Mieminger-, Wetterstein-, Karwendel- und Kaisergebirge, nach Süden in die über 3500 Meter hochragenden Zentralalpen mit Silvretta, Ötztaler- und Zillertaler Alpen und den Hohen Tauern. Über diese Täler sind Dutzende von Ferienorten verstreut, allen voran die großen Fremdenverkehrszentren *Kitzbühel, St. Anton, Seefeld, Zillertal* und *Ötztal*. Allen gemeinsam ist eine anheimelnde dörfliche Atmosphäre – es gibt nirgendwo Betonklötze, auch wenn manche Hotels aussehen wie riesenwüchsige Almhütten –, eine in langjähriger Routine geschulte Gastlichkeit und alle touristischen Einrichtungen, die sich der Urlauber zu erträumen vermag.

Vielen gemeinsam ist die doppelte Saison. Tirol ist nicht nur ein Bergparadies für Sommerfrischler und Wanderer, sondern auch ein Dorado für die Freunde des Sports auf zwei Brettern. Seine Skihänge um *Kitzbühel, St. Anton, Innsbruck, Seefeld, Axams, Hintertux, Sölden, Obergurgl, Ischgl, Lermoos* und im *Stubaital* zählen zu den schönsten und besterschlossenen Europas.

Es sind noch viele Einzelheiten, die den Charme des Tiroler Landes abrunden: Die uralten, trutzigen Burgen auf den Berghängen und Hügelkuppen, der reiche, aus traditioneller Holzschnitzkunst erwachsene Barockschmuck in vielen Kirchen, die urgemütlichen Wirtshäuser in den Dörfern und an der Straße. Da ist, aus Holz und Stein gemischt, das Weiß und Braun der Landhäuser, das Nebeneinander von Blumenwiesen, Wildbächen, Tannenwälder und Felsschroffen, da sind die kleinen Idylle an Bach und Steg, der Hauch der Gletscher und der Geruch von Harz und Heu.

Eine abgeschiedene Welt für sich ist die »vergessene« Landschaft Osttirols, jenseits der Tauern gelegen und vom Tiroler Stammland durch den Salzburgischen Pinzgau getrennt. Ein stiller, einsamer Alpenbereich, schon ein wenig vom Süden bestrahlt. Zwar schleust die Felbertauernstraße seit einigen Jahren etwas Betriebsamkeit ein, aber in den Dörfern der abgelegenen Bergkerben, im Virgen-, Defereggen- und Kalser Tal, scheint das Leben seit Jahrzehnten still zu stehen. *Lienz*, das malerische Hauptstädtchen, von den Felszacken der

Lienzer Dolomiten überragt, hat schöne Kirchen und Kapellen und alte, gemütliche Hotels. In den Dörfern ringsherum findet man in schlichten Kirchen des öfteren überraschenderweise wertvolle gotische Fresken. Sie blieben deshalb erhalten, weil der südöstliche Teil Tirols während der Blüte des Barock wirtschaftlich arm war.

Zum Schluß noch ein paar Tiroler Kuriositäten. Wer glaubt, das Land hätte so ziemlich alles außer einem guten Tropfen Wein, der irrt sich. Unter den Mauern der Martinswand bei Zirl gedeiht in der Föhnsonne seit einigen Jahren ein ausgezeichneter Gewürztraminer! In Wörgl, dem Stadtdorf am Unterinn, gelangte ein Schneidermeister zu weltweiter Popularität; zwar nicht in der Modebranche, doch dafür umso dauerhafter in der Literatur: Denn »vor seinem Haus / floß ein Wasser mit Gebraus« – es war kein anderer als der Schneider Böck in Wilhelm Buschs »Max und Moritz«. Weil wir schon bei den Kindereien sind: Für siebzig Mark kann sich jeder seine Bubenträume verwirklichen und als Lokführer mit einem kleinen Sonderzug der Zillertalbahn eine Stunde lang durch die Gegend fauchen.

Kärnten

Wer Kärnten sagt, meint Wörther See. Wer Wörther See denkt, sieht Bade-
nixen, Strandflirt, Wasserski, Playboys, Luxusboote, Dolce vita, umweht von
einem sündhaft-verführerischen Hauch Leichtlebigkeit und Ausschweifung.
Diese Gleichung ist zu simpel. Kärnten, jenseits des Alpenhauptkamms am
südlichen Rand Österreichs gelegen, ist mehr als »österreichische Riviera«; es
ist ein Land mit vielen Gesichtern und mannigfaltigstem Kolorit. Eine Landschaft der großen Übergänge – topographisch, klimatisch und ethnisch. Schon
die Statistik läßt aufhorchen: In seinem engen Raum liegt Österreichs höchster
Berg, der 3797 Meter hohe *Großglockner*, aber auch des Landes wärmster
Badesee, der kleine Klopeiner See südlich von Völkermarkt mit einer sommerlichen Durchschnittstemperatur von 23 Grad. Es hat zweihundert Seen und
ebensoviele Burgen, aber nur 155 Ortsgemeinden, die ältesten Kulturdenkmäler und Kirchen und die meisten unehelichen Kinder. Es hat drei Haupt-
städte: eine vergangene, St. Veit; eine gegenwärtige, Klagenfurt; und eine
(vielleicht) zukünftige, Villach. Kärnten ist nur über Pässe zugänglich, doch
alle Wasser strömen der dominierenden Drau zu. Es gibt die überfülltesten
und die einsamsten Badeufer, raffiniertesten Luxus und spartanische bäuerliche
Einfachheit. Früher war Kärnten das Land der Fuhrleute, die in den Wirts-
häusern einkehrten und ihre Pferde fütterten, von Dorf zu Dorf Botschaft
brachten und Botschaft mitnahmen – was einen klugen Klagenfurter auf die
Erfindung der Postkarte brachte.

Der Name Kärnten geht sicherlich auf die illyrisch-keltischen Karner zurück,
die in diesem Raume saßen und sich besonders auf die Gewinnung und Verarbeitung von Eisenerz verstanden. Ihre Hauptstadt Noreja wird auf dem Magda-
lenensberg nördlich von Klagenfurt vermutet. Unter den Römern wurde das
Gebiet von Kärnten das Zentrum der um 40 n. Chr. geschaffenen Provinz Nori-
cum. Um 590 besetzten Alpenslawen (Slowenen) das Land. Sie wurden im
8. Jahrhundert von den Bayernherzögen und den fränkischen Karolingern ein-
gedeutscht. 976 wurde Kärnten selbständiges Herzogtum, kam 1286 an die
Grafen von Tirol und 1335 an die Habsburger; Napoleon gliederte es 1809
den Illyrischen Provinzen an. Nach dem Zerfall des österreichischen Kaiser-
reiches am Ende des Ersten Weltkriegs entging Kärnten nur knapp der An-
gliederung an Jugoslawien; schließlich festigte 1920 eine Volksabstimmung den
Verbleib bei Österreich.

② Die Großglockner-Hochalpenstraße, Österreichs großartigste Bergstraße, führt vom Salzburger
Land über den Kamm der Hohen Tauern nach Kärnten. Erste Siedlung an der Südrampe ist das romantische Wintersport- und Bergsteigerdorf Heiligenblut.
Im Bild die sehenswerte gotische Pfarrkirche, dahinter der 3797 Meter hohe Großglockner.

② Am Wörther See bildet die Halbinsel Maria Wörth
einen stimmungsvollen Kontrast zur lebhaft-bunten
Ferienszenerie der jenseitigen Ufer von Velden und
Pörtschach. Die 1155 geweihte Wallfahrtskirche
beherbergt in einem gotischen Schrein Kärntens
schönste Madonnenfigur.

Atemraubend dramatische Landschaftsszenerie findet man in Kärnten – verglichen mit den Westalpen oder den Dolomiten – trotz seines großen Gebirgs-
anteils nur an wenigen Punkten, wie am Südabstieg der Hohen Tauern um
Großglockner, Sonnblick und Ankogel oder an der Südwestgrenze in der Fels-
formation der Lienzer Dolomiten. Gewiß beeindrucken viele Berge und Berggruppen durch ihre Mächtigkeit, doch zumeist herrschen harmonische, weit-
räumige, überschaubare Formen vor, als habe eine weiche, glättende Hand
versöhnlich über das Relief gestrichen. Im nordwestlichsten Zipfel des Landes
liegen die umständlichste und die bequemste Zufahrt unweit voneinander entfernt. Jene verläuft über die bis zweitausendfünfhundert Meter hochgewun-
dene Großglockner-Hochalpenstraße, diese durchstößt als Bahntunnel südlich
von Badgastein das Ankogelmassiv. Beide münden sie in das Mölltal, das sich
mit einigen Umwegen der Drau zuschlängelt. In der obersten Ecke des Tals,
wo unter dem Tauerndom des Großglockners sich erstmals menschliches Sied-
lungswesen regt, liegt das malerische *Heiligenblut*, Höhenluftkurort und Win-
tersportplatz. Sein Blickfang, die stattliche gotische Pfarrkirche St. Vinzenz,
enthält den schönsten spätgotischen Altar Kärntens. Wie Funde bezeugen,
war das Mölltal schon den Römern bekannt. Trotzdem blieb es bis heute
relativ dünn besiedelt. Erst am Unterlauf, nach Obervellach, mehren sich die
Dorfsiedlungen. In *Kolbnitz* klettern Bergbahnen auf die Kreuzeck- und
Reißeckgruppe, in *Möllbrücke* ist eine der schönsten gotischen Dorfkirchen des
Landes zu bewundern. Bei Winklern, wo ein Bergriegel die Möll zur großen
Schleife zwingt, überwindet die Höhenstraße mit kühnem Schwung die
schmale Barriere, bietet auf der Höhe des 1208 Meter hohen Iselsberges eine
prächtige Panoramasicht auf das obere Drautal und die Lienzer Dolomiten.
Unten, am Lauf der Drau, sonnen sich verschlafene Haufendörfer in der weitgeschwungenen Talschale. Daß es hier nicht immer so friedlich zuging, bezeugen die wehrhaften Burgen, die den Talboden umsäumen. Von der Burg Stein,
einem düsteren Steinklotz über dem Laubwaldhang, erzählt man eine wunder-
lich-gruselige Geschichte: Zur Zeit des Ritters Bibernell, so berichtet die Legende, stieß einer der Burgherren seine drei Töchter, die sich hinter seinem
Rücken zum Christentum bekehrt hatten, aus Zorn darüber den steilen Burg-
felsen hinunter. Durch ein Wunder blieben sie unverletzt und wandelten,
fromme Lieder singend, das Drautal hinab.

Südlich der Drau liegt, durch einen schmalen Bergzug von dieser getrennt, das
langgezogene Gailtal. Karnische Alpen und Gailtaler Kette flankieren den
gleichförmigen Grund. Dessen beschauliche Dörfer, vom Tourismus nur dünn
berieselt, führen zumeist ein behagliches Eigenleben mit unverfälschten, lie-
benswerten Zügen. Aufregender geht es im Maltatal, dem »Tal der stürzenden
Wasser«, zu. Der schmale, entlegene Bergtrog steigt vom gletscherübergossenen

㉔ Ein Dorado für Wildwasserkapitäne ist die Enns, die übermütig das steirische Gesäuse durchbricht. Im Hintergrund der 2247 Meter hohe Admonter Reichenstein.

㉕ Eine charakteristische Besonderheit Kärntens sind die überall aufgestellten Bildstöcke, oft mit Figuren, Spruchinschriften und Malereien geschmückt. Sie sind eng mit Religion, Legenden, Aberglauben und Sagen des Volkes verbunden. Blick aus der Drauniederung auf die merkwürdig geformte Koschuta, einen 2100 Meter hohen Gipfel im Zug der Karawanken, Grenzgebirge zwischen Österreich und Jugoslawien.

Ankogelmassiv in abrupten Stufen zum lebendigen Liesertal hinunter, in dem die neue Tauernautobahn, aus dem Salzburgischen kommend, dem Autoreisenden die Mühsal des langatmigen Auf und Ab über Tauernpaß und Katschberg abnimmt.

An das Liesertal schließt sich ostwärts das Nockgebiet an, ein Haufen eigenwillig geformter Buckelkuppen um die zweieinhalbtausend Meter, jede mit kahler Glatze über dem schütter bewaldeten Haarkranz. Diese Eigenart macht sie zum Tummelfeld der Skifreunde, die in Innerkrems, St. Oswald, Bad Kleinkirchheim und auf der Turracher Höhe ihre beliebtesten Stützpunkte haben.

Rings um die Kärntner Täler gruppieren sich noch mehrere Bergreviere mit wenig alpinen Superlativen, aber dafür vielen Freuden für die Liebhaber unverfälschter Natur, wie Gurktaler Alpen, Pack-, Sau- und Koralpe, mit idyllischen Ferienwinkeln für den kleinen Geldbeutel.

Alle Quellen, Bäche, Flüsse, Täler wenden sich – wie durch einen gewaltigen Magnet angezogen – der Drau zu, die sich windungsreich durch die Klagenfurter Senke, das größte Einbruchsbecken der Ostalpen, schlängelt. Die tektonischen Erdbewegungen der Vorzeit haben den Reigen der Seen hinterlassen, auf den sich Kärntens Ruhm als hochrangiges Ferienland stützt. Sie liegen unter den Südausläufern der Tauern, die sie vor den rauhen Nordwinden schützen, sind nur durch die schmale Kette der Karawanken und Karnischen Alpen vom mediterranen Friaul getrennt, das häufig den blauen Himmel und die linde Luft der Adria heraufschickt. Die Durchschnittstemperaturen vieler Seen liegen den ganzen Sommer lang konstant über zwanzig Grad, und mitunter badet man hier noch im Oktober, wenn man nördlich der Alpen schon zum Mantel greift.

Das größte und berühmteste Gewässer ist der 19,4 Quadratkilometer große *Wörther See*, an dessen Ufer sich vielumschwärmte Urlaubsorte aneinanderreihen: Das mondäne *Velden*, das betriebsame *Pörtschach,* das vom Dorf zum Kurort aufschließende *Krumpfendorf* auf der Nordseite, das ländliche *Reifnitz* und die malerische Kulturkulisse von *Maria Wörth* am Südrand. Nächstrangiges Badeziel ist der *Millstätter See,* wo sich – neben dem touristisch aufgeputzten Seeboden – in *Millstatt* das ehrwürdige Benediktinerstift mit der prächtigen Stiftskirche an die sonnseitigen Uferhalden schmiegt. Der *Ossiacher See,* unweit von Villach gelegen und durch imposante Höhenzüge umschlossen, erfreut den Besucher durch seine gedämpfte, bäuerliche Atmosphäre. Ein Geheimtip unter Individualisten ist der in einer Höhenfurche der Gailtaler Alpen versteckte, langgestreckte *Weißensee* mit vielen unberührten Uferzonen und seiner zuweilen türkisblau leuchtenden Farbe. Kenner und Liebhaber schätzen noch eine Vielzahl kleinerer Wasserbecken, wie den dörflichen *Afritzer,* den lieblich verträumten *Faaker* und den warmen *Klopeiner See.*

Doch klimatische Gunst, Seenreichtum und das High-life sommerlichen Ferienbetriebs sind nicht die einzigen Pluspunkte, die Kärntens 200 000 Fremdenbetten alljährlich zu füllen vermögen. Noch höher anzusetzen sind die Schätze an kulturell, geschichtlich und volkskundlich Sehenswertem. *Klagenfurt,* die Hauptstadt des Bundeslandes, überrascht durch sein Ortsbild als Gartenstadt. Seine berühmten Anziehungspunkte sind das Renaissance-Landhaus mit einzigartigem Wappensaal, der aus dem 16. Jahrhundert stammende Dom mit seiner prachtvollen Rokoko-Ausstattung, der Lindwurmbrunnen und mehrere Museen und Sammlungen. In *Villach,* der großen Drehscheibe der Kärntner Seenlandschaft, beeindrucken die Patrizierfassaden am Hauptplatz, die imposante Jakobskirche und das reichhaltige Stadtmuseum. *Spittal* präsentiert mit dem Stadtschloß Porcia das schönste Renaissance-Bauwerk Österreichs und *St. Veit* an der Glan neben wertvollen alten Kirchen einen der schönsten Stadtplätze des Landes. Eindrucksvolle Zeugnisse frühester Kultur finden wir in den Kirchen von *Friesach* und *St. Paul* im Lavanttal; der Dom zu Gurk, erbaut 1140 bis 1200, zählt zu den bedeutendsten Werken romanischer Kunst in Mitteleuropa. An glanzvollen Schlössern und romantischen Burgen ist ebenfalls kein Mangel, angefangen vom Renaissanceschloß Bayerhofen in Wolfsberg bis zur mächtigen, auf einem Felskegel errichteten *Burg Hochosterwitz* aus dem 16. Jahrhundert, dem Prototyp eines befestigten Burgbauwerks. Wessen Bildungsdurst damit noch nicht gestillt ist, der besuche den reizvollen Freizeitpark Minimundus bei Klagenfurt; hier findet er alle großartigen Bauwerke der Welt in verkleinerter Form nachgebildet: vom Eiffelturm in Paris bis zum Kaiserpalast in Teheran und zum Tadsch Mahal, dem traumhaften Marmorpalast im fernen Indien.

Schweiz

Berner Oberland

»Kein Gedanke, keine Beschreibung noch Erinnerung reicht an die Schönheit und Größe der Gegenstände und ihrer Lieblichkeit in solchen Lichtern, Tageszeiten und Standpunkten«, so schrieb Johann Wolfgang von Goethe 1779, von einer Wanderung über die Große und Kleine Scheidegg zurückgekommen, an Frau von Stein über seine Eindrücke aus dem Berner Oberland. Wenn der Dichterfürst, dessen Reiseberichte sonst eher spröde und prosarisch waren, sich zu solchem Lobpreis hinreißen ließ, dann ahnt man, welche hochkarätige Alpenschau diese Landschaft im Herzen der Schweiz präsentiert. Man nennt sie zu Recht einen der schönsten Flecken der Welt.

Aus der weitgeschwungenen, sanften Talregion um den Thuner- und Brienzersee, wo Mandeln und Magnolien blühen, Reben und Feigen reifen, reckt sich übergangslos ein gigantisches, geschlossenes Alpenmassiv himmelwärts, ein Relief von ungeheurer Eindruckskraft. Doch nicht nur die Mächtigkeit seiner Gipfel, deren neun die Viertausend-Meter-Marke überragen, ist imponierend; noch mehr fasziniert die unmittelbare Nachbarschaft von Wildheit und Lieblichkeit, das Nebeneinander von Schrecken und Sanftheit.

Die Geschichte des Oberlandes ist fast identisch mit der Geschichte der Stadt *Bern*. Im Jahre 1191 durch die Zähringer gegründet, wurde sie 1218 freie Reichsstadt und trat 1353 der Schweizer Eidgenossenschaft bei. Seitdem zählen Stadt und Kanton zum Schweizer Staatsgebiet. Das Berner Oberland hat außerdem noch eine eigene Geschichte, jene des Tourismus. Vor hundert Jahren wurde es von den reiselustigen Engländern entdeckt. Sie sind die eigentlichen Gründer des Touristenparadieses, tauften das Land »Playground of Europe«, den Spielplatz Europas, kamen in großen Scharen angereist und ermöglichten damit die Entwicklung zum erstrangigen Fremdenverkehrszentrum. Conan Doyle, der geistige Vater des Superdetektivs Sherlock Holmes, verlegte mehrere Schauplätze seiner Krimis in die Schweiz und ließ seinen Hauptdarsteller in den Reichenbachfällen des Haslitals ertrinken. Viele britische Einflüsse aus jener Pionierzeit, wie Hausdetails, Wortbezeichnungen, Gewohnheiten und in die Sprache eingewebte Ausdrücke, sind heute noch erhalten.

Das Berner Oberland besteht nicht nur aus dem imposanten Alpenmassiv, sondern aus einer Reihe von »Sälen«, »Zimmern« und »Kammern«, unterschiedlich in Größe, Form und Ausstattung. Der anmutigste Raum, einem Vorgarten des Südens gleichend, ist die Landschaft des *Thunersees*. An den milden Ufern gedeihen tropische Pflanzen; entfaltet sich – in der Luftlinie knapp 20 Kilometer von der eisstarrenden Gipfelkrone der Jungfrau entfernt – ein sommerseliges Strandleben mit mediterranen Zügen. Ein Heer von weißleuchtenden Segelbooten, farbenfreudige Ufergärten, sanftgeschwungene Wiesenmatten – eine betörende Symphonie anmutiger Heiterkeit. Ein Straßenband führt rings um den 48 Quadratkilometer großen See, seine Knoten sind idyllische Uferflecken und malerische Städtchen mit geheimnisvollen Schlössern (wie *Oberhofen*, *Thun* und *Spiez*) und weißen, schindelgedeckten Kirchen (wie *Amsoldingen*, *Scherzligen* und *Einigen*). Bezaubernd ist ein Spaziergang durch die altfränkischen Laubengassen der Stadt Thun, die Alexander von Humboldt eine der schönsten Städte der Welt nannte. Traumhaft versponnen liegt Spiez terrassenförmig um eine Bucht; das herrschaftliche Schloß, einst Sitz des Minnesängers Heinrich von Strättligen, ist ein romantisches Relikt aus der guten, alten Zeit. Badefreunden sei besonders das Nordufer zwischen Thun und Merligen empfohlen, das sich die »Oberländische Riviera« nennt.

Halb so groß wie der Thuner See ist der ostwärts nach einer Landbrücke anschließende *Brienzersee;* ein stilles, klargrünes Gewässer von gedämpfter, herber Schönheit. Die Berge treten hier näher an die Ufer heran, an der Südseite teilweise abrupt in den See abfallend. Die Straße verläuft nur entlang der Nordseite, verbindet hübsche, mit rustikalen Oberländer-Holzhäusern geschmückte Dörfer, unter denen besonders Brienz herausragt. Es ist Zentrum der Holzschnitzerei und der Geigenherstellung. Eine pittoreske Dampfeisenbahn schnaubt mühsam auf das 2350 Meter hohe Brienzer Rothorn hinauf, eine der vielen Aussichtslogen vor den Götterthronen der Berner Alpen.

Touristische Hauptstadt des Berner Oberlandes ist *Interlaken*. Manche Städte liegen an einem See, einem Fluß, andere an keinem von beiden. Interlaken hat sich etwas besonderes einfallen lassen: Es liegt zwischen zwei Seen, nämlich auf der vier Kilometer breiten Landzone, dem »Bödeli«, das Thuner- und Brienzersee voneinander trennt. Ein nobles, sympathisches Kleinstädtchen, Pforte in das Grindelwalder und Lauterbrunnental, zentraler Ausgangspunkt zu allen touristischen Zielen der Urlaubsregion; doch nicht nur ein Umschlagplatz, sondern auch selbständiger Erholungsort. Eleganter Treffpunkt ist der Höheweg, ein Promenier-Boulevard mit internationaler Atmosphäre, umsäumt von prunkvollen Hotels, hübschen Boutiquen und prächtigen Parkanlagen. Der Nimbus Interlakens stammt noch aus der Zeit, in der man den Bergen nicht so nahe auf den Leib rückte wie heute, sie lieber aus gebührendem Abstand bestaunte.

In *Wilderswil*, einem südlichen Vorort Interlakens, klettert die Zahnradbahn auf die 2101 Meter hohe Schynige Platte. Deren Gipfel bietet eine geraffte

Totalschau des Dreigestirns Eiger, Mönch und Jungfrau, das aus Matten- und Arvengrün atemberaubend kühn in den Himmel wächst. Unmittelbar davor liegen die Täler von Lauterbrunnen und Grindelwald.

Das *Lauterbrunnental,* ein tief eingesunkener Gletschertrog mit lotrecht hochfluchtenden Felswänden, schiebt sich cañonartig südwärts bis an die Sockel der Bergriesen. Hoch oben, an den Rändern der Felsbrüstungen, von denen stiebende Wasserfälle talwärts flattern, liegen die Ferienorte *Wengen* und *Mürren* – beide ohne Straßenzufahrten und nur per Bergbahn zugänglich.

Von ganz anderem Zuschnitt ist das *Grindelwalder Tal*: Eine weite, offene Schale mit weichen, langgezogenen Hangformen, ein Mosaikteppich aus Alpweiden und Waldparzellen, überstreut mit Hunderten von Berghäusern, Hütten und Stadeln. Zwischen den beiden Tälern, auf begrüntem Vorgebirgswall, liegt die Kleine Scheidegg, Umschlagpunkt der Bergbahnen von hüben und drüben, Startbahnhof zur Fahrt auf das Jungfraujoch. Neun Kilometer lang schraubt sich die Jungfraubahn durch Tunnelröhren bis zum 3454 Meter hohen Gipfeljoch zwischen Mönch und Jungfrau hinauf. Oben, an der höchsten Eisenbahnstation Europas, erwarten uns respektable Attraktionen: Gletschergrotten und Eishöhle, ein traumhaftes Panorama, Hundeschlittenfahrt und Sommerskilauf.

Östlich von Jungfrau und Mönch reckt der Eiger seine düsterabweisende Nordwand 1800 Meter senkrecht in Wolkenhöhen. Ihre Chronik erzählt die dramatische Geschichte des jahrzehntelang währenden Kampfes um den letzten unbezwungenen Gipfel der Alpen.

Eine andere, nicht minder prächtige Stube des Berner Oberlandes ist das von der Grimselstraße durchzogene *Haslital*, das die Hochgebirgsgruppen Dammastock und Finsteraarhorn auseinanderspaltet. Das wilddramatische Oberhasli, von hohem Steingemäuer umklammert und von schaurigen Abgründen zerfurcht, ist reich an Bergkristallen, die früher durch die »Strahler«, einer eigenen Berufsgruppe, systematisch aus dem Granit gesprengt wurden. Die schreckerregende Szenerie wandelt sich bei Innertkirchen zum runden Talkessel; die Aare durchstößt in tiefer Schlucht den Felsriegel des Kirchets, dann weitet sich das Land zum flachen, frischgrünen Boden von *Meiringen*. Dessen größter Anziehungspunkt ist das Hochtal *Rosenlaui*, Dorado der Alpenmaler und Bergwanderer. Rings um den idyllischen Alpwiesengrund, den der hurtige Reichenbach durchplätschert, türmt sich die großartige Kulisse der Berner Alpen auf: das steingewordene Chaos der Engelhörner, die Felsriffe von Wellhorn und Wetterhorn, die drohend herabhängenden Eiswülste des Rosenlauigletschers.

Das *Kandertal,* das sich vom Thunersee südwärts zieht, kann ebenso mit großartigen alpinen Bildern aufwarten – besonders im Talschluß von Kandersteg, wo eine Garde willkürlich gruppierter Urgesteinskolosse den Blick fesselt.

Vielumschwärmtes Ausflugsziel ist der lifterschlossene Oeschinensee, der sich verträumt unter die eisübergossenen Fluchten des Blümlisalpstocks duckt.

Fröhlich, hemdärmelig-volkstümlich gibt sich der Ferienort *Adelboden* im Engstligental, der sich behäbig an eine weitgeschwungene Südhangterrasse schmiegt. Hier, wo fünf Talgründe sternförmig zusammenlaufen, treten die strengen Gebärden alpiner Urgewalt zurück, weichen einer ausgewogenen landschaftlichen Harmonie. Die hohen Gipfel bedrücken nicht mehr, sondern umkränzen.

Eine Landschaft mit liebenswürdigem Charme ist das *Simmental.* Die Felsen sind abgerückt zum schmückenden Dekor, es breiten sich satte, blumenübersäte Weidenmatten aus, belebt durch schattige Waldpartien und verspielt angeordnete Hügelkuppen. Eine Augenweide sind die prächtigen Bauernhäuser – übrigens die schönsten der Schweiz –, rustikale, vereinzelt bis zweihundert Jahre alte Holzblockbauten mit reichem ornamentalem Schmuck.

Im westlichen »Stübli« des Oberlandes, dem *Saanental,* vereinigen sich alle Eigenheiten zum beglückenden Gesamtbild: Wiesenhänge und Waldkuppen, Wildbäche und Bergblumen, rauhes Felsgestein und harmonisch geschwungene Firngrate, pittoreske Bauerngehöfte und die schicken Chalets des Nobelkurorts *Gstaad.*

Wallis

Die geschlossene Front der Alpen, die sich in großem Bogen von Wien bis Nizza spannt, ist an einer Stelle in der Längsrichtung gespalten. Gerade dort, wo sie mit Gipfelhöhen über viertausend Meter ihre Formen ins Gigantische steigert, grub die Rhône eine tiefe Furche, die Massive der Berner und Walliser Alpen auseinanderspreizend. Diese Tallandschaft von der Rhônequelle bis zur Einmündung des Flusses in den Genfer See – seitlich erweitert zu den Gipfelkämmen der Randgebirge – umschließt der Schweizer Kanton Wallis. Die topographische Einheit täuscht über das Wesen dieser Provinz, die eine ungeheuere Fülle von Gegensätzen enthält. Üppiges Feldergrün und karge Karsthalden, die Glut südlicher Sonne und den tödlichen Atem des »Eismeers«, rotverbrannte Weinberge und weißglitzernde Gletschergipfel, das einschläfernde Gezirpe der Zikaden und die in Orgeltönen heulenden Stürme. Vielfältig ist auch die Wesensart der Menschen. Verschlossene, wortkarge Bergbauern, wendige, clevere Hoteliers und Touristikbedienstete, Winzer- und Fischertypen voll südländisch-heiterer Gelassenheit.

Die Geschichte des Wallis berichtet von Kelten und Römern, die das Land besiedelten und beherrschten; von den Burgundern, die über das untere Rhônetal geboten und mit den Wallisern des Oberlandes jahrhundertelang verfeindet waren. Auf diese Erbfeindschaft geht die Sprachgrenze zwischen Deutsch und Französisch zurück, die sich zwischen Leuk und Sierre quer durch das Tal zieht. Im 17. Jahrhundert stritten Fürstbischöfe und Bauernschaften um die Vorherrschaft, 1810 überrollte und annektierte Napoleon das Land, das schließlich zur politischen Einheit fand und sich 1815 der Schweiz als Kanton eingliederte.

Touristisch zählt das Wallis zu den großartigsten Landschaften, die Europa zu bieten hat, unübertroffen in der Gewalt seiner Berge, der Tiefen der Täler, der Kühnheit der Kontraste. Der Korridor der Rhône hat wenig Zugänge; nur ein einziger, jener vom Genfer See her, ist eben. Alle anderen sind Pässe, die sich über die Joche der Hochalpen auf den bis unter fünfhundert Meter Meereshöhe abfallenden Talboden herabwinden: Der liebenswürdige Simplon, der epische Große St. Bernhard, die dramatische Bergstraßengabel von Grimsel und Furka, der großräumige Forclaz und der theatralische Nufenen. Die kürzeste Verbindung mit der Zentralschweiz führt durch den 15 Kilometer langen Lötschbergtunnel, der das Massiv der Berner Alpen durchstößt.

Beginnen wir mit unseren Streifzügen durch das Wallis in der obersten Tal-
kammer der Rhône, die sich *Goms* nennt. In der klar gegliederten, langgezogenen Bergschale, die ein frischer Wind durchstreicht, reiht sich Dorf an Dorf,
jedes blitzsauber, mit weißleuchtendem Kirchturm und dem sanften Tiefbraun
der sonnengerösteten Holzhäuser. *Oberwald, Geschinen, Münster, Reckingen*
und noch ein Dutzend weiterer idyllischer Flecken – eine liebliche kleine Welt,
eingebettet in einen Fleckerlteppich von Wiesen und Feldparzellen. Doch das
Goms ist nicht nur eine Schweizer Bilderbuchlandschaft, sondern auch die
künstlerisch reichste Region des Wallis. Jeden der Orte ziert eine üppig geschmückte, gotische oder barocke Kirche. Unter den vielen Kostbarkeiten ragen
Jörg Kellers Flügelaltar in Münster und die prachtvolle Rokokoausstattung
der Pfarrkirche von Reckingen heraus.

Rhôneabwärts, wo mächtige Felsflanken das Tal einengen, laden in *Fiesch* und
Mörel mehrere Bergbahnen zur Fahrt auf Eggishorn, Rieder- und Bettmeralp
ein, einen zusammenhängenden Höhenzug mit freien Alpterrassen, unter
dessen Nordabhängen sich der Aletschgletscher, mit 24 Kilometern Länge der
größte Eisstrom der Alpen, überaus eindrucksvoll darbietet.

Bei *Brig* weitet sich der Talboden zur breiten Flußniederung. Wahrzeichen des
malerischen, freundlichen Städtchens ist der Stockalperpalast, ein imposantes,
dreitürmiges Bauwerk mit prächtigem Arkadenhof – einst das Privatschloß
des Handelsherrn Kaspar von Stockalper, der im 17. Jahrhundert über den
Simplonpaß und seinem Handelsweg herrschte und daraus Macht und Reichtum gewann.

Großartige Eindrücke vermittelt die Fahrt durch das hier beginnende Haupttal des Wallis. Der brettebene Boden wird zum fruchtbaren Garten mit weitläufigen Weinhängen, Maisfeldern und Obstwäldern, genannt das schweize-
rische »Kalifornien«, ein alpiner Vorhof des subtropischen Südens. An den
beiden Talrändern staffeln sich, Stufe um Stufe emporwallend, die Reben-,
Wiesen- und Laubbaumterrassen bis zu den nackten Felsschroffen und den
schneegekrönten Gipfelketten hinauf. Die Fruchtbarkeit des regenarmen, von
Gluthitze überlagerten Talkessels wird durch ein kompliziertes System Hun-
derter von Wasserläufen genährt, die seit altersher das kostbare Naß von den
Gletschern und Bergbächen talwärts leiten.

Uralte, romantische Städtchen und wehrhafte Siedlungen unterbrechen das
üppige Grün: *Leuk* mit seinen mittelalterlichen Gassen, mit Bischofsschloß
und Herrenhäusern; das malerische Sierre mit Klöstern und Schlößchen auf
den skurril verstreuten Hügelhöckern, die von einem vorgeschichtlichen Berg-
sturz herrühren; das ehrwürdige, stolze *Sion*, Hauptstadt des Wallis, ganz
von Rebenhängen umschlossen, beherrscht von den markanten Silhouetten der
burgengekrönten Felsriffe Valeria und Tourbillon. Weiter talabwärts, am
großen Rhôneknie, am Knotenpunkt der Paßübergänge Großer St. Bernhard

und Col de la Forclaz, liegt das aus einer Römersiedlung entstandene *Martigny*, über das noch heute die aus dem 13. Jahrhundert stammende Burgruine La Bâtiaz wacht. Besonders wirkungsvoll präsentiert sich die Rhônelandschaft von den mächtigen Terrassenhängen über dem Talgrund, die sich, straßentechnisch gut erschlossen, zu beliebten Erholungsregionen entwickelt haben, wie *Crans-Montana, Vercorin, Anzère* oder *Haute-Nendaz.*

Nach ihrem 150 Kilometer langen Lauf durch großzügig geformtes Talterrain durchstößt die Rhône bei *St. Maurice,* dem wehrhaften Brückenstädtchen mit dem ältesten Kloster der Schweiz, die Bergbarriere zwischen Dents du Midi und Dent de Morcles, schlängelt sich behäbig durch die breitgewalzte Flußauenlandschaft und ergießt sich in den Genfer See.

Das Kolossalgemälde des Rhônetals ist nur eines der Szenenbilder aus dem vielgestaltigen Wallis. Dessen unbestrittene Glanzpunkte finden sich in den tief eingekerbten, nach Nord und Süd ausstrahlenden Seitentälern, die sich hoch oben vor dem ewigen Eis verlieren. Die touristisch berühmtesten sind das Saas- und das Mattertal. Sie ziehen sich von *Visp* – zunächst vereint – südwärts, spalten sich bei Stalden, wo hoch oben bei *Visperterminen* bis 1200 Meter der Höllenwein gedeiht, gabelförmig auf und winden sich bis zu den Sockeln der viereinhalbtausend Meter hochragenden Gipfelriesen der Mischabelgruppe, des Monte-Rosa-Massivs und Matterhorns hinauf. Im Talschluß des Saasgrundes liegt *Saas Fee,* Inbegriff des Gletscherdorfes, am Fuß einer überwältigenden Formation der Eisströme. In der weißen Jahreszeit vielumschwärmtes Skiparadies, im Sommer einer der exklusivsten Ausgangspunkte für Hochtouren auf das Dach Europas – zu dem Dom (4545 m), Nadelhorn (4327 m) und Alphubel (4206 m), in die weltenferne, gigantische Hochalpenregion des Wallis.

In *Zermatt,* einem der berühmtesten Dörfer der Schweiz, sieht man vom Tal aus zwar keine Gletscher, doch dafür die majestätische Gestalt des Matterhorns (4478 m), das als schönster Berg der Alpen gilt. Im autofreien Dorf, das nur per Bahn erreichbar ist, entfaltet sich zwischen alten Holzstadeln und modischen Boutiquen, mondänen Hotels und rustikalen Gaststätten eine lebensfrohe Ferienstimmung, vom Gebimmel der Pferdedroschken melodisch untermalt. Zahnrad- und Gondelbahnen klettern zu den klassischen Aussichtslogen Gornergrat und Schwarzsee hinauf, welche die großartigste Alpenschau bieten. Skifreunde können sogar im Sommer auf dem über dreitausend Meter hoch gelegenen Plateau Rosa ihre Schwünge ziehen, Bergfreunde in Wanderschuhen finden ein Netz von mehr als dreihundert Kilometern markierter Wege. Von ganz anderem Charakter ist das nördlich der Rhône in die Berner Alpen hochführende Lötschental, eine einsame, in sich geschlossene Bergoase mit viel Brauchtum und Kolorit, Urlaubsziel für Individualisten. Das im wildzerklüfteten Dalatal genießerisch unter den Felswänden der Lees- und Plattenhörner hingelagerte *Leukerbad* lockt mit seinen Thermalquellen Kurgäste aus aller Welt an. Nicht minder anziehend ist für Bergwanderer der in den Stein gehauene Serpentinenweg zum Gemmipaß, der auf tollkühn angelegtem Felspfad Schönheit und Schrecken der Alpenwelt gefahrlos erleben läßt.

Unter den südlichen Seitentälern der Rhône sind das Val d'Anniviers (Eivischtal) und das Val d'Hérens (Eringertal) besonders vielfältig und interessant. In jenem leben heute noch nomadisierende Bauern, in diesem sind die skurrilen Erdpyramiden von Euseigne, das einem volkskundlichen Freizeitmuseum gleichende Evolène und der großartige Talschluß von Arolla lohnende Ziele.

Die Stichtäler des Unterwallis fallen gegenüber den vorgenannten nicht ab, sie übertreffen diese sogar mit ihren ins Maßlose gesteigerten Dimensionen; so das Val de Bagne, über dem sich das Skidorf *Verbier* in der Bergschale sonnt, und das Trienttal, dessen schaurige Abgründe keine durchgehende Straße zulassen.

Tessin

Die »Sonnenstube der Schweiz« nennt man den Kanton, der sich von den dreitausend Meter hohen Gletschergipfeln der Zentralalpen wie ein Keil bis an den Rand der lombardischen Tiefebene südwärts schiebt. Eine Landschaft, in der Eishauch und Sonnenglut zusammentreffen, in der man italienisch spricht, italienisch lebt und schweizerisch denkt. Doch das sind nicht die einzigen Gegensätze. In dieser Provinz der Kontraste sind auch Wohlhabenheit und Armut, sublimierter Komfort und spartanische Lebensweise, lärmende Betriebsamkeit und weltabgeschiedene Stille dicht benachbart.

Überall im Land finden sich die Spuren seiner reichen, oft recht turbulenten Vergangenheit. Franken und Langobarden, Kaiser Friedrich Barbarossa und die Mailänder Herzöge der Visconti und Sforza, römische Bischöfe und der König von Frankreich rauften um das Territorium auf der Sonnenseite der Alpen, bis schließlich 1512 endgültig die Eidgenossen einziehen und die Vögte von Uri, Schwyz und Unterwalden von den Schlössern Bellinzonas aus das Land regieren. 1803 verleiht Napoleon dem Tessin den Status eines selbständigen Kantons, der sich 1830 eine liberale Verfassung gibt.

Bemerkenswert ist das Verhältnis des Tessin zu Kunst und Kultur. In seinen Tälern wuchsen Generationen von Baumeistern, Bildhauern und Malern heran. Da in der engeren Heimat ihrer künstlerische Entfaltung mangels Geldgeber Grenzen gesetzt waren, zogen sie hinaus an die Höfe der Päpste, Kaiser, Zaren und Sultane und schufen dort, in Rom, Venedig, Moskau, Neapel, Pisa und Konstantinopel prächtige Bauwerke, Fassaden, Skulpturen und Gemälde von weltweitem Rang. Viele von ihnen kamen – wenn der Zenith des Schaffens überschritten war – wieder nach Hause, bauten talauf und talab Kirchen und Kapellen, Villen und Glockentürme, wie sie uns heute noch im Tessin auf Schritt und Tritt begegnen.

Benannt ist das Tessin nach dem Fluß Ticino, der am 3061 Meter hohen Pizzo Gallina, nächst dem Nufenenpaß, entspringt, die Provinz in ihrer ganzen Ausdehnung durchzieht und in der Ebene von Magadino in den Lago Maggiore mündet. Er bildet das tief eingeschnittene Haupttal des Kantons, die *Valle Leventina*; in ihr verläuft das große Sammelband der Touristenströme, die über den Gotthardpaß von Norden kommen. Zu Unrecht wird die Leventina von vielen Autotouristen als Durchzugsland eingestuft, das man – im Drang zum Süden – möglichst rasch hinter sich zu bringen trachtet. Doch es ist durchaus lohnend, den Korridor in den »Midi« näher kennenzulernen.

An der Südrampe des Gotthardpasses, dessen komfortables Autobahnband die
Schrecken der alten Paßstraße im Val Tremola, dem »Tal des Zitterns«, vergessen läßt, empfängt uns der große Talkessel von Airolo. Das Gewirr von
Verladeanlagen und Baustellen erweckt wenig Sympathie, doch wenig später
formt sich das Gelände zur eindrucksvollen Szenerie: Der hurtige Ticino
durcheilt die Sohle der tiefen Talfurche, springt über Felskanten und Geröll,
flankiert von einer mächtigen Garde hoher Berge. Allmählich treten die eng
zusammengerückten Steinflanken auseinander, geben luftige Hochterrassen
und Hangzüge frei, von denen wolkennahe Dörfer und Kirchtürme herunter-
grüßen. Ein einmaliges Erlebnis ist es, in diesem Bereich den Süden schritt-
weise zu »erwandern«. Eine Wanderwegkette, die »Strada alta«, führt auf
halber Höhe zwischen Grund und Gipfeln das Tal entlang bis Biasca, der
Schwelle zur leventinischen Riviera. Wer mit seiner Zeit rationell umgehen
muß, fährt in wenigen Minuten von Piotta mit der kühn hochstrebenden
Zahnradbahn zur 1850 Meter hohen Seenplatte des Lago Ritom, wo sich
Perspektiven großen alpinen Stils bieten.

Bei *Rodi-Fiesso* begegnet man in der talverengenden Piottinoschlucht dem
Chaos alpiner Urgewalt, dann versöhnt das Tal mit grünen Matten, malerischen Wasserfällen, den ersten Kastanien und Weinreben. In *Giornico*, einem
rustikalen levantinischen Dorf, sollte man nicht versäumen, die aus dem 12.
Jahrhundert stammende, in ihrer Schlichtheit eindrucksvolle Kirche San Nico-
lao zu besuchen. Bei *Biasca* weitet sich die schluchtähnliche Talenge zur üppig-
fruchtbaren »Riviera«, die sich nach Bellinzona in der Magadino-Ebene fort-
setzt.
Ähnliche, nicht minder schöne Eindrücke bieten die beiden anderen Alpen-
pforten in das Tessin, der Lukmanier- und der San-Bernardino-Paß. Jener
schlängelt sich unter den weißen Kronen des Adulamassivs durch das malerische Bleniotal, unter dessen verstreuten Bergsiedlungen der Campanile von
Negrentino herausragt; dieser steigt vom Rheinwaldgebirge mit großzügigen
Serpentinen ins Val Mesolcina, das Misox, herunter.

Alle Zufahrten aus dem Norden vereinigen sich in *Bellinzona*, der südlän-
disch-heiteren, von trutzigen Burgen überragten Hauptstadt des Kantons.
Während man sich anderwärts zumeist mit einer wehrhaften Schloßanlage be-
gnügte, schien die besondere strategische Bedeutung der Stadt am Schlüssel-
punkt zwischen dem Gotthardpaß und der Lombardei deren drei zu erfor-
dern: Castello Grande, später »Castello Uri« genannt, Castello Montebello,
das »Castello Schwyz« und Castello di Sasso Corbaro, das »Castello Unterwalden«. Ein Spaziergang durch die imposanten Festungsanlagen veranschau-
licht die kriegerische Vergangenheit Bellinzonas.

78

Nun kommen wir endlich in jenes Teilstück des Tessin, das der Unkundige in seiner Phantasie als den leuchtenden Inbegriff dieser Landschaft sieht: Das sommerselige Ferienparadies um *Lago Maggiore* und *Luganer See*. Durch die fruchtschwere, von Mais und Reben strotzende Magadino-Niederung kommend, besuchen wir zunächst den Lago Maggiore. Nur ein Fünftel seiner 212 Quadratkilometer großen Wasserfläche liegt in der Schweiz, umso mehr sind deren Ufer zur paradiesischen Urlaubslandschaft verdichtet. Da ist alles angeboten, wovon die Sehnsucht nach dem Süden träumt: Weiße Barken auf tiefblauem Wasserspiegel, feinsandige Badestrände, farbenfreudige Bootshäfen, Promenaden unter Palmen, pittoreske Gassen mit schattigen Laubengängen und einladenden Cafétisch-Brigaden, Belcanto in Adagio und Fortissimo, das Dolce-far-niente schlechthin.

Vielumschwärmte Ferienzentren sind die Städte *Locarno* und *Ascona*. Sie liegen, spiegelbildlich einander abgekehrt, auf einer riesigen Schwemmlandzunge, welche die Maggia in Jahrtausenden weit in den See hineingeschoben hat. Trotz intensiver Bebauung hat der kilometerlange Lido Locarnos noch nichts von seiner befreienden Weite eingebüßt, man spaziert stundenlang zwischen Pinien und Zypressen, Zedern und Mimosen, Magnolien und Feigenbäumen. In den Arkaden am alten Markt herrscht unbeschwerte, überschwängliche Urlaubsstimmung bis in den späten Abend. Eine »Funi« (Seilbahn) bringt uns in Minuten zur berühmten Wallfahrtskirche Madonna del Sasso hinauf, von deren Säulenloggia sich der ganze Zauber von Stadt, See und Uferlandschaft entfaltet. – Gegenüber, dem Lago Maggiore nach Süden zugewandt, liegt das kleine, intimere Ascona, früher Kolonie der Künstler, heute Modeort mit pseudo-romantisch verbrämter Kulisse. Kenner und Leute, die den Laufsteg der Eitelkeiten verlassen können, schätzen am Lago Maggiore andere Ziele: Etwa das entzückende *Ronco* auf dem Hangbalkon über den Brissago-Inseln, das stille *Vira* am jenseitigen Ufer oder eines der Dutzend verträumten Dörfer rings um den See.

Ähnlich buntschillernd wie in Locarno ist auch der Stil im jenseits von Gambarogno und Monte Ceneri liegenden *Lugano*, wenn auch mit einigen Abweichungen. Lugano ist als Stadt größer, turbulenter, »italienischer«; dagegen ist sein See kleiner, überschaubarer, ein verwirrendes System verschlungener Wasserbecken. Daß im Luganer See seit einiger Zeit das Baden verboten ist, wirkt sich auf die Art der Gäste aus. Sie sind hier mehr gesetzten Alters, weniger am Strandflirt und mehr an kulturell und landschaftlich Sehenswertem interessiert, wie es in und um Lugano überreich geboten wird. Lugano, das »Rio des Tessin«, amphitheatralisch vom See aus am Hanggrund hochwachsend, hat prächtige Kirchen und Paläste, verführerisch üppige Einkaufsstraßen, besuchenswerte Museen, Theater und Veranstaltungen. Besonderes Plus sind die vielen Ausflugsziele – allen voran die beiden seilbahnerschlossenen Aussichtsberge *Monte Brè* und *Monte San Salvatore,* dann das in subtropischer Lage am Südkap hingeschmiegte Morcote, das malerische Fischerdorf Gandria, in dem die Häuser buchstäblich aus dem Wasser wachsen, und das kokette Campione, eine italienische Enklave am Ostufer, das von seiner stark frequentierten Spielbank lebt. Wer mehr das Ursprüngliche, Unverfälschte liebt, wird von Streifzügen durch die Ortschaften des Malcantone, das Val Colla und das nach Süden abflachende Mendrisiotto begeistert sein.

Außer seinen großen Zufahrtstraßen und seinem Seenparadies hat das Tessin noch ein anderes Gesicht, das nur wenige kennen. Es sind die – abseits der Durchgangsstraßen – nach Nordwesten fächerförmig ausstrahlenden Seitentäler zwischen dem Lago Maggiore und den Tessiner Alpen. Sie haben, weit entfernt von touristischer Tünche, alle ihre herbe, eigenwillige Schönheit: Das weite *Maggiatal* mit Wasserstürzen und schwarzem Felsgemäuer, das wildromantische *Verzascatal* mit den smaragdgrünen Bergbächen, das entlegene *Onsernonetal,* wo vor armseligen Steinhütten emsige Frauenhände Strohwaren flechten, und schließlich das wildzerklüftete *Centovalli,* wo sich über schaurigen Abgründen einsame Bergnester schwindelerregend kühn in den Fels krallen.

Italien

Südtirol und Dolomiten

»Das Land vereint alles, was man Schönes wünschen kann. Dort fällt kein Schnee mehr, und der Sommer dörrt nicht mehr aus. Weite Ebenen und hohe Berge, köstliches Grün, frische Wasser, alte Burgen und fröhliche Menschen. Dort möcht ich wohnen.« Diese Worte sind nicht von einem redegewandten Fremdenverkehrswerber, sondern von dem als »großer Schweiger« bekannten preußischen Generalfeldmarschall Helmuth von Moltke. Es war seine Liebeserklärung an das Tal von Meran, das er vor 130 Jahren aufsuchte. Die Meraner Landschaft ist der Inbegriff dessen, was man sich unter Südtiroler Ferienparadies vorstellt: Eine weite, offene Talschale, von der Sonne verwöhnt, angefüllt mit fruchtschweren Obstwäldern und unabsehbaren Rebengärten, verziert mit schlanken Zypressen und zierlichen Mandelbäumen, umrahmt von hochgestaffelten Terrassenhängen, überragt von nacktem, heroischen Fels. Mittendrin das liebenswert-altmodische Kurstädtchen mit winkeligen Gassen, schattigen Laubengängen und palmenbesäumten Promenaden. *Meran* ist die Ferienhauptstadt Südtirols, einst Weltkurort wie Baden-Baden oder Karlsbad, heute ein Gemütsreservat der österreichischen, der kaiserlichen Zeit.
Wirtschaftliches und politisches Zentrum ist *Bozen*, dreißig Kilometer etschtalabwärts gelegen. Eine imponierende, lebenssprühende Stadt mit sehenswertem historischem Kern, aber durch Industrie und Gewerbe ausgewuchert, vom Fremdenverkehr überfordert. Selbstbewußt und genießerisch beherrscht sie den weiten Talboden, auf dem sich die Wasser von Eisack und Talfer mit der Etsch vereinigen; versöhnt mit einem Reigen anmutiger Berghänge, auf denen die berühmten Weine reifen: der herb-duftige Leitacher, der erdig-kraftvolle St. Justiner, der blumige, rubinrote St. Magdalener. Bozens schönste Perspektiven liegen draußen, auf den Höhen über der Stadt. Auf den Burgen der Landschaft *Überetsch*, *Sigmundskron* und *Hocheppan*, in *Jenesien* und in *Oberbozen* auf dem Bergbalkon des Ritten. Hier steigert sich das weinselige Sonnenland der Talschaften zum gewaltigen Panorama, wachsen aus dunstiger Niederung die Hügel, Bergwälle und Felstürme in gigantischer Anhäufung dem Himmelsblau entgegen. Eindrucksvollster Blickfang sind die steinernen Bastionen der Dolomiten, unter denen sich das klassische Relief des Rosengartens effektvoll präsentiert. Einst taufte man die Dolomiten, diese wunderliche Ansammlung phantastisch geformter Felsriffe über lyrischen Wiesengründen, das »Reich der bleichen Berge«, worin ihr magisches und sagenhaftes Wesen zum Ausdruck kommt. Doch das fahle Gesicht ist nur eine von vielen

36 Der Zauber der Dolomiten liegt in den Kontrasten zwischen sanft hingelagerten Wiesenmatten und jäh hochgetürmten bizarren Felsformationen. Der Confinboden auf der östlichen Seiseralm gegen den 3181 Meter hohen Langkofelstock. Rechts im Bild, von Wolken umspielt, der Plattkofel (2955 m), links die Langkofelscharte, von der nach hüben und drüben Wanderwege und Skipisten talwärts führen.

37 Dolomitenlandschaft großen Stils präsentieren die Berge um Cortina d'Ampezzo: Die steinernen Urweltkolosse Drei Zinnen (3003 m). Ihre Besteigung ist versierten Kletterern vorbehalten; gewöhnlich Sterbliche gelangen vom Misurinasee auf einer reizvollen Bergstraße bis an den Sockel der Felstürme.

Ausdrucksarten; je nach Tageszeit und Beleuchtung wechseln die Farben vom schwefeligen Schwarz über tintiges Blau und Grau bis zum strahlenden Gelb und flammenden Rot. Am schönsten sind diese Farbenspiele zu Zeiten des Sonnenuntergangs. Während sich über die Talgründe schon der Schattenschirm der Dämmerung legt, verwandeln die letzten Sonnenstrahlen den Rosengarten in ein brennendes Felsrelief – man erfand dafür die Bezeichnung »Alpenglühen«.

Die ladinischen Urbewohner der Dolomiten knüpften an solche Erscheinungen geheimnisvolle Vorgänge aus der Götter- und Sagenwelt, und kaum eine andere Landschaft ist so reich an märchenhafter Volkspoesie. Da wimmelt es nur so von Waldprinzessinnen, Wintergöttinnen, Zwergstämmen und Riesengeschlechtern. Die schönste Sage ist jene vom Rosengarten und seinem abendlichen Alpenglühen: Vor langer Zeit, so erzählt man, habe ein König einen mit Rosen bedeckten Berg besessen. Angelockt durch die Rosenpracht, kamen Feinde, bezwangen den König und sein Volk und verwüsteten den Garten. Als der Feind abgezogen war, sagte der König: »Schuld an unserem Unglück sind die vielen Rosen. Sie sollen verschwinden und weder bei Tag noch bei Nacht zu sehen sein«. Und er verzauberte den blühenden Garten in wildgeformtes Gestein. Doch er hatte in seiner Zauberformel die kleine Spanne zwischen Tag und Nacht, die Dämmerung, vergessen. Und so kommt es, daß zu dieser Stunde der Rosengarten wieder aufblüht.

Wer Südtirol – und sei es auch nur flüchtig – kennenlernen will, kommt nicht an seiner Geschichte vorbei. Sie ist hier nicht angestaubte Vergangenheit, sondern lebendige Gegenwart. Nach der Herrschaft der Römer besiedeln im 6. Jahrhundert die Baiern das Land. Im Mittelalter untersteht es den Bischöfen von Trient und Brixen. 1141 bauen Vinschgauer Grafen das Schloß Tirol bei Meran, nennen sich fortan Grafen von Tirol und vereinigen in der Folgezeit die Provinzen diesseits und jenseits der Alpen zur Grafschaft Tirol, die vom Inntal bis zum Gardasee reicht. 1363 kommt Tirol an die Habsburger, wird eines der Stammländer des Kaiserreichs. Während der Zeit Napoleons ist Tirol wenige Jahre an Bayern angegliedert, wird durch den Wiener Kongreß 1814 wieder der österreichisch-habsburgischen Krone zurückgegeben. Die einschneidendste Veränderung in der jüngeren Geschichte erlebt das Land nach dem Ersten Weltkrieg. Tirol wird geteilt: Der Norden bleibt bei Österreich, der Süden kommt zu Italien, der Brenner wird Grenze. Durch Bevölkerungsverschiebungen, durch Unterdrückung von Sprache und Kultur versucht Rom, Südtirol zu italienisieren. Dies erregte den Widerstand des Volkes, es kam zu jahrzehntelangen Spannungen und Unruhen. Umsiedlungsvorhaben, zwischen Hitler und Mussolini vereinbart, scheiterten an den Kriegsereignissen. 1961

bis 1967 flammt der Widerstand der Südtiroler erneut auf, sie versuchen mit Bombenterror die Italiener zu verjagen. Erst seit 1969, mit der Einigung über das sogenannte »Südtirol-Paket«, zeichnet sich das friedliche Nebeneinander ab; Südtirol bekommt vermehrte Rechte, einen autonomen Verwaltungsstatus. Bei den Weinbauern um Bozen und Meran gilt der alte Spruch: »Wer rechtens Herr des Schlosses [Tirol] ist, dem gehört das Land.« Schloß Tirol wurde 1973 Eigentum der Südtiroler Landesregierung.

Mag sein, daß den Urlaubsgast dies alles wenig interessiert. Er fährt dorthin, um Berge, Sonne und Wein zu genießen. Doch die Unterschiede der Sprachen, Kulturkreise, Wesens- und Lebensarten werden selbst dem oberflächlichen Gemüt spürbar, wenn es eine urgemütliche Wirtsstube in Brixen mit Holzdecke und Butzenscheiben und eine laute Caféteria in San Martino di Castrozza mit Steinfußboden und Plastikstühlen miteinander vergleicht. Trotz aller nivellierenden Tendenz des Tourismus zieht sich eine unsichtbare Grenze quer durch den Raum Südtirols und der Dolomiten.

Wer auf dem großen Band der Südautobahn über Brenner, Eisack- und Etschtal das Land durchfährt, erhascht nur winzige Streiflichter. Kurvt man aber die kleinen Bergsträßlein hinauf – von *Sterzing* zum *Penser Joch,* von *Brixen* zur *Plose,* von *Waidbruck* nach *Kastelruth* oder von *Meran* zum *Gampen-Joch* –, dann beginnt die Landschaft zu leben und zu wachsen, blättert sich auf wie ein mehrdimensionaler Panorama-Atlas. Der ganze Bereich ist mit einem Labyrinth dieser kühnen Gebirgsstraßen bespickt; manche sind hochberühmt, wie Mendelpaß, Pordoi-, Sella- oder Grödner Joch, andere haben noch nie ein deutsches Autokennzeichen gesehen. Allen gemeinsam ist, daß sie die Hochgebirgswelt in einem Ausmaß und einer Vielfalt erschließen, wie dies in keinem anderen Teil Europas geboten wird.

Das Land hat viele, frappierend unterschiedliche Gesichter: Am *Reschenpaß,* der mit langer Hangtraverse aus dem Inntal hochklimmt, ragt aus dem kalten Stausee die Kirchturmspitze des in ihm versunkenen Dorfes; südlich davon versetzt uns der Marienberg mit gewaltigen, abgeplatteten Terrassen in eine »tibetanische« Landschaft. Gegenüber ragt die Spitze des *Ortlers,* mit 3902 Meter höchster Gipfel des Landes, in makellosem Weiß in den blauen Himmel. Der *Vinschgau,* von der jungen Etsch durcheilt, überrascht mit seinem herben Charakter; ab Meran ist das Etschtal bis nach Trient und Rovereto hinunter ein einziger üppiger Garten, von mächtigen Felszügen begleitet. Westlich davon liegt der Dolomitenstock der *Brenta,* eine der wildesten Formationen der Südalpen, mit seinen Gipfeln Cima Tosa, Cima Brenta und dem vielgerühmten Bocchette-Kletterweg. Östlich des Eisack, der sich gemeinsam mit Straße, Eisenbahn und Autobahn durch den schluchtartigen Talkorridor zwängt, wachsen aus dem Alpenblütenmeer der *Seiseralm* die Südtiroler Dolomiten in Wolkenhöhen: Der majestätische Dom des *Langkofels,* die trutzige Felsfestung der *Sella,* die mächtige Eisburg der *Marmolada.* Dahinter die Gigantengarde der *Ampezzaner Dolomiten* um Cortina, im Süden die Fassaner Alpen mit der wildzerklüfteten, bizarr geformten *Pala-Gruppe.* Der imposanten Bergarchitektur im Norden vorgelagert, spannt sich um die Ufer der Rienz das sanftgewellte *Pustertal,* eine verhaltene Landschaft mit viel ländlichem Dekor.

Doch nicht nur die Schöpfung, auch Menschenhände schufen hier Meisterwerke, In jeder Stadt, fast in jedem Dorf stehen prächtige Kirchen mit wertvollen Fresken, Statuen und wunderschönen Flügelaltären, Zeugnisse der Fleimstaler und Belluneser Maler und der Holzbildhauer des Grödner Tals. Aus dem Heer der Künstler und Kunsthandwerker, die hier gelebt und gewirkt haben, ragen die Namen von Tizian, Andrea Brustolon, Hans Multscher, Friedrich und Michael Pacher und Hans Klocker heraus.

Von allen Hängen, Hügeln und Bergen grüßen Burgen ins Tal, 250 an der Zahl, alle pittoresk und uralt. Noch älter aber ist der Weinbau, der schon in hoher Blüte stand, ehe die Römer ins Land kamen. Als Kaiser Domitian im Jahr 90 n. Chr. den edlen Tropfen zu probieren bekam, war er davon so angetan, daß er gleich den Rebenanbau in anderen Provinzen verbot. Ein solches Gesetz wäre wohl der einzige Grund, der die Südtiroler dazu bewegen könnte, für einen römischen Kaiser zu stimmen.

Oberitalienische Seen

So alt wie das Reisen auf dieser Welt ist auch der Streit darüber, welches wohl ihr schönstes Fleckchen sei. Im 16. Jahrhundert wollte Agostino Brenzone diese Meinungsverschiedenheiten ein für allemal schlichten, indem er kategorisch feststellte: »Die ganze Welt besteht aus drei Teilen: Afrika, Asien und Europa. Der schönste Teil ist Europa, und davon ist Italien der schönste Teil, von Italien wiederum die Lombardei, und von dieser der Gardasee, und an diesem San Vigilio. Ergo ist San Vigilio der schönste Ort der Welt.« Er ließ es nicht bei der Schwärmerei bewenden, sondern baute auf der vorspringenden Halbinsel am Rand der Bucht von Garda seine Villa Guarienti, eine prächtige Anlage mit zauberhaftem Garten.

Inzwischen hat es sich herumgesprochen, daß die Welt aus mehr Teilen besteht mit einer Vielzahl ›schönster‹ Orte. Doch immer noch vermag der *Gardasee* mit seinem gerafften Bild aller Schönheiten Europas die Illusion zu erwecken, er sei der paradiesischste Erdenwinkel. Er steht gleichsam stellvertretend für eine ganze Reihe von Seenbecken am Südrand der Alpen, die von vorzeitlichen Gletschern in die Böden der Talfurchen gegraben wurden. Gardasee, *Lago Maggiore* und *Comer See* sind die großen, *Luganer See* und *Lago d'Iseo* die mittleren, *Lago di Varese* und *Lago d'Orta* führen die Reihe Dutzender kleinerer Wasserbecken an. Allen gemeinsam ist die Gunst des Klimas, das die Mittelmeerzone zweihundert Kilometer nach Norden verschiebt, wo sich im Schutz der Alpenkette subtropische Wärme und Vegetation entfaltet. Allen gemeinsam ist auch der reiche kulturelle Hintergrund, der bis in die Antike zurückreicht und an den zu allen Zeiten beliebten Seeufern viele Spuren römischer und lombardischer Kunst und Tradition hinterließ.

Die Geschichte des Seenlandes deckt sich weitgehend mit jener der Lombardei, die seit altersher eine der meistumkämpften Provinzen Europas war. Vor unserer Zeitrechnung, etwa um das 6. Jahrhundert v. Chr., besiedelten die Etrusker Norditalien, das 400 v. Chr. von den Galliern erobert wurde. Von 200 v. Chr. bis 400 n. Chr. herrschten die Römer. Nach dem Untergang ihres Reiches rauften Byzantiner, Germanen, Hunnen und Ostgoten um das Land. Im 6. Jahrhundert fiel der Langobardenkönig Alboin, aus Nordeuropa kommennd, ein und errichtete seine zweihundertjährige Herrschaft. Den Langobarden folgten die Franken; Karl der Große verleibt die Lombardei seinem fränkischen Weltreich ein, Otto der Große vereinigt sie 951 mit dem Deutschen Reich. Im Mittelalter blühen die großen Städte auf, zerspalten das Gebiet in Feudalstaaten. Der östliche Teil des Landes kommt unter die Herrschaft Venedigs, der westliche zum Herzogtum Mailand. Im 18. Jahrhundert erobert Österreich die Po-Ebene, der Wiener Kongreß von 1815 errichtet das Lombardisch-Venezianische Königreich unter der Hoheit des Habsburger Kaiserhauses. Fünfzig Jahre später tritt Österreich die Lombardei an die italienische Krone ab.

Alle Straßen, die aus dem Norden über die Pässe kommen, berühren – mit der einzigen Ausnahme der Etschtalroute – einen der Seen am Südabstieg der Alpen. Dem Gast aus dem Norden sind sie mit dem neuen Licht, der wohligen Wärme, der üppigen Flora und der anderen Lebensart der Bewohner die ersten Vorboten der mediterranen Welt.

Der *Gardasee*, Inbegriff der Seenlandschaft, ist mit 52 Kilometern Länge und 370 Quadratkilometern Fläche das größte und eindrucksvollste Gewässer. Plinius und Catull, Goethe und D'Annunzio haben ihn besungen. Er ist ein Stück phantastischer Welt, eine fortwährend wechselnde Kulisse aus Sonne, Wasser, Blüten, Felsen und Bergen; an seinen Ufern verschwistert sich der strenge Atem der Dolomiten mit dem weichen Belcanto Venedigs.

Der langgestreckte Nordteil, von hohen Bergzügen flankiert, gleicht einem norwegischen Fjord; im Süden wandelt sich der See zum weiten, meerähnlichen Becken, um das die sanften Weinhügel ausklingen zur großen Ebene. Unvergleichlich ist das Panorama, das man, von Norden über die Höhenstraße von Nago kommend, genießt, wo sich unter dem monumentalen Felsriff des Monte Brione das alte Städtchen Riva an die Ufer schmiegt. Im Westen, wo sich die steilen Felswandfluchten anmaßend ans Wasser drängen, fädelt sich die ›Gardesana Occidentale‹ durch siebzig Tunnels und über fünfzig Brücken am schroffen Ufer entlang; eine Prachtstraße ersten Ranges – nur leider zu schön, um einsam zu sein. Fünfzig Kilometer lang belagern die Steilwände den Strand, in den wenigen Nischen nisten kleine, rustikale Dörfer: Limone mit seinen Zitronenterrassen, das nüchtern-sachliche Campione, das verschlafene, hoch oben auf einem Bergsporn liegende Tignale. Bei Gargnano wandelt sich das rauhe Feltsterrain zum üppigen Garten, und in Gardone Riviere heißen die Wirtshäuser nicht mehr Albergo, sondern ›Grand-Hotel‹ und ›Savoy‹. Nach der Bucht von Salo wird die Landschaft sanft, die Straße trennt sich vom See, durchzieht verträumte Siedlungen, die in Wein- und Olivengärten ertrinken. Von der Mitte des weiten, flachen Südufers aus schiebt sich eine langgestreckte Landzunge ins Wasser. An deren Ende entzückt das pittoreske Sirmione mit uralten Gassen, der mächtigen Scaligerburg und prächtigen Badeufern nach allen Seiten hin. Vor dem Ort sind ausgedehnte Ruinenfelder aus römischer Zeit zu besichtigen, die man in touristischer Unbescheidenheit die »Grotten des Catull« nennt.

Landschaftlich nicht so dramatisch wie die Westseite ist das Ostufer. Hier be-
stimmen die langgezogenen Hänge des Monte Baldo, auf dessen Schultern
schmale Bergsträßlein hinausklettern, das Bild. Am südlichen Seende erschrek-
ken die wehrhaften Bastionen von Pesciera, trutzig-abweisende Festungsanlagen aus der Zeit der Scaliger, der Grafen von Mantua, aus venezianischer,
napoleonischer und österreichischer Epoche. Nordwärts schließt sich das mittelalterliche Lazise, dann das weinberühmte Bardolino an. Nach der weit ins
Land greifenden Bucht von Garda reihen sich auf schmalem Uferstreifen reiz-
volle Fischerdörfer und dichte Olivenhaine aneinander. In Malcesine, einem
stattlichen Dorf mit imposanter Scaligerburg, finden wir viel urbanes Kolorit.
Hier wurde einst Goethe, weil er seine Eindrücke auf dem Zeichenblock fest-
hielt, als Spion verdächtigt und kurzzeitig eingekerkert. Das nördlichste Stück
des Ufers ist von rauhem Gestein geprägt, dann weitet sich das Land zur
Bucht von Torbole, das noch ein Hauch von österreichisch-lässiger Vertraut-
heit umweht, und beschließt mit dem Übergang nach Riva den großartigen
Uferreigen.

Von gleichem südländischem Zuschnitt, wenn auch in anderer Gestalt, ist der
Comer See. Er zwängt sich wie ein auf den Kopf gestelltes Y in die Furchen
der Bergamasker Alpen. Sein Wasserspiegel erreicht nirgends die meerähnliche
Weite des Gardasees, seine fjordartigen, vielverzweigten Arme sind schmal,
wirken intim. Die nördliche Hälfte ist von arkadischer Heiterkeit, der Ausläufer des Lago di Lecco wirkt elegisch und schwermütig, der nach Como rei-
chende Arm ist ein einziger tropischer Garten mit Hunderten weißer Villen,
unter denen die Villa Carlotta, die Serbellioni, die d'Este und die Villa Mo-
nastero mit ihren prächtigen Parks herausragen. Jahrhundertealte romanische
Kirchen thronen auf den grünen Hängen, und im Wasser spiegeln sich die
trutzigen Burgen der alten Herrschergeschlechter, der Sforza, Medici, Visconti. Wie ein Keil schiebt sich der Monte San Primo von Süden heran, spal-
tet den See in zwei Teile; an der vordersten Bugspitze sonnt sich das zauberhafte Bellágio in paradiesischer Umgebung. Obgleich viele Teile des Ufers be-
baut sind, bleibt noch genügend Raum für verträumte Buchten, für Camping-
plätze und Badestreifen. Der bunte Bilderbogen zeigt auch sehenswerte Beson-
derheiten: Die Grotta Verde, die grüne Grotte von Lézzeno, die Wasserspiele
der Villa Pliniani in Torno, die Felsstürze von Bellano und den Fiumelatte,
den kleinsten Fluß der Welt, nur ganze 250 Meter lang; er entspringt plötzlich in jedem Frühling und lebt nur bis zum Herbst.

Den *Lago Maggiore* könnte man eine Mischung aus Gardasee und Comer See
nennen. Das nördliche Fünftel seines Bereichs liegt im schweizerischen Tessin;
seine ganze Pracht entfaltet er in der großen Westbucht, die zwischen Verba-

43 Pinienidyll, aquamarinklares Wasser und sonnengebleichte Felskulissen kennzeichnen die Landschaft des südlichsten Italien. Blick vom Festland zur Insel San Nicola in Apulien.

44 Das griechische Theater bei Taormina auf Sizilien gewährt einen prächtigen Blick auf das alte Seebadstädtchen und die Uferlandschaft der Ostküste, die sich in großräumigem Stil bis zum schneebedeckten, 3296 Meter hohen Ätna hinaufzieht, dem höchsten tätigen Vulkan der Welt.

nia und Stresa ins Tal des Toce-Flusses ausgreift. Hier liegen die berühmten Borromäischen Inseln: die Isola Bella, ein in Form eines Schiffsdecks gestalteter Barockgarten; die Isola dei Pescatori, die Fischerinsel, mit holperigen Gassen und malerischen Weinkneipen; die Isola Madre, ein Eiland verhaltenen Charmes mit weitläufigen Parkanlagen und brüchigem Palast. Hübsche Städtchen säumen die Ufer, das attraktive Pallanza, das hypermoderne Stresa, das südländisch-turbulente Arona und drüben am Ostufer, wo noch viel Unverfälschtes vorherrscht, das wehrhafte Maccagno, das platanenumhüllte Luino, das urwüchsige Ispra.

Abseits dieser Seenziele liegen die kleineren, wenig bekannten, doch nicht minder schönen Gewässer. Im blanken Wasser des *Lago di Varese* spiegelt sich das Massiv des Monte Rosa; vom nahen Aussichtsberg, dem Campo dei Fiori, überblickt man sieben Seenbecken. Die Südseite des *Luganer Sees,* dessen Hauptanteil zur Schweiz gehört, bietet immer noch viel Einsamkeit. Der *Lago d'Orta,* westlich des Lago Maggiore gelegen, träumt unter grünen Berghängen, und der *Lago d'Iseo,* dessen Ränder ländlich-beschauliche Dorfflecken zieren, ist stolz auf seine Isola Montisola, die größte Binnensee-Insel Italiens. Am *Lago di Ledro,* einer kleinen Wasserschale im Felsmassiv über dem Gardasee, kann man seine Zelte gar unter Tannen aufschlagen und anheimelnden Harzgeruch unter südlicher Sonne genießen.

45 Nahe der sizilianischen Hauptstadt Palermo
liegt Monreale, dessen Kathedrale aus dem zwölften
Jahrhundert als prächtigstes Beispiel arabisch-
normannischen Kirchenbaustils gilt. Im Bild der
stimmungsvolle Kreuzgang und der südliche Turm.

Sizilien

»Geben Sie uns drei Wochen Ihrer Zeit und wir geben Ihnen dreitausend
Jahre unserer Geschichte« – dieser Werbeslogan übertreibt nicht; Sizilien ist
eine der erhabensten klassischen Kulturlandschaften, zu reich und außerge-
wöhnlich, um nur schön zu sein. Wer gewohnt ist, das Land bloß als eine zu
Italien gehörende Mittelmeerinsel einzustufen, muß umdenken lernen. Drei-
einhalb Kilometer breit ist die Meerenge von Messina zwischen dem Festland und der Insel; im Denkschema unserer Zeit ein unbedeutender Zwischen-
raum. Ethnologisch ist sie eine Kluft, die Welten voneinander trennt. Phöniker, Griechen, Römer, Araber, Normannen, Spanier, Österreicher, Franzosen
und Italiener beherrschten die Insel; alle nahmen, alle gaben auch. Ihre
komplexen Einflüsse schufen das ungewöhnliche Profil dieses Landes, formten
das sizilianische Wesen, ein Gemisch aus Stolz und Askese, aus verzehrenden
Leidenschaften und frommer Demut – Spiegelbild einer gewaltigen, heroischen
Landschaft mit schroffem Felsgestein und lieblichen Meeresbuchten, ausgedörrten Karsthügeln und verzaubernden Mandelblüten, sanftmütigen Strand-
dünen und drohenden Vulkanen.

Tausend Jahre vor unserer Zeitrechnung siedelten die Sikaner auf der Insel,
wurden durch die einwandernden indogermanischen Sikuler nach Westen ge-
drängt. Im 8. Jahrhundert v. Chr. landeten die Griechen, gründeten die
Städte an der Ostküste, formten Sizilien zum westlichen Mittelpunkt der
griechischen Kultur. Zweihundert Jahre später drangen die Karthager ein,
kämpften mit den Griechen um die Vorherrschaft. Im 1. Punischen Krieg, 264
bis 241 v. Chr., vertrieben die Römer die Karthager und gliederten die Insel
ihrem Reich ein. Während der Völkerwanderung wurde Sizilien 440 n. Chr.
von den Wandalen, 493 von den Ostgoten, 535 von den Byzantinern erobert.
Eine wirtschaftliche und kulturelle Blüte erlebte das Land vom 9. bis zum
11. Jahrhundert unter der Herrschaft der Araber, die Palermo zur Hauptstadt machten. Den Arabern folgten 1061 bis 1091 die Normannen, dann kam
Sizilien zum Königreich Neapel unter der Herrschaft der Staufer. Den Kriegen mit dem französischen Haus Anjou und dem blutigen Volksaufstand der
»Sizilianischen Vesper« folgte 1442 die Wiedervereinigung mit dem König-
reich Neapel, als dessen Teil die Insel in der Folgezeit den Savoyern, den
Österreichern und den spanischen Bourbonen unterstand. Der Berufsrevoluzzer
Garibaldi stürzte 1860 die Bourbonen, seit 1861 gehört Sizilien zum König-

reich Italien. Mehrmals, vor allem im 19. Jahrhundert, erstrebten die Sizilianer mit Revolutionen eine politische Selbständigkeit, wobei der noch heute wirkende Geheimbund der Mafia eine oft tragende, zwielichte Rolle spielte.

Aus den vielen Wirren seiner dreitausendjährigen Geschichte erwuchs das sizilianische Bewußtsein, das alle fremden Einflüsse aufsog und integrierte; alle eingedrungenen Völker wurden in wenigen Generationen zu Sizilianern. Man zählt die Tempel der Griechen, die Paläste der Normannen und den Barock der Spanier ebenso zum sizilianischen Kulturgut wie die Marionettenspiele über die Heldentaten Karls des Großen und spricht etwas herablassend vom Kontinent, dem restlichen Europa.

Dem Reisenden bietet Sizilien eine ungeahnte Fülle kultureller Sehenswürdigkeiten und landschaftlicher Schönheit und Eigenart. Wirtschaftlicher und kultureller Mittelpunkt ist die Hauptstadt *Palermo,* deren Alter man auf siebentausend Jahre schätzt, und das Zeugnisse aller Epochen und der unterschiedlichsten Kulturen aufweist. Dom und Palast zählen zu den Meisterwerken arabisch-normannischer Kunst; sie wurden noch übertroffen vom Dom im nahegelegenen *Monreale,* der schönsten Normannenkirche Siziliens, mit stimmungsvollem Kreuzgang aus dem 13. Jahrhundert. »A Ziz«, die Herrliche, tauften die Araber Palermo, das ebenso ehrwürdig wie lebendig ist, das Richard Wagner zum zweiten Akt des »Parsifal« inspirierte, in dessen Standbild sich Europa und der Orient begegnen und verschwistern. Touristische Attraktionen sind die bunten, quirlenden Märkte, an arabische Souks erinnernd, die Katakomben von San Giovanni degli Eremiti mit den mumifizierten toten Aristokraten der Stadt und der Palast des Fürsten Lampedusa, dessen Roman »Der Leopard« (auch deutschen Literaturfreunden ein Begriff) einen Einblick in das rätselvolle Wesen Siziliens gewährt.

Einer der Schwerpunkte des Fremdenverkehrs ist *Taormina* an der Ostküste, das über der weiten Bucht terrassenförmig die Felshänge hinaufwächst. Sein Glanz stammt noch aus der Zeit vor dem Ersten Weltkrieg, als es eines der klassischen Reiseziele des bürgerlichen Europa war. Gegen die Strandidylle der Zitronen- und Orangenhaine setzt der mächtige, 3263 Meter hohe Ätna, größter tätiger Vulkan der Welt, einen wirkungsvollen Kontrast. Unter den wenigen baulichen Sehenswürdigkeiten genießt das Griechische Theater, Relikt aus römisch-hellenischer Zeit, besonderen Rang. Es liegt auf einem Bergwall, von dem sich ein großartiger Blick auf Stadt und Meer bietet.

Für die Landschaft Siziliens typisch ist *Catania,* eine betriebsame Stadt mit großem Hafen, malerisch an der Felsküste unter dem Ätna, der Riviera dei Ciclopi, gelegen. Sein Castello Ursino, unter dem Staufenkaiser Friedrich II. erbaut, gilt als hervorragendes Beispiel deutscher Festungsbaukunst.

46 Bevor die Alpen zum französischen Mittelmeer ausklingen, demonstrieren sie im Pelvoux-Massiv letztmalig ihre gewaltige Schönheit. Höhepunkt dieser Landschaft ist die 3983 Meter hohe Meije, die »Königin der Dauphiné«, ein großartiges Gebilde aus Fels und Gletscher, Türmen und Zacken. Blick auf La Meije aus dem Tal der Romanche, durch das die Straße von Grenoble nach Briançon führt.

47 Durch eine aus Olivgrün, Rostbraun und Schiefergrau komponierte alpine Urwelt windet sich die Straße zum 2556 Meter hohen Col du Galibier hinauf, einer der strapaziösen Höhepunkte der alljährlichen Tour de France. Blick von der Scheitelhöhe auf die Nordrampe, gegenüber die Rochers de la Grande Paré. Siehe Seiten 109 u. 110

Um *Syrakus*, die Metropole der hellenischen Welt, zu erfassen, bedarf es eines besonderen historischen Verständnisses. Wenige Kilometer entfernt liegt die Totenstadt Pantalica, mit dem makabren Reiz einer Nekropole: fünftausend Felshöhlen, bewohnt bis zum Mittelalter, mit byzantinischen Kapellen über schaurigen Abgründen.

Eindrucksvoll und packend ist Agrigent an der Südküste mit dem Concordia-Tempel, einem der besterhaltenen griechischen Kulturdenkmäler. – *Marsala* hat außer dem penetrant süßen Wein und Italiens wichtigsten Fischereihafen wenig zu bieten. Interessanter ist *Trapani*, die wohlhabende Stadt an der Westküste mit maurisch-spanischer Note und honiggelben Sandsteinpalästen. Hamilkar, der Vater Hannibals, errichtete hier 260 v. Chr. einen Flottenstützpunkt, der im 1. Punischen Krieg heiß umkämpft war.

Während im Nordosten der Insel die Peloritanischen Berge mit dramatischen Formen, mit schroffen Wänden und Granitspitzen das Bild beherrschen, überwiegt im Landesinnern die statische Ruhe großräumiger Landschaftsszenerie mit kalen, durstenden Karstbergen, tafelförmigen Schwefelplateaus und weltentlegenen Dörfern.

Ein Ausflugsziel besonderer Art sind die Sizilien im Norden vorgelagerten *Liparischen* oder *Äolischen Inseln*, weltentrückte Eilande mit weißen Stränden, trostlosen Mondkrater-Landschaften und bizarr geformten Vulkanfelsen. Deren berühmtester, Stromboli, spukt alle paar Minuten gischtenden Dampf und Feuerflammen zum Himmel, über die Felshänge wälzt sich glühende Lava ins tiefblaue Meer – vor allem bei Nacht ein faszinierendes Schauspiel.

Die schönsten Badestrände bieten die Umgebung *Catanias*, das vom Club Mediterraneè erschlossene Ufer von *Cefalù* im Norden und die »afrikanischen« Küstenstreifen von *Gela* im Süden; Dorado der Tauchsportler ist die *Insel Ustica* mit ihrer märchenhaften Unterwasserwelt.

Frankreich

Französische Alpen

Südlich des Genfer Sees, wo die Alpen mit großem Bogen nach Süden schwenken, erreichen sie im Mont-Blanc-Massiv ihre gewaltigsten Formen und höchsten Gipfel. An Höhen nur wenig abnehmend, in der Masse noch kompakter, setzen sie sich südwärts mit den Gebirgsgruppen von Vanoise und Pelvoux fort, ehe sie in den ›Seealpen‹ zum Mittelmeer ausklingen. Ihr Hauptanteil liegt in den französischen Landschaften Savoyen und Dauphiné.

In der Vergangenheit waren die beiden Territorien der französischen Hochalpen politisch nicht so einheitlich verbunden, wie sie uns heute erscheinen. Das ursprünglich von Kelten, später von Burgundern besiedelte Savoyen war über acht Jahrhunderte Stammland der italienischen Krone und wurde erst 1860 – als Dank Italiens für französische Waffenhilfe – an Frankreich abgetreten. Die Dauphiné, deren geschichtliche Rolle unbedeutend war, fiel bereits 1349 durch Verkauf vom deutschen Reich an Frankreich.

Die klassische Hochgebirgswelt von Savoyen und der Dauphiné glänzt mit vielen Superlativen – mit dem Mont Blanc, mit 4807 Meter höchster Berg Europas; dem größten zusammenhängenden Gletschergebiet der Alpen um den Glacier du Géant, die Vallé Blanche und die Mer de Glace; mit Europas längstem Straßentunnel unter dem Mont Blanc-Massiv; mit der höchsten Seilbahn der Welt auf die 3842 Meter hohe Aiguille du Midi; mit Briançon, der höchstgelegenen Stadt des Kontinents, und mit Saint-Véran, dem höchstgelegenen Dorf.

Bevor wir uns die Französischen Alpen als Urlaubslandschaft näher betrachten, stellt sich die wichtigste Frage, welche Art von Ferienfreuden wir erwarten. Hier liegen nicht, wie wir das vom deutschen, österreichischen oder schweizerischen Alpenanteil her gewohnt sind, einladende Badeseen, blumenbunte Almwiesen, tannenumsäumte Wanderwege und g'führige Skihänge nachbarlich nebeneinander. Vielmehr weist eine in großräumigsten Formen und Klimazonen gegliederte Landschaft jeder Ferienart ihre spezifischen Gebiete zu. Wer einmal über die großen französischen Hochalpenpässe gefahren ist, wird schwerlich ersehnen, die chaotischen Urgesteinswüsten – in denen er tagelang weder Almhütte noch Berggasthaus antrifft – in Wanderschuhen zu durchmessen. Selbst passionierte Pistenfans, denen die endlosen Hangweiten von Val d'Isère und Courchevel ein Paradies in Weiß bedeuten, verspüren wenig Neigung, die alpinen Ödlandwiesen zur Sommerzeit in monotonen

48 Die Grandes Jorasses in den französischen Hochalpen, 4208 Meter hoch, gehört zur Trabantengarde des Mont Blanc. Der 1868 erstmals bestiegene Bergriese steht auf der Wunschliste vieler Alpinisten. Während er von Chamonix aus in eine kolossale Gletscher- und Felsszenerie verpackt ist, steigen aus dem italienischen Val Ferret seine Flanken atemraubend himmelwärts.

49 Der Mont Blanc, mit 4807 Metern höchster Berg der Alpen, wie er sich von der 3842 Meter hohen Seilbahnstation der Aiguille du Midi über Chamonix dem Auge bietet. Jaques Balmat bestieg ihn 1786 zum ersten Mal, heute gibt es rund 40 Anstiegsrouten jeden Schwierigkeitsgrades.

Tagesmärschen abzuspazieren. Andererseits weiß der Skifreund in den großartigen Schluchten des Verdon – des wandernden Weltentdeckers größtes Entzücken – mit seinen Gleitbrettern recht wenig anzufangen.

Als Ferienlandschaft im weiteren Sinn wurden die französischen Alpen erst in den letzten Jahren entdeckt. Traditionelle Gebirgsdörfer, wie etwa Mittenwald, St. Anton oder Zermatt, sind hier nie entstanden; die Landschaft schien dafür zu rauh und lebensfeindlich. Es gab nur altersgreise, graubemooste Steinhütten, die sich schwerlich zu Touristenunterkünften umfunktionieren ließen. In den letzten dreißig Jahren wurde an vielen Orten rege gebaut, wobei das Schwergewicht auf der Erschließung riesiger Skigebiete lag. Es entstanden die berühmten »Retorten-Stationen« Courchevel, Tignes, La Plagne, Flaine, Les Arcs – Großstadtsiedlungen im Gebirge, mit viel Komfort und wenig Gemütlichkeit. Was wir in den Hochalpen Frankreichs an menschlichen Siedlungen antreffen, ist zumeist entweder uralt oder brandneu.

Eine Alpenlandschaft, die am ehesten unseren gewohnten Vorstellungen entspricht, finden wir im nördlichen Savoyen, das an den Genfer See und das Schweizer Wallis anschließt. In der reich gegliederten Voralpenlandschaft des Chablais erfreuen uns sattgrüne Wiesenmatten, die forellenreichen Dranses (Wildbäche), tiefe Laubwälder und ein Reigen von Berggipfeln um die zweitausend Meter. Touristisches Zentrum ist das Dorf *Morzine* mit seinen supermodernen Fortsetzungen *Avoriaz* und *Les Gets*. In den abgeschiedenen, kleinen Tälern begegnen wir viel ursprünglichem Kolorit; kurios sind die pfeifenrauchenden Frauen in *Bellevaux*, deren Urahnen einst nach Südamerika ausgewandert und die Stadt Sao Paulo gründeten. Wo die Berge mächtiger werden, versteckt sich in weltentlegener Einsamkeit, nur auf 23 Kilometer langer Bergstraße erreichbar, die avantgardistische Skistation *Flaine*, bestehend aus einer Handvoll Hotelhochhäusern und paradiesischen Skigefilden. Liebenswürdig und malerisch gibt sich das südwestlich davon gelegene Land um die beiden Seen *Lac d'Annecy* und *Lac du Bourget*, übrigens (vom Genfer See abgesehen) Frankreichs einzige natürliche Alpenseen nennenswerter Größe. An deren grünen Ufern – die Berge abgerückt zur fernen Randkulisse – wird Wassersport in allen Varianten großgeschrieben. *Aix-les-Bains* am Lac du Bourget ist zudem ein vielbesuchter Heilkurort. *Annecy*, der Hauptort am gleichnamigen See, entzückt mit seinem alten, malerischen Stadtbild, besonders mit romantischen Sujets am Thiou-Kanal. Trotz vieler, geschickt versteckter Industrieanlagen wird der Lac d'Annecy als einer der saubersten Seen Europas gerühmt; man entnimmt ihm auch das Trinkwasser für 100 000 Menschen.

Die bisher beschriebenen Landschaften sind freilich nur hübsches Randdekor der Hochalpenwelt par excellence, die sich um *Chamonix* entfaltet. Aus dem tiefen Talgrund der Arve türmt sich das Massiv des *Mont Blanc* gigantisch himmelwärts, die zerklüfteten, blaugrün schillernden Gletscherströme schieben sich dreieinhalbtausend Meter bis auf den Talgrund herunter. Gegenüber, nicht minder gewaltig, steht die steinerne Garde der *Aiguilles Rouges*, eine Staffage bizarr geformter, spitz aufragender Felsnadeln. Von diesen aus – etwa vom seilbahnerschlossenen, 2526 Meter hohen Brévent – hat man den schönsten Blick auf den ›Monarchen‹, wie der Mont Blanc genannt wird. Eine andere, auf der Welt konkurrenzlose Attraktion ist die Seilbahn auf die 3842 Meter hohe *Aiguille du Midi*, einem Vorgipfel des Mont Blanc, eine starre Klippe inmitten der Brandung einer phantastisch geformten Welt aus Eis und Fels. Von diesem Gipfel aus spannt sich eine Seilbahnbrücke über Europas mächtigstes Alpenmassiv hinweg bis ins jenseitige, italienische *Entrèves* im Aostatal. Im Tal, den Mont Blanc halbkreisförmig umschließend, präsentiert sich Frankreichs größte alpine Ferienregion mit den Hauptorten *Chamonix, Saint-Gervais, Megève* und *Contamines* und einem Dutzend kleinerer Erholungsorte. Typisch französisch kann man diese Gegend nicht nennen – sie ist international; die Bauernkinder haben englische Vornamen und trinken am liebsten Tee.

Südlich des Mont-Blanc-Massivs unterbricht eine tiefe Kerbe, das ›Tarentaise‹ genannte Tal der Isère, die geschlossene Alpenfront. Ähnlich wie in vielen anderen französischen Alpentälern überrascht auch hier den Gast aus dem Norden der ungeheuere Vegetations- und Klimaunterschied zwischen den Tal- und Hochlagen. Während unten Wein und Feigen reifen, selbst im Winter kaum Schnee fällt und zu keiner Jahreszeit ein Mantel nötig ist, tragen die gewaltig hochgereckten Bergmassive auch im Hochsommer ihre weißen Schneehauben.

Zwischen dem Isèretal und der nächsten Alpenfurche, dem Tal des Arc, liegt das kompakte *Massiv der Vanoise*, gipfelnd in dem knapp viertausend Meter hohen *Grande Casse*. Der riesige Block fällt nach allen Seiten schroff ab; auf seinem weitläufigen Dach herrscht eine rauhe Urgesteins- und Ödlandschaft vor. Diese für den Wintersport nützend, haben sich in den wenigen Stichtälern berühmte Skistationen etabliert: *Val d'Isère, Tignes, Les Arcs, La Plagne, Courchevel, Méribel, Val Thorens*.

Südlich des Arctals, *Maurienne* genannt, folgt eine zusammenhanglose, chaotisch verstreute Anhäufung von Berggruppen und Einzelgipfeln mit Höhen um die dreieinhalbtausend Meter. Diesen Bereich durchziehen die großen Alpenpässe Galibier, Col de la Croix de Fer und Col du Lautaret. Dann recken sich die Alpen, letztmalig vor dem Mittelmeer, im *Pelvoux-Massiv* noch einmal über viertausend Meter empor, demonstrieren mit Nadeln, Zacken, Wänden und Gletschern ihre ungeheuere Dramatik. Schönster Berg dieser Gruppe ist die 3983 Meter hohe La Meije, die »Königin der Dauphiné«.

Rings um diese drei Hauptblöcke der Französischen Alpen ranken sich noch einige Massive, Gruppen und Grüppchen, unter denen die Chartreuse, westlich der Isère und nahe Grenoble gelegen, einen Sonderrang einnimmt: Ein geschlossener Gebirgsblock, dessen helle, zerfressene Kalkklippen senkrecht aus dunklen Tannenwäldern hochsteigen, mit feuchten, düsteren Klüften, ein Dorado für entdeckungsfreudige Berggänger.

Der Streifzug durch die Französischen Alpen wäre unvollständig ohne Besuche in den sehenswerten Städten. Allen voran *Grenoble,* ein imponierendes Stadtwesen mit Altstadt-Romantik und Hochhaus-Fassaden, Austragungsort der Olympischen Winterspiele 1968, eine Mischung aus kleinem Paris und großem Bozen, dessen Kulisse sich mit Alpenstädten wie Innsbruck oder Salzburg durchaus messen kann. Dann das ehrwürdige *Briançon,* die kühn auf einem Felshügel thronende Vauban'sche Festungsstadt; das lebhafte *Albertville* und das alte *Chambéry,* Residenz der Herzöge von Savoyen mit imposantem Schloß und prächtigen Kirchen; das rustikale *Embrun* im Durancetal mit seiner berühmten, romanisch-lombardischen Kathedrale; schließlich die ungezählten kleinen Orte und Dörfer, vom halb verfallenen *Bonneval* im Arctal bis *Assy* unterhalb des Mont Blanc, dessen moderne Kirche von den größten Künstlern unseres Jahrhundert ausgestattet wurde.

Provence und Côte d'Azur

Provence und Côte d'Azur, im französischen Süden zwischen den Alpen und
dem Mittelmeer gelegen, bilden geographisch und politisch eine Einheit. In
ihrem Wesen sind die beiden Landschaftsbegriffe höchst unterschiedlich. Dies
drückt sich augenfällig darin aus, daß Marseille, die mit einer knappen Million Bewohner größte Stadt des Bereichs, nie die politische oder symbolische
Hauptstadt der Provence war; diesen Rang teilten sich das nur dreißig Kilometer landeinwärts gelegene, nur ein Zehntel so große Aix-en-Provence und
das noch kleinere Arles am Rhônedelta. Die Provence, deren Blick nie dem
Meer, sondern dem Landesinneren zugewandt war, ist eine uralte Kultur-
landschaft (eine der ehrwürdigsten Europas), im Schatten der Vergangenheit
stehengeblieben. Die Côte d'Azur, die Blaue Küste, ist – abgesehen von den
Relikten seiner Seefahrertradition – ein Produkt der Zivilisation, ein Kind
unserer Zeit.

Die lange Geschichte des Landes ist verwirrend, voller Ruhelosigkeit und Dra-
matik. 600 v. Chr. gründen seefahrende griechische Kaufleute Massalia, das
heutige Marseille; 125 v. Chr. erobern die Römer das Land, errichten die
Provinz Gallia, verbreiten die römische Kultur. 470 n. Chr. herrschen die
Westgoten, 509 die Ostgoten, 536 die Franken, im 9. Jahrhundert fallen die
Sarazenen ein. Dann wird die Provence burgundisches Königreich unter der
Oberhoheit des Kaisers des Heiligen Römischen Reiches. Im 10. Jahrhundert
entwickeln sich selbständige Herrschaftsbereiche; deren bedeutendste ist die
Grafschaft Provence mit der Hauptstadt Aix. 1246 kommt die Provence –
die in der Folgezeit ihren Oberherren eine gewisse Unabhängigkeit abtrotzt –
an das Haus Anjou und 1481 an die französische Krone. 1309 bis 1377 ist
Avignon Residenz des Papstes und Mittelpunkt der damaligen Welt. Einer
langen kulturellen Blütezeit seit dem Spätmittelalter setzt die Pest von 1720
ein Ende. In unserem Jahrhundert hat die Provence noch einmal fremde
Herrschaft zu erdulden: Sie wird von 1942 bis 1944 von deutschen Truppen
besetzt.
Alle Herren der Vergangenheit haben ihre Spuren hinterlassen, glorreiche und
grausame, angefangen von der Zerstörung Entremonts, der antiken Hauptstadt der Keltoligurer, durch den römischen Feldherrn Sextius über die Entfaltung päpstlicher Macht in den Prachtpalästen von Avignon bis zur Schlei-
fung der Hafenviertel Marseilles während des Zweiten Weltkriegs. So ist die

Provence ein lebendiges Geschichtsbuch seiner zweieinhalbtausend Jahre Vergangenheit, für Freunde von Kunst, Kultur und Tradition eine schier unerschöpfliche Fundgrube.

Aus der Fülle historischer Sehenswürdigkeiten, deren eingehende Beschreibung ansehnliche Bände füllt, seien hier wenigstens einige Glanzpunkte herausgestellt. In *Avignon,* das vom Fremdenzustrom zuweilen überlaufen ist, fasziniert der einer Kirchenfestung gleichende Papstpalast; unweit davon liegt die berühmte, vielbesungene Rhônebrücke, der Pont d'Avignon, von dessen einst 22 Steinbögen noch vier erhalten sind. Die Altstadt mit prächtigen Kirchen kuschelt sich innerhalb der mächtigen Stadtmauer aus dem 14. Jahrhundert eng zusammen. Der Stolz von *Orange,* unweit von Avignon im Rhônetal gelegen, ist das zweitausend Jahre alte römische Theater, das besterhaltene der Antike, das 15 000 Personen faßt und heute als effektvolle Stätte von Theater- und Musikfestspielen dient. Die Via Agrippa wird abgeschlossen vom gedrungenen römischen Triumphbogen, den Cäsar im Jahr 49 v. Chr. errichten ließ. In *Arles,* dem vorrömischen Handelsplatz der Griechen, fasziniert die antike Ruinenwelt; Hauptanziehungspunkt ist der Steinkrater des Amphitheaters, das einst 21 000 Besuchern Platz bot. In dem von Ruinengalerien umkränzten Rund finden jeden Sommer die ›Corridas de muerte‹, an die Zeit der Gladiatoren erinnernde Stierkämpfe statt. Bezaubernd ist *Aix-en-Provence,* eine ehrwürdige, zeitlose Stadt, kulturelles Zentrum, Geburts- und Sterbeort des Malers Paul Cézanne, mit der uralten Kathedrale St. Sauveur, seinen 24 bemoosten Steinbrunnen und dem platanenüberwölbten Prachtboulevard Cours Mirabeau. *Marseille,* selbstbewußter Außenseiter unter den französischen Städten, hat an altertümlichen Werten wenig bewahrt, die meisten Sehenswürdigkeiten stammen aus dem 18. und 19. Jahrhundert, wie die monströse Kathedrale ›La Major‹ (sie faßt 12 000 Personen) und die auf beherrschendem Aussichtsberg aufragende Basilika Notre-Dame-de-la-Garde mit ihrer überdimensionalen Madonnenstatue auf dem Turm. Dafür überrascht das ruhelose, sich in der Geschichte fortwährend erneuernde Stadtwesen mit seinem imponierenden, weltstädtischen Rhythmus, der sich besonders eindrucksvoll in der ›Canebière‹, der Hauptgeschäftsstraße beim Alten Hafen, demonstriert. Toulon, Stadt der Purpurproduktion und der Galeerenschiffe, einst blühendes Seefahrer- und Handelszentrum, erzählt mit seinen verödeten Kaianlagen vom Untergang einer Schiffahrtsmetropole.
Neben diesen großen städtischen Zentren sind es in der Provence oft Kleinstädte, Dörfer, abgelegene Einöden, deren Bauten nicht minder eindrucksvoll von der einstigen Größe des Landes zeugen. So in *Sisteron,* der Pforte zur Provence im Norden, wo über der schluchtartigen Verengung der Durance die Zitadelle, der Prototyp einer wehrhaften Festungsanlage, hochragt; in *Taras-*

con, der Stadt des Sagenungeheuers Tarasque, dessen mächtiges Schloß am Rhôneufer, im 15. Jahrhundert vom legendären provenzalischen König René erbaut, heute oft als Schauplatz glanzvoller Historien- und Ritterfilme dient; oft im einsamen *Sénanque*, dessen romanische Zisterzienserabtei seit acht Jahrhunderten unversehrt inmitten einer ausgedörrten Karstlandschaft steht; in den geheimnisumwitterten Schloßruinen von *Les Baux*, deren Herkunft und Bedeutung bis heute nicht enträtselt werden konnten; in der einstigen Bischofsstadt *Vaison-la-Romaine*; im verstümmelten *Manosque*; im Schloß Forcalquier, dessen Töchter auf die Throne der europäischen Kaiser- und Königreiche geradezu abonniert waren, und in vielen ungezählten Tälern und Bergwinkeln.

Doch die Provence zeichnet nicht nur geschichtlicher Reichtum aus, sie ist auch ein Land vielfältigster Natur-Szenerie, die triste Öde und üppigste Farben und Formen dicht aneinandersetzt. In der Crau, der Steinwüste um das Durancetal, entfaltet sich neben nacktem, von der Sonne gebleichten Felsterrain das satte, fette Grün der Obst- und Gemüsegärten, bei Apt überziehen flammende Lavendelfelder Talgrund und Hänge. *Roussillon*, die »Hauptstadt des Ockers«, steht auf einem ganzen Berg des gelbbraunen Farbstoffes, *Châteauneuf-du-Pape* an den Rampen des Rhônetals in einem Meer von Weinreben. Den feuchten, verwilderten Flußauen im Tal der Sorgue steht der Mont Ventoux gegenüber, dessen zweitausend Meter hoch aufragender Gipfel aus einem Gebirge der Sahara stammen könnte. Korkeichenwälder und Tabakpflanzungen, Reisfelder in der Marschlandschaft der Camargue, Mandelblüten um Aix, Olivenhaine um Salon, Pinienforste im Massif des Maures, Blumenteppiche an den Hängen der Küste, die heroischen Schluchten des Verdon, die den Canyons der Rocky Mountains gleichen und die leuchtenden Felsabbrüche von Les Baux in den Alpilles, die dem Bauxit, dem Aluminiumerz, seinen Namen gaben – ein mannigfaltiger Bilderbogen der Eindrücke und Stimmungen.

Ihr eigenes Gesicht hat die Côte d'Azur, der Strand des Mittelmeers, der mit einer Länge von vierhundert Kilometern diesen Bereich im Süden begrenzt. Aber auch hier, wo der Tourismus seit hundert Jahren die Szene beherrscht, bildet die urbane Topographie den glanzvollen Rahmen.

Im Rhônedelta liegt die *Camargue*, eine Wüste aus Wasser und Land, mit Schilfsümpfen und Salzdünen, Pferdeherden und Flamingoschwärmen. Inmitten der endlosen Weite, in dessen flimmerndem Licht Meer, Sumpf und Erde ineinander verschwimmen, liegt *Saintes-Maries-de-la-Mer*, der Wallfahrtsort der Zigeuner. Alljährlich am 24. und 25. Mai strömen sie aus ganz Europa herbei, um ihr großes Fest zu zelebrieren, eine Mischung aus religiöser Tradition, mystischer Verzückung und folkloristischem Brauchtum.

54 Im Herzstück der Costa Brava, der »Wilden Küste«. Unter dem wehrhaften Kastell aus dem 14. Jahrhundert duckt sich das mittelalterliche Tossa de Mar. Die Küstenstraße zwischen Tossa de Mar und San Feliú zählt zu den eindrucksvollsten Panoramastrecken des Mittelmeerraumes.

55 Eine stolze Garde monolithartiger Felsriesen überragt das weltberühmte Kloster Montserrat bei Barcelona, obligater Wallfahrtsort aller Spanienbesucher. Die heroische Felskulisse, inzwischen längst seilbahnerschlossen, inspirierte einst Richard Wagner zur Szenerie seines »Parsifal«.

Siehe Seiten 125 u. 126

Der riesigen, häßlichen Industriezone von Fos-sur-Mer an der Rhônemündung schließt sich ostwärts die Küste der Calanques an, ein felsiger Strandabschnitt von wilder Schönheit; mit steil ins Meer abstürzenden Klippen und einsamen, fjordartigen Buchten, nur wenige Kilometer von der Weltstadt Marseille entfernt.

Einer der letzten ursprünglich erhaltenen Schätze des nördlichen Mittelmeerstrandes sind die der Steinküste von Toulon vorgelagerten *Iles d'Hyères*, die Goldinseln; wildromantische Eilande, aus denen der französische Staat die Baulöwen und Immobilienmakler verbannt hat. Die berühmteste der vier Inseln, die insgesamt dreitausend Hektar umfassen, ist die *Iles du Levant*, seit langem in aller Welt bekannt als Paradies der Nudisten.

Nordöstlich davon, wo in die behutsam zum Meer herabsteigenden Hänge des Mauresgebirges die Weinhänge trapezförmig in die Kniefernwälder einschneiden, liegt in weiter Bucht *Saint-Tropez*, der ›Fliegenfänger der Welt‹, skandalumwittertes Playboydomizil, Laufsteg der Eitelkeiten. Unweit davon – besonders raffinierte Spielart des Tourismus – das Pseudo-Venedig von *Port Grimaud*, ein Pfahlbaudorf aus Beton mit Kanälen und Bogenbrücken und Bootshafen vor jeder Haustür. Zur großartigen Szenerie steigert sich die Küste um *Saint-Raphaël*, hier wachsen die roten Porphyrfelsen Korsikas aus dem Wasser. Der große Rest des französischen Mittelmeerufers, die achtzig Kilometer lange Küste von *Cannes* über *Nizza* bis *Menton*, ist ebenso berühmt wie gleichförmig: eine schmale, endlose Ferienstadt am Meer, die ihre Eskalation im gigantisch hochwachsenden Häuserhaufen von *Monaco* erfährt.

Spanien

Katalonien, Costa Brava und Costa Dorada

»Das fröhliche Meer, die fruchtbare Erde, die klare Luft«, so sang und jubelte Don Quijote, der »Ritter von der traurigen Gestalt«, Cervantes' ebenso lächerliche wie ergreifende Romanfigur, als er von der weiten, ausgebrannten Hochlandschaft Kastiliens an die Küste von Barcelona herunterkam. Sicher hätten er und sein »Kontrastkumpan« Sancho Pansa noch einige mehr ihrer skurrilen Abenteuer erlebt, hätte es damals schon Barcelonas »Rambla« gegeben. Die Rambla, das Entzücken aller Touristen aus dem Norden, ist Barcelona Lebensnerv: Straße der Tavernen und gotischen Kirchen, der Luxusgeschäfte und Blumenmärkte, der Antiquitätenhändler und der Liebe gegen bar; Reeperbahn und »Kö« und Drosselgasse in einem.

Barcelona, mit 1,8 Millionen Einwohnern Spaniens zweitgrößte Stadt, ist eine vitale, lebenssprühende Metropole, oft mit New-York verglichen, ein Schmelztiegel der Temperamente, für den Fremden ein südländisches Feuerwerk von schillernder Vielfalt. Seine Nächte sind ebenso berühmt wie seine Bauwerke, mit seinem ausgeprägten Sinn für Wirtschaft und Geschäft war es allen anderen spanischen Städten stets eine Nasenlänge voraus und die schwerblütigeren Südspanier sagen neidvoll, Barcelona wüßte »aus Steinen Brot zu machen«.

Sein mannigfaltiges Gesicht ist von der Geschichte geprägt, in der wechselweise die Einflüsse von Nord und Süd wirkten. Um 550 v. Chr. landeten griechische Kaufleute an der heutigen Costa Brava und gründeten Ampurias, 200 v. Chr. wird Barcelonas eine bedeutende Kolonie der Römer. 415 n. Chr. überfluten die Westgoten das Land, 713 erobern es die arabischen Mauren. Knapp hundert Jahre später schlagen die Franken die Mauren zurück, Barcelona wird Hauptstadt der spanischen Mark. Durch Heirat kommt es 1137 zum Königreich Aragonien und entwickelt sich in der Folgezeit zum blühenden Wirtschafts- und Handelszentrum. Im Spanischen Erbfolgekrieg von 1701 bis 1714 entscheidet sich Barcelona für die Habsburger, wird aber durch die Bourbonen unterworfen und gehört seitdem zu Spanien.

Dem Spürsinn Barcelonas und der Aufgeschlossenheit der Katalanen ist es zu danken, daß die dreihundert Kilometer lange Küste von der französischen Grenze bis Alcanar – Costa Brava und Costa Dorada – in den fünfziger Jahren als erste Landschaft der Iberischen Halbinsel zur Urlaubsregion er-

schlossen wurde. Die Sehnsucht nach dem Süden, des italienischen Klischees etwas müde, hatte ein neues »Paradies« entdeckt: Mit Pinien und Wein, Sandstränden und Felsklippen, Flamenco und Toreros, dem Zauber lauschiger Nächte und dem Klang der Gitarren. Ein Land zudem, das auch Urlaubern mit kleinem Geldbeutel die Erfüllung ihrer Träume bescherte. Inzwischen haben sich die Wogen des ersten Ansturms geglättet, weil das Zeitalter der Düsen-Jets viele andere Ziele entdeckte und näherrückte. Mag sein, daß da und dort die touristische Entwicklung das Ursprüngliche übertüncht hat, doch nach wie vor ist die katalanische Küstenlandschaft voll bezwingender, klassischer Schönheit.

Südlich von Perpignan, an der französisch-spanischen Grenze, wo der schier endlose Flachstrand des Golfs von Lion endet und die letzten Ausläufer der Pyrenäen ins Mittelmeer verklingen, beginnt bei Argelés die *Costa Brava*, die »Wilde Küste«; eine herbe, urbane Uferregion mit steil abfallenden Felsklippen, windverrenkten Kiefern und Pinien, dazwischen einsame, traumhaft schöne Buchten und Wasserwinkel. Aus dem Schiefergrau der Landschaft und dem silbrigen Grün der Olivenwälder löst sich als erste Siedlung *Cadaqués*, das weiße Fischerdorf, jahrhundertelang nur über das Meer zugänglich. Dahinter öffnet sich der Golf von Rosas, eine weite, freie Bucht, touristenumschwärmt, einladend und modern. In der Nähe lebt Salvador Dali, der ebenso skurrile wie berümte Maler, Don Quijotes würdiger Nachfolger. *Gerona*, im Hinterland, ist ein ehrwürdiges Städtchen mit vielen Treppen und brüchigen Mauern, von Sonne und Blumen zärtlich bedeckt und verklärt. Weit draußen, an der Küste zwischen *Aiguablava* und *Tossa de Mar*, entfaltet die Costa Brava ihre großartigste Szenerie: Wildromantische Felsufer, alte Fischerdörfer, die man nur zu Fuß erreicht, rötlicher Sand und das tiefblaue Meer. *Palamos*, die alte Küstensiedlung vor den Korkeichenwäldern, blickt gelassen auf seine vielen Gäste; es ist Besuch gewöhnt: Kaiser Karl V., Cervantes und maurische Seeräuber weilten schon in seinen Mauern. In der Johannisnacht feiert man hier das Fest von San Juan: Der Legende nach rettete er einst die Stadt, weil er die anrückenden Piratenschiffe in Felsriffe verzauberte. Sie liegen noch heute vor der Küste, ein Schwarm winziger Steineilande, »Ameiseninseln« benannt; und mancher Tourist sieht, vom katalanischen Wein verwirrt, wie sich nachts die steinernen Schiffe bewegen.

San Feliu de Guixols gebärdet sich als Hauptstadt der Costa Brava, glänzt mit attraktiven Hotels, verführerischen Boutiquen, Promenaden und Stierkampfarena. 24 Kilometer lang ist die Straße von San Feliu nach Tossa de Mar; mit ihren 370 Kurven gilt sie als eine der schönsten europäischen Küstenstraßen. Umhüllt von Korkeichen- und Pinienwäldern reckt sich die alte

Festung von *Tossa de Mar* auf einem Felssporn gegen das Meer. Ein bezauberndes Stück Land, Paradies der Maler und Romantiker. Außerhalb des Städtchens liegen die modernen Hotels und Ferienhäuser; in den engen, schattigen Gassen spielt sich der Alltag wie seit Jahrhunderten auf kleinen Stühlen ab, die dutzendweise vor den altersgreisen, weißgetünchten Häusern stehen. Nach dem vornehmen *Lloret de Mar*, dem rustikalen *Calella* und dem überlaufenden Fischerdorf *Blanes* weitet sich das Land zur großen Sandbucht von Barcelona.

Südwestlich der katalanischen Hauptstadt dehnen sich die breiten, goldgelben Sandstrände der *Costa Dorada* bis zum weitläufigen Mündungsdelta des Ebro. In den beliebten Badeorten, wie *Sitges, Calafell, Torredembarra* und *Salou* tummelt sich zwischen vielreihigen Sonnenschirmspalieren das Heer der Bräune- und Wasserhungrigen. Mittelpunkt dieser Region ist *Tarragona,* eine stolze Stadt, einst Hauptstadt des römischen Spanien, mit vielen Zeugen seiner alten Tradition. Ringsherum wächst der süße, berauschende Wein.

Daß im Hinterland Kataloniens, in den Pyrenäenwinkeln von *La Molina, Nuria* und *Vallter* eine gut erschlossene Skilandschaft existiert, wissen die Wenigsten. Alle aber kennen *Montserrat,* den Heiligen Berg mit seinem legendären Kloster, eine Festung des religiösen Kults. Einst Eremitagen einsamer Mönche, dann Hochburg des geistig religiösen Lebens, heute Wallfahrtsort der Touristen aus aller Welt. Zu Hunderten kurven die Busse die fast tausend Jahre alte Bergstraße hinauf zu dem weitläufigen Klosterkomplex mit der wundertätigen Schwarzen Madonna, wo über dichten Pinienwäldern die riesigen Monolithen gleichenden Felstitanen eine phantastische Kulisse bilden.

Andalusien, Costa Blanca und Costa del Sol

»Torre . . .«, »Torre Annunziata«, »Torre del Greco«, »Torrens-See« – im Großen Brockhaus von 1930 sucht man es vergeblich: »Torremolinos«, Turm und Mühlen, Fischerdorf an der südspanischen Mittelmeerküste bei Málaga. Fischerdorf? Eine Feriengroßstadt mit 100 000 Sommerbewohnern, ein Super-Saint-Tropez mit Hotelhochhäusern, Appartementzeilen, Bars, Dancings, Luxusläden, Chrom und Neon, mit der ewig lachenden, wärmenden, bräunenden Sonne, ein »Pigalle« am Mittelmeer.

Torremolinos, nur ein Punkt aus Dutzenden ähnlichartiger, symbolisiert stellvertretend das »spanische Wunder«, die Entwicklung der Sonnenküsten Costa del Sol und Costa Brava von der einsamen Strandregion zur vielumschwärmten Ferienlandschaft. Vor 40 Jahren gab es am 900 Kilometer langen Uferabschnitt zwischen Valencia und Gibraltar nicht einmal einen ländlichen Gasthof; heute reiht sich, wo das herbe Land dazu Raum läßt, Hotelkette an Hotelkette . . .

Dahinter, landeinwärts, liegt Andalusien, eine verlockende, geheimnisvolle Welt, in der Europa und der Orient ineinander verschmelzen: Glutäugige Zigeunerinnen, die zum Stakkato des Flamenco ihre berüschten Tanzröcke wirbeln; schwarzhaarige Caballeros mit breitkrempigen Sombreros, die hoch zu Roß mit langen Lanzen ihre Stier- und Pferdeherden dirigieren; weite Ebenen und welliges Hügelland mit Oliven- und Zuckerrohrpflanzungen, Korkeichenwäldern und Weinfeldern; rote Erde und die schneeglitzernden Gipfelkronen der 3500 Meter hohen Sierre Nevada. Dazwischen die uralten, glanzvollen Städte: Granada, Córdoba, Sevilla.

So wie der immerwährende Schirokko einen Gluthauch Afrikas herüberträgt, so liegt auch im Land und seinen Menschen ein Einschlag des Orient, ein Stück afro-semitischer Kultur. Achthundert Jahre lang betete man hier mit dem Blick nach Mekka, heidnischer Mythos und christlicher Glaube sind noch heute ineinander verwoben, das Antlitz Mariens durchschimmern die Züge Fatimas, der Tochter Mohammeds, und die bedeutendsten Kulturbauten stammen aus der arabischen, der maurischen Zeit.

Ein Jahrtausend vor unserer Zeitrechnung besiedelten seefahrende Phöniker und Griechen das heutige Südspanien, 600 v. Chr. eroberten die Karthager das Land. Von 206 v. Chr. bis 409 n. Chr. herrschen die Römer, ihnen folgen die germanischen Wandalen, diesen die Byzantiner, die im 6. Jahrhundert

⑤⑧ *An der spanischen Mittelmeerküste südlich von Valencia. Eine felsige Landzunge stößt weit nach Osten vor, bildet mit Cap San Antonio die Grenze zwischen Costa del Ahazar und Costa Blanca. Entdeckungsfreudige Urlaubszigeuner finden zwischen den rauhen Uferriffen Hunderte einsamer Bade- und Sonnenplätzchen.*

⑤⑨ *Die Küstenstraße zwischen Motril und Nerja, bekannt als »Balkon de Europa«, zählt zu den schönsten Panoramarouten des spanischen Mittelmeerufers. Darunter liegen, vom Tourismus noch unberührt, zwischen wilden Strandfelsen abgelegene, sandige Buchten mit dem urtümlichen Kolorit der Boote und Fischerhütten.*

der Westgotenkönig Leowigild besiegt und vertreibt. Ihre einschneidendste geschichtliche Wende erfährt die Iberische Halbinsel von 711 bis 756, als die Araber über den Brückenkopf Gibraltar das ganze Land erobern und islamisieren. Achthundert Jahre lang, viel länger als in den nord- und mittelspanischen Bereichen, regieren in Málaga, Córdoba und Granada die Kalifen; erst 1492 fällt mit der Eroberung Granadas durch die katholischen Könige die letzte Bastion des Islam auf europäischem Boden, wird das letzte Maurenreich zerstört.

Vor diesem dramatischen geschichtlichen Hintergrund entrollt sich heute die Urlaubsszenerie unserer Zeit. Manche Völker, wie die Venezianer, verbündeten sich mit dem Meer, bezogen durch es ihre Größe und ihren Reichtum. Die Südspanier mißtrauten ihm. Vom Meer kam der Schrecken, das Unheil, kamen Kriegsflotten und Eroberer, maurische Seeräuber, Piraten aus dem Berberland. Dreitausend Jahre lang wandten sie sich von der See ab, bauten Befestigungen, Mauern, Signaltürme, um das Land vor den Gefahren des Meeres zu schützen. Nun ist dieses gefürchtete Meer schlagartig zum Spielplatz der Zivilisation, zum Brennpunkt des Lebensgenusses geworden. Das Land am Meer, das von den Früchten seiner Sonne mehr schlecht als recht leben konnte, hat die Genießer seiner Sonne zu sich gerufen.

Die Costa Blanca, die »Weiße Küste«, beginnt südlich von Valencia, wo die üppige, fette Fruchtbarkeit der Huerta mit Orangen- und Zitronenhainen, Bohnen und Mais, Hanf und Getreide ans Meer grenzt. Hier ist der Strand mehr grün als weiß. Bei Denia, das mit Funden aus der Römerzeit, einer maurischen Zitadelle und der gotischen Kirche die Vielfalt spanischer Geschichte umreißt, greift das Land weit nach Osten aus, wandelt sich zu den grauschwarzen, gischtumtosten Felsklippen von *Cap Náo* und *Cap San Antonio.* Dahinter krönt der einsam aus dem Wasser hochragende Zuckerhut des Penon de Ifach, Rest eines Vulkanberges aus glattem, seifigem Gestein, die wilde, herbe Landschaft. Wenige Kilometer landeinwärts steht auf mächtigem Felsblock *Guadalest,* ursprünglich ein weitläufiges maurisches Kastell, das die späteren Bewohner in ein Dorf verwandelt haben. In den düsteren Mauern scheint die Zeit vor Jahrhunderten stehengeblieben zu sein. Im krassen Gegensatz dazu präsentiert sich draußen an der Küste *Benidorm* als Prototyp des modernen Seebades; ein babylonisches Wolkenkratzerdorf, Freihafen für die Urlaubsfreuden unserer Welt. Die spanische »Côte d'Azur« nennen es die einen; andere reden wehmutsvoll vom »verlorenen Paradies«. Kilometer um Kilometer ziehen sich die Hotels und Feriensiedlungen den Strand, die »Playa«, entlang, verschlucken die alten Fischerdörfer, enden erst vor den Hafenmolen von *Alicante.* Hier vermischt sich der Duft des frischen Meeres

mit den Gerüchen von Olivenöl und Gesalzenem, Kaffee und Benzin. Die stolze, selbstbewußte Stadt rühmt sich als südlichster Hort katalanischer Sprache und Geschäftstüchtigkeit.

Südöstlich davon begegnet man einem Stück Afrika, dem Dattelpalmenwald von Elche. Von den Phönikern angelegt, standen hier einst eine Million Palmen; heute sind es noch 170 000, einzelne sind bis zu 40 Meter hoch und 250 Jahre alt. Vor 80 Jahren fand man hier die »Dame von Elche«, eine der wenigen Skulpturen der alten Iberer aus dem 4. bis 3. Jahrhundert v. Chr., die jetzt im Prado-Museum in Madrid steht. Dem Meer abgewandt, weit im Landesinnern, liegt *Murcia,* im 9. Jahrhundert von den Mauren gegründet und zu einer der prächtigsten Städte des muselmanischen Spanien ausgebaut. Die gotische Kathedrale Santa Maria, 1358 über einer Moschee errichtet, beeindruckt durch ihre imposante Barockfassade und dem 95 Meter hohen Turm. Murcias berühmtester Künstler, Francisco Salzillo, schuf viele spanische Heiligenfiguren, »Pasos« genannt, die als schönste Volkskunsterzeugnisse der iberischen Halbinsel gelten. Rings um die Stadt dehnt sich, vom Wasser der Stauseen gespeist, eine subtropische Gartenlandschaft aus, zieht sich hinaus bis an die flache Küste des Mar Menor, einem binnenseeartigen Lagunengewässer, durch eine 22 Kilometer lange Dünenlandzunge vom offenen Meer getrennt, in afrikanisch flimmerndes Licht getaucht. *Cartagena,* von den Karthagern gegründet, war viele Jahre die wichtigste Stadt Spaniens; noch heute ist sie ein bedeutender Kriegs- und Exporthafen.

An der Küste vor Cartagena löst die Costa del Sol die Costa Blanca ab, die Landschaftsfolie wird gewaltiger, urtümlicher, die Szenerie geheimnisvoller. In *Almeria* thronen die grauen Rundtürme des Alcazaba, eines riesigen arabischen Kastells, über den weißleuchtenden, spartanischen Steinhäusern, der wuchtigen Kathedrale und dem altersgrauen Kloster, in dem Garcia Lorca erzogen wurde. Östlich der Stadt, um Adra und Berja, drängen die Ausläufer der Sierra Nevada an die Küste, stürzen mit zerklüfteten Felsflanken ins tiefblaue Meer. Nur wenige Besucher verirren sich in das Hinterland der Sierra de Gadór, einer rauhen, weltenfernen Felswüstenei, wegen ihrer Verwandtschaft mit dem amerikanischen Colorado oft Schauplatz spannender Italo-Western.

In *Motril* ist alle Schwermut vergessen; da sind unter den Schneegipfeln der Sierra Nevada tausend emsige Hände mit der Verarbeitung von Zuckerrohr beschäftigt. Die Höhenstraße zwischen Motril und Nerja gilt als eine der schönsten Promenadenstrecken der iberischen Küste: Zwischen Palmen, Agaven und Oleander öffnen sich zauberhafte Blicke auf die buchtenreiche Ufer-

137

landschaft; an den silbrig-grauen Hängen und Höhen liegen die Häuser der Dörfer wie verstreuter Würfelzucker. Nach Nerja beginnt das große Ferienreich der Costa del Sol. *Málaga*, Stadt der Fische und Meeresfrüchte, der Orangen und Kakteen, der Palmen, Gärten und Blumen, der vielen Kirchen und Kulturbauten aus griechischer, römischer, arabischer und christlicher Vergangenheit, Geburtsstadt Pablo Picassos. Dann, vor den in bläulicher Ferne verschimmernden Bergkulissen, von Eukalyptuswäldern umschlossen, die Parade der Seebäder – *Torremolinos*, das »Las Vegas« des spanischen Südens; *Fuengirola*, eine Nuance gedämpfter, urtümlicher; *Marbella*, die »Schöne am Meer«, gleichermaßen altertümlich und luxuriös; *San Pedro de Alcántara* und *Estepona*, die Fischerdörfer mit den Palasthotels der spanischen Aristokraten – ein hundert Kilometer langer Ferientraum bis zum Felsblock von Gibraltar, der wehrhaften Trutzburg zwischen Europa und Afrika.

Ein paar Kilometer vom internationalen Getriebe der Küste entfernt lebt das unverfälschte, alte Andalusien; in winkeligen, kaum schulterbreiten Gassen, die Wände bis unters Dach mit Geranientöpfen behängt, mit verträumten, gründurchwucherten Patios, in denen die Zeit stillsteht; mit uralten Gebräuchen und Riten. Weiter im Landesinnern die stolzen Städte: Das vielbesungene *Granada*, von der Alhambra, der größten Araberburg Europas, überragt; *Córdoba*, Stadt der Matadore, mit der Mezquita, der größten islamischen Moschee auf spanischem Boden mit ihren 856 Säulen; *Sevilla* mit dem Alcázar, dem festungsähnlichen maurischen Herrscherpalast. Schließlich, zwischen Karst und Steppe, Wein und Wüste, die vielen namenlosen Orte, in denen das Gestern dem Heute begegnet, wo Stierkämpfer mehr gelten als Kriegshelden, wo in Fernsehkrimis die Romantik der »Bandoleros«, der andalusischen Räuber, lebt, und an den Wänden der Kneipen das Pin-up-Girl neben dem Bild der Schwarzen Madonna hängt.

Portugal

Land am Atlantik

Das Ritual und die Kulisse sind fast gleich: Eine Arena voll erhitzter Gemüter, Fiesta-Stimmung, Cavalheiros in Rokokokostümen auf edlen Pferden, Toureiros und Stiertreiber. Der Stier trabt auf den Schauplatz, der Matador plaziert mit Grandezza seine buntbebänderten Pfeile im Nacken des Tieres, fordert es, Auge in Auge, zum Kampf, schwingt kraftvoll den Degen und stößt zu — symbolisch. Dann ringen acht Männer den »erlegten« Stier mit bloßen Händen nieder; schließlich trottet er, begleitet von einer Schar Jungtiere, willig aus der Arena zurück auf die Weide.

Das ist »spanischer« Stierkampf auf portugiesisch. Diese liebenswürdige Abwandlung ist symptomatisch für den Unterschied zwischen Spanien und Portugal – für die Menschen wie für die Landschaft. Das Wesen Portugals ist weicher, sanfter, versöhnlicher. Die Sprache klingt – im Gegensatz zum harten, prägnanten Spanisch – mit den gebrochenen, verschwimmenden Nasallauten und den schwelgerisch ineinander verwobenen Silben und Sätzen melodisch und einschmeichelnd, obwohl beide aus dem gleichen Wortmaterial schöpfen. Statt des knatternden Flamencos tönt hier der melancholisch-schluchzende Gesang des »Fado«, und das portugiesische Gemüt kennt einen Begriff, der in keiner Sprache übersetzbar ist – »Saudade«, die Sehnsucht nach dem Unbekannten und Unerfüllbaren, eine Art von genießerischer Traurigkeit. Auch die Formen des Landes sind weich und voll großräumiger Übergänge, von den Höhen Kastiliens sanft nach Südwesten zum großen Ozean hinunterfließend. Die Häuser der Fischerdörfer scheinen – bei aller Einfachheit – sauberer und gepflegter zu sein, die Farben klarer und leuchtender als jene des sonnendurchtrieften Mittelmeerraumes, als hätte die frische Brise des Atlantik alle Unreinheiten weggefegt.

Aus oberflächlicher mitteleuropäischer Sicht ist Portugal ein kleines Land am Rand des Kontinents, ein Anhängsel Spaniens. Gewiß sind die geschichtlichen und kulturellen Wurzeln der beiden iberischen Nachbarländer annähernd die gleichen. Hier wie dort siedelten tausend Jahre v. Chr. die Kelten, errichteten Phöniker und Griechen an den Küsten ihre Stützpunkte. Um 200 v. Chr. brachen die Römer ein, eroberten nach und nach die ganze iberische Halbinsel. In dieser Zeit finden sich die ersten Anzeichen einer Trennung der beiden Völkerschaften. Die Römer teilten das Land in das Spanien »oberhalb des Ebro« und in das westspanische Lusitanien zwischen Douro und Minho. Un-

62 Der Kreuzgang des Klosters Belém bei Lissabon, ein Höhepunkt des manuelinischen Stils. Das zu orientalischer Pracht entfaltete Zierwerk aus Ornamenten und Arabesken stammt aus Anregungen, die im 15. und 16. Jahrhundert portugiesische Seefahrer aus aller Welt mit nach Hause brachten.

63 Ein Urlaubstraum aus tiefblauem Meer, feinem Goldsand und phantastischen Felsgebilden ist die südportugiesische Algarve-Küste am Atlantischen Ozean. Im Bild der Strand bei Praia da Rocha.

ter der Herrschaft der Westgoten, die um das Jahr 500 n. Chr. beginnt, gab es bereits eine burgundische Grafschaft »Portocalle«, das Land um den Hafen Oporto. Nach 711 überfluteten die Araber in einem Blitzkrieg das ganze Land. Bei der Rückeroberung zeichnete sich 1136 Afonso Henrique durch einen Sieg über die Mauren aus und wurde der erste portugiesische König. In der Folge entwickelte Portugal, das gleichzeitig gegen Kastilien und die Mauren kämpfte, den trutzigen Geist eines eingeschlossenen Volkes, verbündete sich mit England und legte damit den Grundstein zur Unabhängigkeit vom spanischen Nachbarn. 1147 wurde Lissabon erobert, um 1250 wurden die letzten Araber aus Südportugal vertrieben, 250 Jahre früher als in Südspanien. Portugal wurde zur ersten europäischen Nation und behauptete seine Grenzen – abgesehen von einer vorübergehenden, sechzigjährigen spanischen Herrschaft von 1580 bis 1640 – durch die letzten siebenhundert Jahre. Seit diesen Ereignissen besteht eine gemäßigte Art von Feindschaft zwischen den beiden Staaten; heute steht man sich zwar nicht feindselig, aber mit gemessener Distanz gegenüber. Die Grenzübergänge zwischen Spanien und Portugal sind die am wenigsten frequentierten in Europa.

Portugal richtete schon früh seinen Blick aufs Meer. Doch sein Interesse galt nicht – wie jenes der Griechen, Genueser und Venezianer – dem begrenzten Mittelmeerraum, sondern der lockenden Weite des Atlantik. In der ersten Hälfte des 15. Jahrhunderts schickte der Infant Heinrich der Seefahrer die Kapitäne an die Küsten Westafrikas, widerlegte die Theorie des Aristoteles, nach der die Tropen wegen ihrer Gluthitze unbewohnbar seien. 1498 erreichte Vasco da Gama auf dem Seeweg über die Südspitze Afrikas das sagenhafte Indien. Dieses Ereignis war damals viel bedeutungsvoller als die Entdeckung Amerikas sechs Jahre vorher. Die Tragweite von Kolumbus' Seefahrten war noch nicht faßbar, er fand ja nur unerforschte Inseln mit primitiven Naturvölkern; Vasco da Gama aber brachte kostbare Gewürze und Edelsteine mit. Fernando Magellan umschiffte als Erster die Südspitze Südamerikas (Magellan-Straße) und entdeckte 1521 die Marianen und Philippinen. Portugal errichtete Stützpunkte und Kolonien in allen Erdteilen, wurde zum Weltreich ungeheueren Ausmaßes. Doch es verströmte seine Kraft in alle Welt, dem Land kam wenig zugute. Die wenigen Reichen wurden noch reicher, die vielen Armen blieben arm, und so ist es im Wesentlichen bis heute geblieben.

Der glanzvolle Mittelpunkt des Landes ist die Hauptstadt *Lissabon,* einst als schönste Stadt der Welt gepriesen. 1755 zerstörte ein Erdbeben die Stadt und damit auch – trotz großartigem Wiederaufbau – seine legendäre Ausstrahlung. Das Juwel der Stadt ist *Belém* – Sperrfestung, Kloster, Kirche, ein Kreuzgang, der zu den festlichsten der Welt zählt. Hier begegnet man – wie auch

in Caminha, Coimbra, Batalha – den faszinierenden Höhepunkten des manuelinischen Stils, eine durch Ornamente, Arabesken und phantastische Zierformen sublimierte Spätgotik – steingewordenes Märchen aus Tausendundeiner Nacht.

Für den mitteleuropäischen Urlaubsgast hält Portugal zwei Strandregionen bereit: Die Costa do Sal und die Küste der Algarve. Die *Costa do Sal,* die »Salzküste«, liegt westlich von Lissabon an der Mündung des Tejo in den Atlantischen Ozean. Der Bereich, mit dem Mittelpunkt des luxuriösen Seebades *Estoril,* erinnert etwas an die Côte d'Azur: Hunderte prunkvoller Villen am Felshang, Kasinos, Golfplatz, Tennisplätze, Reitparcours – Tummelplatz von Portugals oberen Zehntausend.

Von ganz anderem Charakter ist die Küste der *Algarve,* die im Süden des Landes ihre volle Breitseite der Sonne zuwendet. Ein 180 Kilometer langes Ufer mit phantastischen Felsgebilden und feinem Goldsand, pittoresken Fischerdörfern und weinlaubengedeckten Tavernen; ausreichend erschlossen und noch nicht überlaufen. Man verliebt sich auf den ersten Blick in diese klassischschöne Landschaft mit dem tiefblauen Meer, dem wolkenlosen Sommer, den malerischen Windmühlen mit weißen Flügeln, der köstlichen Frische der Farben, überlagert von einem Hauch Griechenland und Afrika. Weit draußen im Westen, wo die iberische Halbinsel eine spitzwinkelige Kante bildet, umtosen die Meereswellen *Cap San Vincente* und das Städtchen *Sagres.* Darüber, auf der Serra de Monchique – für viele schönste Kanzel Europas – residierte einst Heinrich der Seefahrer, dirigierte seine Schiffe in alle Welt. Dahinter, nach Osten zu, schmiegen sich die kleinen Städtchen und Dörfer in die Buchten: *Lagos,* wo man die ersten Karavellen baute und von Sardinen lebt; *Portimao* mit dem skurrilen Felsstrand von Praia da Rocha; *Lagôa* mit seinen duftenden Weingärten; *Albufeira,* das lebhafte Städtchen, in Mandelblüten versinkend; *Faro,* Hauptort und Drehscheibe der Küste; *Olhao,* eine Fata Morgana aus weißen, kubistisch aufeinandergetürmten Fischerhauswürfeln; schließlich, vor der Grenze gegen Spanien, *Tavira,* alt und rustikal, mit römischer Brücke und maurischer Burg.

Jugoslawien

Dalmatinische Adria

Wissen Sie, wo »Omas Popo« liegt? Wo der »Ziegenbauch«, der »Schwalben-flügel« und die »Hure« liegen? Um es ganz genau zu erfahren, müßten Sie nach Betina auf der Insel Murter fahren und einen alten Fischer befragen. Er wird Ihnen erzählen, daß dies einige der dalmatinischen Kornaten-Inseln sind, die »zahlreicher sind als die Tage des Jahres«. Wieviele genau? Er weiß es nicht, niemand weiß es, nicht einmal – man hält es in unserer total erfaßten, registrierten, computergesteuerten Welt kaum für möglich – das jugoslawische Vermessungsamt in Belgrad. Es können 150 sein, vielleicht auch 300. Einst kam ein kaiserlich-österreichischer Admiral, um sie in eine Seekarte aufzuneh-men. Um ihn zufriedenzustellen, erfanden die Fischer die launigen Namen, und die gelten hier noch heute.
Die Kornaten-Inseln, der dalmatinischen Küste vorgelagert, sind eine Armee von steinernen Tropfen; ausgebleichtes, tristes Gestein und Geröll, mit dürfti-gem Grün betupft, keine dauernd bewohnt, aus der Flugzeugsicht eine un-wirkliche, surrealistisch-graphische Vision. Die Legende erzählt, sie seien »von den Göttern aus Sterntränen und Meereshauch geschaffen«.

Dalmatiens Küste ist eine der wildesten und bewegtesten Europas. In grauer Vorzeit falteten Urkräfte die Landmassen, mit gewaltigem Sturz versanken die westlichen Bergketten in der Adria, aus der sie heute mit über tausend Gipfel, Rücken und Klippen herausragen. Doch die titanische Wüstenei ist nur eines von vielen Gesichtern des Landes. Gewiß, tonangebend ist die pittoreske Szenerie der bleichen Steininseln im tintigen Blau des Wassers, der verkarsteten Uferhänge, die sich, vielfach zerklüftet, »zum Brandungsstreifen niedersenken und sich dort wie geschmolzenes Blei verästeln«. Dazwischen aber erweckt die südliche Sonne an den Küstenrändern eine üppige Pflanzen-pracht mit Pinien und Zypressen, Oliven und Weinreben, Palmen und Aga-ven, Feigen und Lavendel; nisten in den Felsnischen, auf Landvorsprüngen und Inseln uralte Städte und Siedlungen von bezwingender Originailität, in vollkommener Harmonie mit der Landschaft verwachsen.
Von der Geschichte wurde das Land nie verwöhnt. Urbewohner waren, über weite Teile des Balkans verstreut, die indogermanischen, kriegerischen Illyrier. Um 230 v. Chr. drangen die Römer an die ostadriatische Küste vor, bekämpf-ten in vielen Kleinkriegen das uneinheitliche Seeräubervolk, unterwarfen es schließlich im Jahr 9. n. Chr. völlig und verleibten Illyrien ihrem Reich ein.

146

Wiederholt waren Illyrier große Kaiser des Römischen Reichs, so Aurelian, Diokletian, Konstantin. Nach der Reichsteilung fiel das Land an das oströmische Byzanz, später beherrschten es Ostgoten und Awaren. Im 6. und 7. Jahrhundert drangen die südslawischen Serben und Kroaten vor, drängten die romanische Bevölkerung in die Küstenstädte und auf die Inseln. Diese aber wurden um das Jahr 1000 zur Beute der Venezianer. Zwischendurch kämpften sich die ungarischen Magyaren bis an die Küste durch, wurden aber dort 1420 wieder vom Dogen Venedigs vertrieben. Venedig behauptete sich, wiederholten Türkenanstürmen trotzend, bis zum Ende seiner Machtepoche: Erst 1797 wurde Dalmatien Kronland der Habsburger-Monarchie; nach dem Ersten Weltkrieg kam es 1920 zum neugeschaffenen Mehrvölkerstaat Jugoslawien.

Eine Ausnahme in diesen geschichtlichen Wirren bildete Ragusa, das heutige *Dubrovnik*. Es war im 15. Jahrhundert eine weltbedeutende Seefahrermacht, trotzte dem mächtigen Venedig, schwang sich gar zu dessen Rivalin auf dem Weltmarkt auf, unterhielt 70 Konsulate und befuhr alle Meere der Erde. Doch schließlich mußte auch die »Perle der Adria« die Segel streichen, weil die Geschicke des Kontinents es geboten. Tragisch und historisch einmalig ist sein Untergang: Als es 1815 zu Habsburg kam, beschloß der Adel Ragusas Kinderlosigkeit und verurteilte damit die stolze Stadt zum Tod.

Heute ist Dubrovnik auserwähltes Objekt der Reisesehnsucht. Die kompakt auf einem ins Meer vorspringenden Felssporn erbaute Stadt hat einen voll erhaltenen, bis ins 10. Jahrhundert zurückreichenden Mauerring mit trutzigen Befestigungswerken, prächtige Kirchen und Paläste im venezianischen Stil; in den mittelalterlichen Gassen erzählt jeder Stein von vergangener Größe.

Doch Dubrovnik ist nur eines der vielen besuchenswerten Ziele, die das 800 Kilometer lange Küstenstraßenband der Adria-Magistrale miteinander verknüpft. Der schönste Abschnitt beginnt, von Norden her, in *Zadar*, das fast ganz von Wasser umschlossen ist. *Šibenik*, im 10. Jahrhundert von den kroatischen Königen gegründet, wird von drei mächtigen Forts bewacht; seine Kathedrale ist eine der bedeutendsten Kirchen Dalmatiens. Ein mittelalterliches Juwel ist *Trogir*, aus einer griechischen Siedlung des 4. Jahrhunderts v. Chr. hervorgegangen und auf einer künstlichen Insel erbaut; unter seinen vielen sehenswerten Bauwerken ragt die Kathedrale (13.–15. Jhd.) mit prachtvollen Skulpturen heraus. Wirtschaftliches Zentrum Dalmatiens ist *Split*, eine moderne Stadt in antiken Kulissen: Keimzelle und Herzstück ist der 310 erbaute Palast des römischen Kaisers Diokletian: Altersruhesitz, Verbannungsort und Fluchtburg für die Bewohner des nahen römischen Salona (Solin), das 615 von Slawen und Awaren zerstört wurde. Südlich von Dubrovnik, dem »dalmatinischen Florenz«, wandelt sich an der Küste Montenegros die zerrissene und zerklüftete Uferformation zu weiten, langgezogenen Hangfluchten, auf denen das Grün der Oliven- und Pinienwälder die elegischen, grau-violetten Schattierungen des Karsts verdrängt. Reizvolles Kleinod in diesem Bereich ist das Felsinseldorf *Sveti Stefan,* das – unter Erhaltung der alten baulichen Substanz – zu einem modernen Feriendorf umgestaltet wurde.

Der reich gegliederten Küste vorgelagert ist eine Vielzahl von Inseln aller Größen, manche kahl und unbewohnt, andere mit dichtem Bewuchs, auf denen noch Mungos, Schakale und hunderterlei Kriechtiere leben. Einige der größeren Inseln tragen malerische alte Städtchen mit passablen Straßen – wie *Brač, Korčula, Hvar, Pelyešac* und *Pašman.* Die Uferlängen der Küste und der vielen Inseln ergeben aneinandergereiht eine Strandlänge von über sechstausend Kilometern – Platz genug für jede Art von Badefreuden, Wassersport und hüllenlosem Robinsonleben in paradiesischer Einsamkeit. Der größte Teil der Ufer ist felsig, wird aber immer wieder von feinkiesigen Flachstränden unterbrochen. Mehligen Goldsand findet man nur selten, Ausnahmen sind die Ufer von *Crikvenica, Budva, Petrovac* und *Ulcinj.* Große Zonen sind noch unerschlossen und unberührt, in vielen gewinnt touristischer Service erst langsam Boden; einige Punkte aber, wie *Makarska* oder *Cavtat,* haben sich schon zu modernen Seebädern gemausert. Großes Plus der dalmatinischen Küstenlandschaft sind die menschenfreundlichen Preise: hierin übertrifft sie alle Strandregionen Europas.

Griechenland

Hellas und seine Inselwelt

Im Reigen der europäischen Urlaubs- und Reiseziele hat Griechenland, auch sinnbildlich gesehen, das letzte Wort. Es ist die Krönung dessen, was man auf unserem Kontinent an Reiseerleben mit nach Hause nehmen kann. Nach landläufigen Ferienmaßstäben ist Griechenland weder schön noch lieblich – eine phantastische, unwirkliche Welt aus Licht, Wasser und Stein.
Rudolf Hagelstange sagt darüber: »Das Land ist nackt, nackt in seinem äußersten Sinn. Wo sich die Geschlechter am innigsten und ungestümsten begegnen, begegnen sie einander schmucklos, nackt. Darum scheut der Mangel, das Gebrechen die Nacktheit. Wenn Griechenland nackt ist, so, weil es schön ist. Auf der letzten Stufe ist der äußerste Schmuck der Schönheit die Nacktheit ... Wer dem Tand der Zivilisation nachläuft, wird Griechenland nicht finden. Es ist nicht die Perle, mit der man sich schmückt, an der man sich weidet, sondern die Muschel, die sie gebar.«

Griechenland ist die Wiege Europas; alles, was das Abendland an Ideen, Formen, Gedanken und Entwürfen hervorbrachte, ist aus den Wurzeln griechischer Kultur erwachsen. Lange vor unserer Zeitrechnung blühten Wissenschaften und Künste: Homer schuf seine klassischen Epen, Pythagoras – jedem Quartaner bekannt – die Grundlagen von Mathematik und Geometrie, Hippokrates jene der wissenschaftlichen Medizin. Archimedes entdeckte die Zusammenhänge von Mechanik und Astronomie, Sokrates entwickelte seine auf Stärkung von Körper und Geist zielende Sitten- und Tugendlehre, Sophokles schuf mit seinen Tragödien die Grundlagen des abendländischen Dramas. Architektur und plastische Kunst brachten Meisterwerke im Tempelbau und in der Darstellung des menschlichen Körpers hervor. Höchstes Streben galt dem Gemeinwesen, und die Volksherrschaft wurde praktiziert, lange bevor man dafür den Begriff Demokratie erfand.
Griechenlands Geschichte, beginnend im III. Jahrtausend vor unserer Zeitrechnung, ist so komplex und vielschichtig, daß sie in einigen Zeilen nicht ausführlich darzustellen ist. Hervorgegangen aus den Völkern der Ionier, Achäer und Dorer, erlebte das Land im I. Jahrtausend v. Chr. seine große Zeit. Aus dieser Epoche stammen die meisten der heute bewunderten Bauwerke. Doch es gab damals kein einheitliches griechisches Reich, sondern die Machtblöcke von Athen, Theben, Korinth und Argos, die sich zwar zeitweise – wie in den Kriegen gegen die Perser und unter der Hand Alexanders

des Großen – zusammenfanden, doch zumeist stritten, verbündeten, bekämpften und besiegten; nur während der olympischen Wettkämpfe schwiegen die Waffen. Durch Uneinigkeit geschwächt, erlag das Land 197 v. Chr. den Römern; dies war auch das Ende der glanzvollen Zeit. 395 n. Chr., mit der Teilung des römischen Reiches, geriet Griechenland unter die byzantinische Herrschaft Konstantinopels. Machtpolitisch bedeutungslos, kam es in der Folgezeit in die Hände der Araber, Bulgaren, Normannen, Albaner, Venezianer und schließlich der Türken. Fast hundert Jahre, von 1821 bis 1913, dauerte es, bis Griechenland seine heutigen Grenzen erkämpfte. Selbst in unserer Zeit schwelt noch die Erbfeindschaft gegen die Türken, wie sich am Beispiel Zyperns zeigt.

Topographisch ist Griechenland ein Phänomen. Dem Festland, an den Rumpf der Balkanhalbinsel »angehängt«, sind über dreitausend Inseln vorgelagert, von denen nur 150 bewohnt sind. Befährt man auf dem Schiff die griechischen Meere, verliert man oft jede Orientierung: Die vielen Inselsilhouetten narren den perspektivischen Sinn, täuschen geschlossene Ufer vor und man wähnt sich auf einem See. Eindrucksvoll ist diese Verzahnung von Wasser und Land vom Flugzeug aus; da erscheinen die Felsriffe wie Gipfel eines vom Meer überfluteten Gebirges. Statistiker haben ausgerechnet, daß die Küste des Festlandes und aller Inseln zusammen eine Länge von 15 000 Kilometern ergibt; demnach entfallen auf jeden Einwohner Griechenlands zwei Meter Ufer. Hier liegt das große Reservoir des mediterranen Tourismus, auf das er zwangsläufig ausgreifen wird, wenn eines Tages die Strände Italiens, Spaniens und Jugoslawiens bersten. Das Überraschende: Jede dieser Inseln ist anders in ihrer Form, ihrer Vegetation, ihren Bauten, ihren Menschen und deren Bräuchen. Allen gemeinsam sind ihre Gastfreundschaft und ihre Armut. Doch diese Armut ist nicht der Not am Rand der Industriestaaten oder im übervölkerten Indien gleichzusetzen; hier ist sie genügsam, spartanische Selbstzufriedenheit, geprägt nach uralten Maßstäben, die den Begriff »Sozialismus« nicht kennen.

Das individuelle Reisen auf den griechischen Inseln – abseits der touristischen Förderbänder – ist ein Spiel mit der Zeit und dem Zufall. Irgendwann wird ein Schiff ankommen, abfahren, vielleicht ein »Kaiki« (seit Odysseus' Zeiten der gedrungene, einheimische Bootstyp), das Früchte oder Schafe zur Nachbarinsel bringt. Fahrpläne? Nein, so etwas kennt man nicht, aber irgendwann . . . Schiffe und Schiffchen sind die Fäden zur Welt, Übermittler, Boten, Lebensbringer; ihr Anlegen und Auslaufen ist das große Ereignis im eintönigen Inselalltag. Kommt gar ein Schiff mit Touristen, erwacht das Eiland zu ameisenhafter Regsamkeit. Da werden die Windmühlen ange-

168 Rembrandt. Detail of *Portrait of a woman*. X-ray photograph. Paris, Louvre.

During his period which one might call 'worldly', Rembrandt, especially when painting portraits, concealed the impetuosity of his technique behind a surface appearance of 'bourgeois' handling.

Spanish contemporaries give us fewer clues to his character than can be gleaned from a study of his pictures. One such comment, though, describes him as a 'knight in grand style,' and it not difficult to imagine him infatuated by the idea of nobility, and rendered all the more eager to climb the social ladder by the conviction that he was an aristocrat by nature.

An ambiguous remark about him by Philip IV has continued to provoke discussion. On an occasion when the king had sent him to Italy to buy paintings, and he had lingered there longer than seemed necessary, the king, writing to his ambassador in Rome urging him to persuade his court painter to return home, said that he was fully aware of the latter's '*flema*'. Some have interpreted this word as meaning that Velázquez was of a stable, 'phlegmatic' temperament; others see it as an accusation of selfishness and thoughtlessness. Each is a facet of the probable truth. A non-committal attitude suited the artist very well; during that era, it was an aristocratic characteristic, signifying a refusal to commit oneself, a disinclination to emerge from a state of silence, that 'sanctuary of prudence' as Baltasar Gracián called it in *El héroe*, adding that 'one should, then, imitate the procedure of God who holds mankind in suspense'. Velázquez assumes the role of demiurge, setting up brilliant appearances above the abyss of nothingness, deigning to confer on them existence of a sort but not true being. The duel between subject and object, which at one moment had appeared to have reached a solution, ends in the annihilation of both.

At the other end of Europe, in the newly created 'United Provinces' which were diametrically opposed to Spain both politically and culturally, another artist was developing a method of handling paint that was as uniquely his own as was that of Velázquez. But whereas Velázquez mastered his style so rapidly that in the absence of documentation it is difficult to classify his works chronologically, Rembrandt continued throughout his life, until the very end, to invent new means of expressing more effectively his creative desires, and the body of work he produced certainly represents the richest fund of technical experimentation in the history of painting. From the very beginning he created his own style through the way he worked his paint. Although the handling in his earliest paintings is very clumsy, he quickly acquired an astonishing virtuosity, painting small-scale pictures in which the pigment, treated minutely but in thickness, with a fine brush, contains a concentrated force (*The Artist's mother*, Amsterdam; *Saskia as Flora*, Hermitage).

Rembrandt soon entered his baroque period, during which he set himself the task of painting large-scale dramatic compositions of a boldness unparalleled until the advent of the cinema (*Blinding of Samson*, Frankfurt; *The man with the bittern*, Dresden; the *Company of Captain Frans Banning Cocq*, better known as the *Night Watch*, Amsterdam). Until 1648, the date when he painted the admirable *Pilgrims of Emmaus* (Louvre), his handling was powerful and calm, displaying progressively all the riches of the most generous impastos combined with the subtle use of glazes; he innovated ceaselessly, sometimes using – particularly for landscapes – sized mahogany panels, allowing the fruity tone to show through the brown tints, sometimes tracing the image on this foundation by scratching in the colour with the back of the brush.

Between the years 1630 and 1645 Rembrandt painted a series of far more conventional portraits of dignified burghers, but even here X-rays have revealed that the evenly spread blandness of this artificial impasto conceals the battle of brushstrokes which preceded the conquest of the image (*pls 167–8*). In his final period, Rembrandt expressed himself entirely in terms of this impassioned movement, and the paintings took shape just as they came, throbbing, from his imagination. During the last ten years of his life, pigment became as malleable in his hands as clay is for the modeller, and he abandoned the spatial researches of his baroque period to concentrate entirely on the ductility of matter.

The *Flayed ox* of the Louvre, painted in 1655, displays to us the splendour of its blood-streaked flesh and fat. This extraordinary work should be viewed as a kind of anatomy lesson: it springs from the same desire to explore the depths of carnal nature, but apprehended at a stage beyond analysis, as a kind of primordial matter forming the basis of life. This particular work is, in a sense, the antithesis of the cubist drawings of Dürer, Cambiaso and Poussin, who all responded to the spirit of the Renaissance in seeking truth beyond rather than within appearances. Rembrandt accomplished his boldest feat of all in his immense *Conspiracy of Julius Civilis* (*pls 170–1*), commissioned for Amsterdam Town Hall and then rejected by the municipal council who failed to understand that the vastly exaggerated handling allowed for the fact that the picture was due to be positioned at a considerable height and viewed from a distance.

Rembrandt had, for many years, manipulated his paint with palette-knife as well as brush; in his last works, he even worked the thick impasto with his fingers, as though he could not bear any intermediary to come between his hand and the pigment

169 Gillis van Coninxloo (1554–1607). Detail of *Elijah fed by the crow*. Brussels, Musée Royal d'Art Ancien.

Anticipating Rembrandt, the Fleming van Coninxloo gives the impression, in his landscapes, of wishing to probe into the material substance of things.

170 Rembrandt. *The Conspiracy of Julius Civilis*. Stockholm, Nationalmuseum.

Commissioned for Amsterdam Town Hall, this colossal canvas was judged to be scandalous and returned to the artist who, in order to preserve the principal part of it, was obliged to cut it up.

he loved to knead (the *Jewish bride*, Amsterdam; *Family portrait*, Brunswick; *Tobias*, Hermitage). Released from all descriptive servitude, this colour-drenched paint possesses an astonishing evocative force that is all the more suprising in that, truly transfigured, it no longer expresses anything but the infinite capacity for love of an old man overwhelmed by the blows of fate and condemned by bereavement to face death alone.

In his passion for the expressive virtue of matter, Rembrandt was preceded by a strange artist who lived like a hermit, Hercules Seghers. Rembrandt himself owned examples of the work of this painter, whose aim seems to have been to transcend the purely visual aspect of nature which had been all that interested landscape painters, and so to penetrate, in all its mineral density, the very matter of which the world is made. He expressed himself in etchings, in which he did not hesitate to work in negative, and to invent entirely new biting pro-

cedures to render the appearance of the earth's crust. His rare paintings reveal similar pre-occupations, and these fantastic visions, rendered with finely worked pigments, certainly inspired Rembrandt's landscapes. A Flemish painter of the previous generation, Gillis van Coninxloo, may be considered the pioneer of this approach to landscape: all the elements in his marshy forests appear to blend into a kind of primordial matter, an aqueous substance which evokes the Amazonian jungle rather than Europe's orderly vegetation (*pl. 169*).

Another painter who undoubtedly influenced Rembrandt was Adam Elsheimer, a curious man whose researches into light effects also inspired that very different artist, Claude Lorrain. As Willi Drost has pointed out (*Adam Elsheimer als Zeichner*, 1957), Rembrandt made a close study of Elsheimer's work; he seems to have been particularly struck by the latter's drawings which he may have seen

at Leyden, or else at Amsterdam, where the sister of Elsheimer's pupil Hendrick Goudt had had to sell those which had belonged to her brother. The young Rembrandt must have been deeply impressed by Elsheimer's brilliant manner of coaxing forms from the depths of the imagination and revealing them by means of a swirl of forcefully applied strokes often executed in wash-tint (*pls 172–3*).

The aesthetic theories of the seventeenth century are so impoverished that it is pointless to turn to the writings on art of the period for enlightenment about this new attitude on the part of artists. Seventeenth- and eighteenth-century aesthetic opinions were far less subtle than those of the six-teenth century, which had benefited greatly from the refinements of neoplatonism. It is a strange paradox that at the moment when painting was abandoning the literal imitation of nature, the pundits who wrote about art insisted ever more

vehemently that its aim was to imitate nature! If these authors went beyond the Aristotelian concept of *mimesis*, imitation of nature, it was only to advocate a different sort of imitation, that of antiquity. Pacheco could think of no better way of bragging about his son-in-law Velázquez than to praise his talents as a perfect imitator. So no useful purpose would be served by consulting these dusty theses. Since artists have always agreed secretly with the major intellectual developments of their own time, it may be more profitable to examine the ideas of seventeenth-century philosophers.

In addition to the importance, which I have already emphasized, of the heliocentric theory, other contemporaneous scientific investigations are relevant to an understanding of the vision of seventeenth-century painters. Certainly, the ex-pansion of the human horizon to infinity, made possible by Copernicus, Galileo and Kepler, is reflected in the fascination with space experienced

171 Rembrandt. Detail of *The Conspiracy of Julius Civilis*. Stockholm, Nationalmuseum.

Towards the end of his life, Rembrandt produced marvellous transfigurations of colour and texture from the pigment that he explored so deeply.

195

172 Rembrandt. *The Denial of St Peter*. Madrid, Biblioteca Nacional.

by the painters of that era. But, as we have seen, these spatial aspirations degenerated into a sort of intellectual equivalent of angel-worship, resulting in a withdrawal of interest from this earth, which now appeared to be nothing more than a speck in the vastness of space.

Parallel with advances in cosmology, the seventeenth century gave fresh impetus to geological research. A number of scholars sought to determine the history of the earth; it was at this point in time that the Dane Nils Steensen, making a study of Tuscany, succeeded in describing the structural evolution of this region and founded the science of

stratigraphy, noting his observations in a short treatise which he published in 1669 and the title of which started significantly with the words *De solido*. This conception of the world as a play of forces had previously attracted Descartes, whose strange cosmogony had attempted to explain the formation of universal matter by postulating forces acting by means of vortices, contacts, shocks, pressures, tractions: this cosmic malaxation conjures up the image of Rembrandt kneading the pigment on his picture surface.

But the dividing line between the Renaissance and the seventeenth century may perhaps be

located more precisely. However incompatible they may seem to us today, aristotelianism and platonism had finally converged in an abstract conception of the world. It was not by chance that Raphael united the opposite but complementary gestures of the two masters of Greek thought at the centre of his *School of Athens*. In a stabilized intellectual universe, Plato's Idea and Aristotle's Essence, both deprived of substance, had merged as pure concepts. From the Middle Ages to the end of the sixteenth century these philosophical abstractions had resulted in the supremacy in painting of a purely visual world. Sight being the sense which is most easily amenable

to intellectualization, the speculations of the artists of the fifteenth century had bestowed a geometrical framework upon this world; although the mannerists had succeeded in smashing this framework, they had allowed the forms thus released to drift aimlessly.

The creation of new structures was to be accomplished in the seventeenth century in a different direction. The great victory was the destruction of the hegemony of aristotelian and scholastic causality, which was replaced by a *Novum Organon* based upon direct experimentation with phenomena. Since scientific knowledge no longer derived from

173 Adam Elsheimer (1578–1610). *The Murder of Abel*. Frankfurt-on-Main, Städelsches Kunstinstitut.

Elsheimer was an experimentalist who influenced painters as different as Claude and Rembrandt. Rembrandt was particularly impressed by the forceful line employed by Elsheimer in his drawings.

197

174 Jan Vermeer (1632–75). Detail of *The Milkmaid*. Amsterdam, Rijksmuseum.

In Vermeer's paintings, pigment is a luminous fluid which turns that ideal of the Dutch, the mirror-picture, into a mirror of the soul.

the *formal* and the *efficient*, the former being absorbed eventually by the latter, which was more immediately responsive to experimental data.

Seventeenth-century science was less concerned with setting up systems than with studying the properties of things and so enabling man to act upon them. In this way, things were analysed in terms of their matter and substance, their differential and specific qualities. Once the human mind had been liberated from the old classifications of the four elements, chemistry received its initial impetus and the list of known elements continued to grow throughout the century.

During the seventeenth century, philosophy, like science and painting, represented a devastating attack upon *form*, the category which had imprisoned minds for centuries, had impeded the advance of the sciences, but had inspired the masterpieces of art of the Renaissance era.

The painter, like the scholar, no longer sought for the transcendental reality behind appearances. Appearances were sufficient for him, but he was able to apprehend them only through his senses. His motto became 'I paint as I see' (not 'as one sees') and his vision therefore grew essentially subjective, addressing itself likewise to the spectator's subjectivity. The generalized objective aspect of things ('as one sees') was no longer evoked except as a framework of reference, serving, for the spectator, to evoke memories of which he would seek to grasp the proper meaning. Painting, no longer form but symbol, had become a dialogue between individuals.

The things of this world take an unconscionable time to die. While free thought sprang to life in the seventeenth century, scholastic thought continued to be taught at the Sorbonne until the eighteenth century, and in that era Père Castel was still at pains, in the Jesuit *Journal de Trévoux*, to refute the theories of Leibniz and Newton. The same sort of situation existed in painting: the formalist conception crossed the barriers of the baroque, came to terms with it, and continued its career throughout the seventeenth century, parallel with the tendency which one might call 'phenomenalist' or materialist.

France remained more obstinately faithful to artistic formalism than any other European country, and even in the eighteenth century Watteau's and Chardin's efforts to break away remained unsupported. In Holland, on the other hand, it is possible to understand how the aesthetic of image-as-form, evolving from a tradition established solidly on the basis of bourgeois taste, finally produced its antithesis in the person of Vermeer. Vermeer made use of the same fund of images, soul-

logic but from observation, it came within the field of sensibility and so became, in a sense, subjective: throughout the century, man invented instruments to supplement his inadequate senses. Descartes, Spinoza and Leibniz destroyed scholasticism's system of the four causes, retaining only two of them,

less reflections of everyday life, as the run-of-the-mill society painters of his time, but transformed them through his magical handling of paint. He breathed life into this inert substance, this thin film of colour, working the paint in depth, disintegrating it into pin-point elements, 'pearls of colour', which made it vibrate. He was able to express the nature of the soul through this living quality of his paint.

Vermeer's lack of success among his contemporaries proves how deeply engrained was their attachment to what one might call 'scholastic painting'. The same innovations which they were just able to accept, reluctantly, when used by Rembrandt in developing themes of the imagination, must have seemed intolerable when applied to their own daily life (*pl. 174*).

175 Claude Lorrain (1600–82). *Ulysses restores Chryseis to her father*. Paris, Louvre.

Claude foreshadowed the impressionists in the way he made light the very substance of things.

199

176 Francesco Maffei (active 1620–60). Detail of *The Translation of the bones of the saints of Brescia*. Brescia, Duomo Vecchio.

In Spain, it was Velázquez who put an end to 'scholastic painting'. Those who inherited his discoveries – his son-in-law Juan Bautista del Mazo, Claudio Coella, Juan Carreño de Miranda – thought themselves competent to handle paint with an equal freedom, but this over-confidence led them, more often than not, into confusion. One of these, however, Carreño de Miranda, drew from his brush effects of such richness that they anticipate Goya's generous use of colour. Carreño de Miranda sometimes collaborated with Velázquez, and it seems that he must have been somewhat inhibited by the latter's greatness, since it was only after the master's death that he painted his first great works. One of them is an immense altarpiece, painted in 1666 for the Trinitarian monks of Pamplona, representing *The Foundation of the Order of Trinitarians by St John of Matha (pl. 157)*. The splendid movement of the heavens which animates its upper part makes this picture undoubtedly the supreme example of baroque in the art of Spain, a country whose traditions in painting have always run counter to the baroque depiction of the supernatural world by means of free-flowing forms.

177 Sebastiano Mazzoni (*c.* 1611–78). *The Temple of Janus*. London, collection Lady Aberconway.

The provincials of seventeenth-century Italy, especially the Venetians, countered the classical or baroque formalism of Rome and Bologna with a romanticism characterized by free treatment and colour and by bold layout.

The treatment of this work was so bold that the Trinitarians of this remote provincial city, not at all accustomed to such novelties, were quite scared by it. Palomino relates that 'when the monks saw the picture close up they disliked it so much that they were reluctant to take delivery of it, and it was only the approval of the picture by Vicente Berdusan (a well-known painter of this region) that induced them to accept it'. Carreño de Miranda's treatment is much more subjective than that of his master. However free it may be, Velázquez's handling never violates the duty of 'likeness' incumbent on the portrait-painter; Velázquez's intention is not to transgress appearances but, rather, to render them as subtle as a mirage. A picture by Velázquez remains an image, an image about to vanish, crossing our field of vision for a single moment, borrowing from some form of the real its own evanescent appearance.

For Carreño de Miranda, on the other hand, the act of painting simply represents an opportunity to create a fictional world. Individual forms disappear in the rich brew; swirls of colour give birth to a miraculous universe drawing its essential unity from the original matter of painting. This masterpiece, unique of its kind in the Spanish school, belongs to the baroque lineage of Rubens. We know, in fact, that its author had been profoundly impressed by the work of Rubens, many of whose pictures had entered into the Spanish royal collection. It does not seem unreasonable to suppose that Carreño de Miranda, frustrated by the stiff portraits his post as court painter obliged him to produce, welcomed this commission from an obscure monastery in a distant province as a splendid chance to display a greater freedom of expression. And so, in one stroke, he invented this magnificent handling which, after an eclipse of more than a century, was to be rediscovered triumphantly by Goya in his frescoes for the church of San Antonio de la Florida, Madrid.

In Rome, even Poussin, who had continued to apply the principles of form established by Raphael and Titian, allowed himself to be won over by the new current during the last twenty years of his life. It was when he started painting landscapes that, by a plastic use of paint, he, too, sought to suggest some cosmic substance. The preference of French painters for landscape has always provided them with the best field for experiment and research. It led Claude Lorrain to conceive of the different aspects of the world as being produced by the infinite motions of light, thus anticipating the impressionists (*pl. 175*).

While the Roman school, rooted in the Carracci and Caravaggio, maintained aesthetic formalism

during the seventeenth century, the other Italian schools allowed themselves to be tempted by the idea of experimenting with the substance of paint. However, this approach to painting was so foreign to the Italian temperament in art that artists went no further than the destruction of formal texture, accomplished in a twilight atmosphere; they remained incapable of re-creating substance *from within*, as Rembrandt and Velázquez had done. Only a few isolated painters. Giovanni Serodine, Francesco Maffei, Sebastiano Mazzoni (*pl. 177*), really succeeded in penetrating the secrets of substance. In Verona, Maffei, inheriting the Venetian tradition, created for himself a subtle technique, animated by an iridescent colour, which can be compared to that of Velázquez (*pl. 176*). In Naples, two painters from Lorraine, whose works have been jumbled together under the single name Monsù Desiderio, worked a livid pigment into stucco-like texture to produce visions of the end of the world (*pl. 178*).

The eighteenth century, in France as well as in Italy, witnessed a strange retrogression. Formalism reassumed its supremacy. Tiepolo's technique, for example, was no more than a method of rapid execution, a *fa presto* which was still based on a principle of formal composition. Francesco Guardi was alone in being able to express the atmosphere of the lagoon through vibrating colours; Gian Paolo Panini remained a precise and accurate recorder of images. As for France, artists seem to have decided finally to confine painting within the traditional limits of academic technique, exemplified by Jean-Baptiste Oudry's masterpiece, the *White duck*, which is a *tour de force* of academicism. There was nothing to indicate that in the following century the future of painting was destined to lie in France's hands.

In England, Sir Joshua Reynolds was obsessed by technical problems, copying the masters, especially Rubens and Rembrandt, and even, allegedly, destroying some of their paintings in order to discover their secrets (there exists a so-called Rembrandt *Self-portrait*, withdrawn from the 1950 Katz sale, which might well be a pastiche by Reynolds). However, whereas objective treatment is perfectly transmissible, the same is evidently not true of subjective style, which obliges the painter to create a personal technique. Delacroix was to make the same error; and Reynolds's imitative paintings already anticipate certain aspects of the romantic painter's work. Goya, on the contrary, although formed in the classical aesthetic, was capable of freeing himself by personal effort and so creating his own handling.

178 Monsù Desiderio (17th century). Detail of *St George slaying the Dragon*. Vienna, Graf Harrach'sche Gemäldegalerie.

Monsù Desiderio achieved his fantastic effects by treating paint as though he were working in stucco, moulding it in depth.

13 Conquest of space

Long convinced that *perspectiva artificialis* was based upon a scientific truth, art historians have at last come to realize the relative character of this conception of vision which could not, in fact, be real except for a one-eyed man whose eye is not only immobile but equipped with a flat retina. Until recently it was considered unthinkable to question the validity of a theory, and a practice, which were founded by Brunelleschi and Alberti and taught for three centuries in the schools and academies.

Erwin Panofsky was the first to challenge the dogma: in 1924–5, he demonstrated that this famous geometric perspective which imposed on the picture a single point of sight – that of the individual – expressed the spatial perception of fifteenth-century Italians and was not applicable to other artistic civilizations. It would be going too far to deny all objective reality to this *perspectiva artificialis*: although it does not correspond exactly to the physiology of vision, it does provide the greatest possible approximation to it, relative to the two dimensions of a picture. Certain artists – principally those who specialized in decorative schemes – were conscious of the artificiality of this single point of sight offered to the eye for the exploration of these painted surfaces. Their solution was to use more complex systems with several secondary sources which were nevertheless adapted to a general point of sight: Raphael took this approach in the *School of Athens*, and so did Veronese in the *Marriage of Cana*.

The treatment of space by painters of the modern age certainly involves a far richer approach than could be obtained simply by the application of the *perspectiva artificialis* to which nineteenth-century artists returned, and the complexity of these problems is only now receiving belated recognition. The facilities offered by numerous museums and illustrated art books may, indeed, be held partially responsible for the backwardness of art history in this field, since they tend inevitably to reduce the object to its image and cut off the spectator from direct contact with the work of art. Those paintings in which the idea of space is expressed most effectively, namely those executed in buildings and preserved *in situ*, remain largely unknown to art lovers today except in the form of flattened miniatures which deprive them of all substance. Curved surfaces, in particular, lose their natural qualities in photographic reproduction. Baroque art, which is essentially the modulation of spaces, cannot, in fact, be appreciated except in the countries which created it, and even then it would require more than a single glimpse to appreciate the full significance of these works: the sensations they provoke cannot readily be fixed in the memory except as a result of repeated examination.

Photography can produce only inaccurate results: a photograph of a church interior, such as Vierzehnheiligen near Bamberg, for instance, would give this complex, multipolar structure an axial appearance. And it would be impossible to photograph the ceiling of the staircase painted by Tiepolo at the Würzburg Residenz except in separate units, which would completely destroy the work's significance. This is one reason why the monumental paintings of the modern age, apart from Michelangelo's frescoes in the Sistine Chapel and those by Raphael in the Vatican Stanze, have not yet taken their place in the imaginary museum of our times. Another reason, no doubt, is that, in the case of ceiling paintings in particular, the many marvels they display can be appreciated properly only at the cost of a degree of physical effort which the impatient visitor is seldom willing to expend.

Leaving aside antiquity, about which the experts differ, one can say that the awakening of spatial feeling coincides with the reinvigoration of Western civilization after a period of several centuries when man's relations with the external world seemed to have been reduced to a sort of groping for immediate values. During those centuries, values had been apprehended by a series of discontinuous sensations, analogous to those through which a small child discovers the existence of objects around him. The co-ordination of these perceptions, from which sprang the concept of a multidimensional environment as the framework for human life, did not affect all the arts simultaneously; and the two great thirteenth-century civilizations, the French and the Italian, applied the new thinking in different areas of experimentation.

180 Uccello (1397–1475). *The Deluge*. Florence, Santa Maria Novella.

Sacrificing all verisimilitude to his passion for perspective, Uccello shows Noah's ark twice in the same composition, aligning it like two walls so as to obtain an effect of depth through the convergence of horizontals.

The first speculations on space were those of the architects of the Gothic cathedrals. They achieved in their naves the effects of perspective from which the Italians of the Quattrocento were to deduce the theoretical principles in order to apply them to painting. These architects were fully conversant with all the virtuosities of spatial design, including slowed-down and accelerated perspectives; but if the central nave provided a concrete demonstration of the thrust towards the future symbolizing the progress of Western man, the secondary effects of perspective obtained by a multiplication of aisles, tiers and columns expressed a confused aspiration towards a multidimensional space. During the same era, in France, all the arts apart from architecture remained the slaves of platitude and of superficial imagery.

The problems of pictorial space were to be born with painting itself, that is to say with Giotto. He succeeded in organizing empirically the shallow, horizonless space bequeathed him by the Middle Ages, and peopling that space with the actors of the sacred drama. In the fourteenth century the Italian painters tried to break out of this partitioned space, but could find no solution to the problem of how to deal with the horizon. The problem was solved simultaneously by van Eyck in Flanders, thanks to the observable process of aerial perspective,

and by the Florentines using the intellectual method of geometrical perspective. The medieval prison cell, from which the only escape had been by supernatural means, was opened up by the removal of one of its walls; now, Renaissance man, in his yearning for the Beyond, was able to see terrestrial horizons, luring him on to explore his existence here below. This geometric perspective which allowed the gaze to travel along the surface of the earth reflects the first action of space upon an earth which had hitherto been regarded as motionless and the centre of the universe. Now that the earth's boundaries were known, man's gaze was lifted above the horizon and into the heavens.

The century of great geographical discoveries was succeeded by the astronomical explorations of the sixteenth, seventeenth and eighteenth centuries. In 1543, the publication of Copernicus's system forced man to look beyond his terrestrial limitations; then, Tycho Brahé, Kepler, Galileo, Gassendi, Herschel, Newton, Laplace all proposed that men should face the challenge of infinity, either through observation or through calculation. It was perfectly normal that, in their own sphere of action, painters should have been eager to explore space, too. It is interesting to note that this quality is entirely absent from nineteenth-century painting, when the preoccupations of artists reverted to terrestrial and

human horizons; their century was a great era of progress and discovery in the fields of geography, biology and psychology rather than in that of astronomy.

The most significant example of the intoxication with perspective to which the Florentines of the Quattrocento succumbed is the *Deluge* in the Chiostro Verde of Santa Maria Novella (*pl. 180*). In this composition, Uccello, at the risk of making it incomprehensible by juxtaposing two moments of a single action, conjures up two Noah's arks with walls battlemented like castles and from which fleeing figures are streaming towards the horizon.

The virtuosity with which Mantegna applied the Florentine principles in order to derive completely original effects, especially in making the point of sight vary, went as far as situating that point below the level of the horizon. These innovations were symptoms of new processes of self-questioning, through which, following Leonardo and Fouquet, he achieved an understanding of the theoretical principles of *perspectiva communis*, based upon retinal

181 Andrea Mantegna (1431–1506). Detail of *The Crucifixion*. Paris, Louvre.

Mantegna is one of the very few painters who seem to have had a presentiment of the true principles of human vision, involving the appearance of a curved space.

182 Andrea Mantegna. Lunette of the *Camera degli Sposi*.
Mantua, Palazzo Ducale.

Mantegna was the first painter to conceive the bold idea of
showing figures upright and looking straight down on the
spectator.

curvature (*pl. 181*). In 1474, Mantegna took a
giant step in freeing the painter from his bondage
to terrestrial surroundings: in the Camera degli
Sposi of the Gonzagas' Palazzo Ducale at Mantua
he turned his gaze vertically upwards and had the
audacity to conceive the first *sotto in sù* illusionistic
perspective in the history of painting, decorating the
dome in the ceiling with figures looking straight
down from behind a simulated balcony on to the
spectator below (*pl. 182*).

Mantegna, using *perspectiva artificialis* in a vertical
context, had demonstrated that architecture was the
indispensable adjunct to this approach. Correggio
was the first who dared to show figures floating in
mid-air on the concave surface of a cupola, without
making use of any of those architectural lines of
perspective which help to direct the eye through
space towards some imaginary vanishing-point.
This *Ascension*, painted on the cupola of San
Giovanni Evangelista in Parma (*pl. 118*), provided
an ideal theme for Correggio's imagination, which
thus envisaged a celestial orbital motion long before
Copernicus published his *De revolutionibus orbium
coelestium*.

Until the end of the eighteenth century artists
used one of two methods of ceiling painting, either
geometrical perspective expressed in architectural
terms, or spatial perspective in which hovering
figures are seen through the dome's hollow base.
The first of these two methods is known as *quadratura*.
This was first perfected during the second half of the
sixteenth century by mannerists such as Pellegrino
Tibaldi in Bologna and the brothers Cristofano and
Stefano Rosa in Venice; later, it became the preserve of specialists who were called in to provide
the backgrounds for painters of figures who had
been commissioned to decorate ceilings.

The greatest of all the *quadraturisti* was the Jesuit
lay-brother Andrea Pozzo; he achieved the masterpiece of illusionist perspective with his painting,
the *Glory of St Ignatius*, on the ceiling of San Ignazio
in Rome (1691–4), celebrating the founder of his
Order. In this theme, fictive architecture continues
the actual architecture so cunningly that the eye is
unable to discern the transition, and is prolonged
into a limitless sky which is a true vision of paradise.
The heavenly purpose of this triumphant monument
soaring up into the clouds is revealed by the successive arcades, which house a variety of allegories,
saints, angels and *putti*, a countless host filling with
its swirling flight this ideal space suggested by the
curvature of what once constituted a kind of lid,
confining the faithful within the sacred precincts.

The dizzy perspective of the ceiling of San
Ignazio is rigorously centred on a single point of

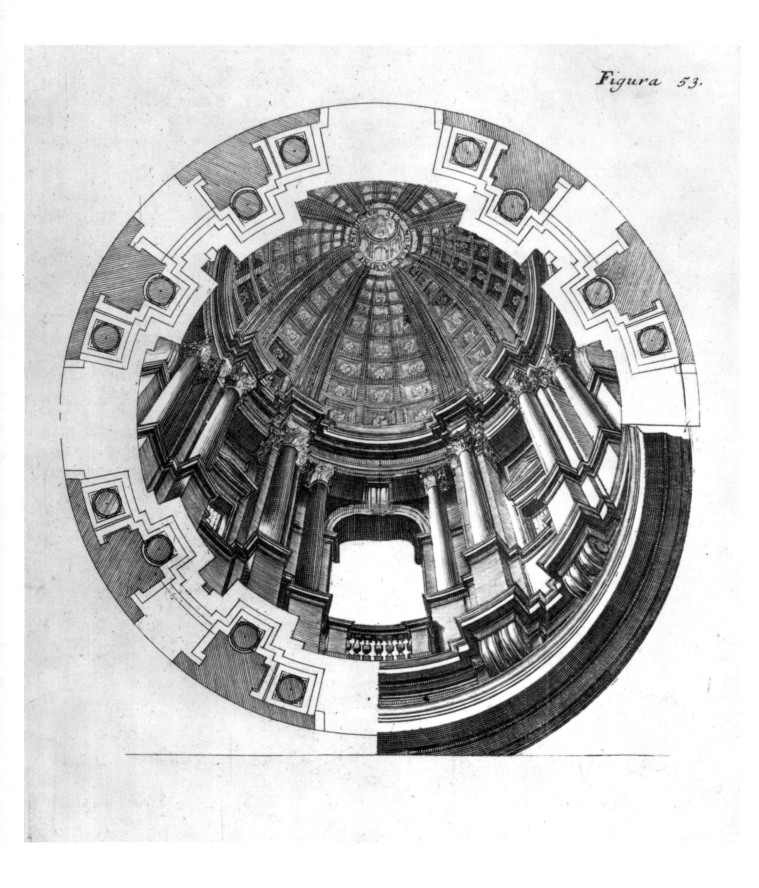

Figura 53.

183 Andrea Pozzo (1642–1709).
The cupola of San Ignazio, Rome.
Engraving from *Prospettiva de' pittori
e architetti* . . ., the treatise on
perspective by Pozzo.

sight situated in the centre of the nave at a spot marked by a circle of white marble. Padre Pozzo had gone even further in 1676, at San Francesco Saverio in Mondovi (Piedmont), where he had depicted on the curved surface of the central cupola the interior of an octagonal edifice opening up on to the sky, seen in oblique perspective from the nave of the church. But his *tour de force* as a *quadraturista* was accomplished at San Ignazio where the fathers, wanting to save themselves the expense of constructing a cupola, had asked him to simulate one, seen from the nave, on a canvas stretched above the

To suggest on a horizontal surface the curve of a cupola seen in perspective, as Pozzo did in San Ignazio, must be considered one of the great masterpieces of *trompe-l'œil.*

184 Pietro da Cortona (1596–1669). Frescoes in
Santa Maria in Vallicella, Rome.

185 Sebastiano Ricci (1659–1734). Detail of *Hercules
received on Olympus*. Ceiling in the Palazzo Marucelli,
Florence.

While Andrea Pozzo was making use of architectural
devices, Pietro da Cortona was following Correggio in
making his figures seem to float in mid-air.

Together with Piazzetta, Sebastiano Ricci introduced to
Venice the audacious innovation of an apparent gap in a
ceiling composition, through which a whole world can be
seen swirling around in the clouds.

186 Cosmas Damian Asam (1686–1750). Cupola of the church of Weingarten.

During the eighteenth century, artists in the German-speaking countries endowed ceiling painting with its full expressive power. The most influential of them, Cosmas Damian Asam, was a follower of the school of Andrea Pozzo.

transept. This astonishing example of Pozzo's virtuosity, which has always attracted great admiration, was at one time damaged by fire, but has recently been restored and is now back in place again (*pl. 183*).

German artists of the eighteenth century were to achieve surprising effects from this soaring perspective, producing vertical illusions of simulated architecture which, when looked at from a particular vantage-point, seen *sotto in sù*, appear to be resting upon the ceiling (*pl. 186*).

At the same time as Padre Pozzo, a Genoese

painter, Giovanni Battista Gaulli, known as Il Baciccia, obtained very fine effects by letting his hovering figures be seen through an apparent gap in the vault, a form of spatial expression which had already been used in Rome by Pietro da Cortona (*pl. 184*), Giovanni Lanfranco and Domenichino. This manner had the advantage of being less rigid than *quadratura*, deformations of bodies being far less apparent than deformations of architecture when viewed from a point other than the obligatory one; the whole spatial scaffolding evolves from anatomical foreshortenings, and this style of ceiling

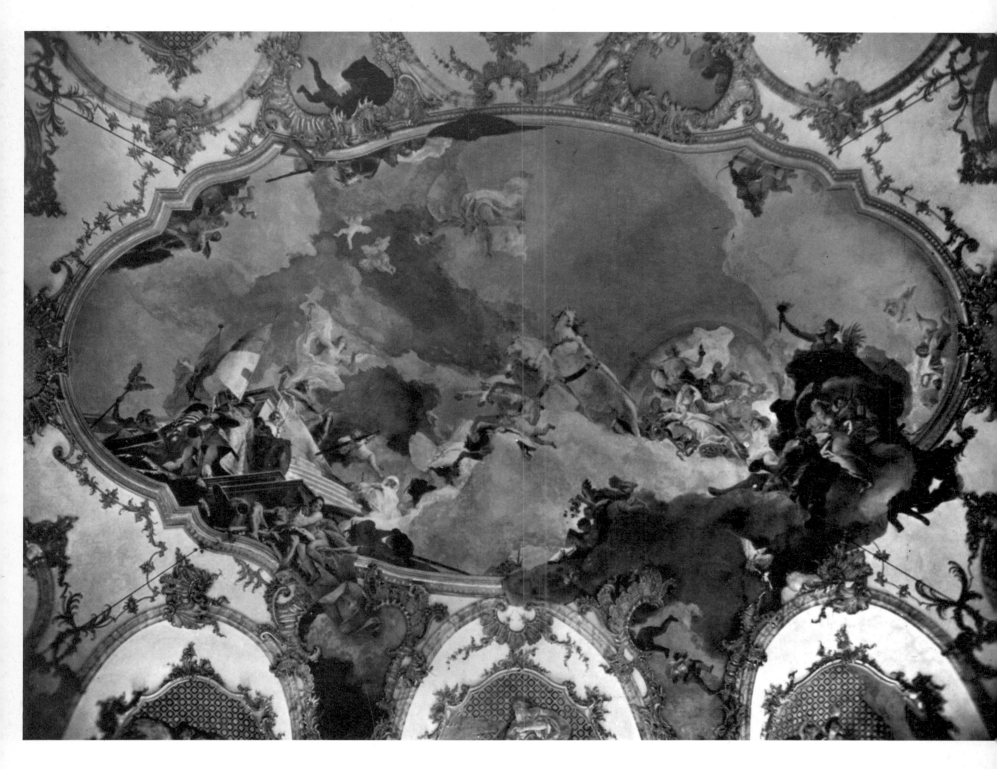

painting thus descends directly from Michelangelo's Sistine frescoes.

Pozzo's *quadratura*, like Il Baciccia's figural foreshortenings, demonstrated the inability of the Rome-based artists to conceive space in terms other than those defined by human attributes, living figures or works of architecture. It was left to the Venetians, traditionally responsive to atmospheric values, to express flight in pure space. Sebastiano Ricci, Giambattista Crosato and Giambattista Piazzetta reinforced the resources of perspective with those of colour and light; by firmly eliminating all

architectural references they allowed the spectator's imagination to soar away from the ground and hover in space (*pls 179, 185*). An effect of spatial depth is obtained by gradation of light, the lightest parts of the composition being the most distant, while shadows are extended over the nearest parts, around the rim of the opening where gesticulating figures, silhouetted against the background, serve as a foil for the distant figures. The sky, in which clouds with dark under-sides and luminous crests are floating, is traversed in breadth and depth by oblique streams of flying figures; these figures grow increasingly

187 Giambattista Tiepolo (1696–1770). *Apollo leading Beatrix of Burgundy to her betrothed, Frederick Barbarossa.* Fresco in the dome of the great hall of the Würzburg Residenz.

It was in the ceilings which he decorated at Würzburg that Tiepolo gave expression most happily to his cavalcades of forms apparently vanishing into luminous clouds.

213

disembodied with distance, becoming finally transformed into impalpable forms blending into the play of luminous light.

In his *Glory of St Dominic* at Santi Giovanni e Paolo in Venice (*pl. 179*), Piazzetta, by using a diagonal point of sight, situates the foregrounds on the part of the ceiling which is furthest away but first to come into view, whereas the distances loom up gradually on the nearer part of the ceiling as the spectator moves forward. In this way, the worshippers are immediately confronted by the vision as they enter the church. German artists were to exploit this illusionistic procedure with great virtuosity.

Throughout Europe, Venetian painters were called upon to enliven palaces and churches with their visions. Tiepolo, the greatest of all these magicians of spatial enchantments, painted his masterpiece on the ceiling over the stairway of the Würzburg Residenz (*pl. 187*). No architectural setting could have been more appropriate for the expression of this spatial theme of ascension. At San Ignazio in Rome the spectator contemplates the Almighty as from the bottom of a well, symbolizing the condition of the Christian plunged in the darkness of his terrestrial existence, for whom the light appears as an ideal vision of the after-life. At Würzburg, on the other hand, the spectator's soul is seized by a kind of intoxication as he mounts the steps leading to the empyrean. This cinematic unfolding of space is made possible by the combination of several successive vanishing-points. The depiction of the four quarters of the world around the rim of the opening leads the spectator's imagination towards the limits of the earth's horizon before projecting it into the glittering light in which the gods of Olympus are bathed.

One may well be astonished at the ease with which the Venetians abandoned the resources of oil-painting to which they were traditionally attached, in favour of fresco through which they were able to obtain effects of aerial transparency. While oil had allowed them to express the delicate shadings of the earth's atmosphere, fresco gave them the means to imagine that crystalline purity of absolute space which man was to discover much later when he started flying above the clouds with his own wings.

The Venetians may be said to have inaugurated a new kind of spatial invocation. The centred space of Padre Pozzo had been the symbol of eternity; the actuating forces of the Venetian ceilings seemed to thrust the spectator into a quest for the infinite.

The art of ceiling painting, elaborated in Italy, was practised extensively, later on, in the rococo palaces and churches of the German-speaking countries. The treatise written by Andrea Pozzo in 1698, *Prospettiva de' pittori e architetti . . .* , was soon translated into a number of languages, including English (*Rules and Examples of Perspective . . .*, London 1707), and served to spread the methods of *quadratura*. These methods were used as alternatives to aerial perspective, and often in combination with it, by Austrian and German painters. The finest light effects were achieved by the Austrian artist Paul Troger, whose silvery colour scheme at the Altenburg monastery has transformed the Apocalypse into a glorification of the Virgin Mary. The most proficient manipulators of space were doubtless the Asam brothers of Munich who worked in collaboration, Egid Quirin doing the stucco-work and Cosmas Damian the painting (*pl. 186*). Their most astonishing creation is perhaps the chapel of Maria de Victoria at Ingolstadt. The problem here was that they had only a very low ceiling to work with. The simulated architecture, in which the Virgin appears on the threshold of a palace, retains its vertical position only from one particular point of sight, indicated at the entry to the nave by a disc of white stone. Once this point is passed, the architecture vanishes above the spectator's head and the figures come into view in the foreground. In all these Bavarian churches, the ceiling's illusionistic space is designed to be seen by a perambulating spectator who can see figures disappear and others suddenly appear in a play of multiple perspectives; the compartments of space develop like the movements of a symphony.

By taking increasing liberties with pictorial space, German painters ended by destroying it altogether, an evolution comparable to that which saw cubism succeed impressionism. Exaggerating the obliqueness of perspectives, Matthäus Gunther dissolved space by allowing the planes to glide away from each other; Franz Josef Spiegler twisted space in the spasm of a nebula (*pl. 188*); Johann Baptist Zimmermann made it as stormy as the sea; Carlo Carlone slashed it into strips like rocaille ornament. With most of the Bavarian painters the colour becomes smoky and sulphurous; in the paintings of Anton Maulpertsch, the Magnasco of ceiling painting, the light can only pierce the thick clouds in thin shafts. As soon as it reached Germany, ceiling painting ceased being a feast for the eyes and became dramatic. Tiepolo's solar splendour, Paul Troger's delicate shades of dawn, gave way to the fires of a twilight which foreshadowed the eclipse of ceiling painting itself, about to disappear for ever after having created so many breathtaking spectacles for three centuries.

188 Franz Josef Spiegler
(1691–1757). *Vision of St Benedict*.
Fresco in the nave of the church of
Zwiefalten.

In the compositions of the German
ceiling-painters of the rococo period,
space twists and swirls like a nebula.

189 Jacques-Louis David (1784–1825). *Self-portrait*. Paris, Louvre.

216

14 Romantic conflict

In 1775, the French architect Nicolas Ledoux received a commission for an industrial building, the saltworks at Chaux; although the practical details were laid down in advance, he was given complete freedom to decide on the style, being instructed simply that it should reflect 'the simplicity of a factory'. It might have been thought that the social, humanitarian and physiocratic ideas which haunted his imagination would have inspired him to heights of inventiveness corresponding to the originality of the theme. But not at all: the design he produced was Palladian neo-Greek.

Ledoux showed rather more courage in his project for an ideal city which was to be built round the Chaux saltworks, although certain ideas, such as having the piers of the bridge look like triremes and giving a forge the shape of a pyramid, were merely eccentric. Some of his designs were so visionary that a modern German historian, Emil Kaufmann (in his *Ursprung und Entwicklung der autonomen Architektur*, Vienna 1933), has hailed him as a precursor of Le Corbusier; but these dreams of a new architecture never got beyond the theoretical stage, any more than did those of other architects of the time, such as Etienne-Louis Boullée, François-Joseph Bélanger, Louis-Jean Desprez, Pierre-Jules Delépine, studied more recently by the same author (*Architecture in the Age of Reason*, Cambridge, Mass., 1955). Ever since the fifteenth century, there has existed, alongside real architecture, a 'paper architecture' of pure speculation produced by artists and engineers; this phenomenon became particularly conspicuous towards the end of the eighteenth and beginning of the nineteenth century, but little of it was translated into fact.

After a few isolated experiments, architecture resumed the yoke of antiquity from which it did not manage to free itself again until the end of the nineteenth century. The occasional nineteenth-century attempts at liberation were designed simply to impose a different antiquarian aesthetic, that of Gothic. The German architect Karl Friedrich Schinkel, equally adaptable to Gothic and neo-Greek principles, is perfectly typical of this antiquarian horizon which limited the vision of nineteenth-century architecture.

The situation in painting was equally strange. In Rome, in 1785, the great French painter Jacques-Louis David unveiled before a stupefied public a picture that was to have a profound and lasting effect on aesthetic attitudes. This was the *Oath of the Horatii*. Inspired by a performance of Corneille's play *Horace*, and drawing admittedly upon Poussin, this picture must be considered one of the most astonishing applications of the antiquarian aesthetic of all time. More than three centuries after the dreams of Alberti, it seemed that art was still limiting its aims to the restoration of antiquity, and this on the eve of an earth-shaking revolution. But the revolution itself was undertaken in the name of antiquity; what the members of the National Convention wanted was to restore the idea of a republic based on the best possible model, that of the ancient Romans. Brutus was honoured as one of the heroes of humanity, until the establishment of the First Empire made Brutus's victim Caesar a more appropriate hero.

Humanity's capacity to project its thoughts and its conscience into the future is a contemporary phenomenon. Although the sense of spiritual adventure has always been an essential factor in Western civilization, even those most clearly driven by this sense have always masked it with curiously regressive motivations inspired by some confused dream of a golden age buried deep in our collective unconscious. Even the Christian, his whole being directed towards a future life, is in fact aspiring to rediscover primal innocence. In the fifteenth century, Italian thinkers were unwilling to admit that all their new ideas constituted more than a rebirth of Graeco-Roman civilization, a 'Renaissance', just as Luther, Calvin and Zwingli viewed their activities as simply a 'reform'. In 1793, the *sans-culottes* invoked the shades of Cato, Brutus and Scipio. Napoleon, the genius who assumed the reins of power, made Plutarch's parallel *Lives* his bible, and it remained so on St Helena. David, exiled to Brussels, advised Antoine-Jean Gros: 'Reread your Plutarch'. Indeed, the unhappy Gros, torn between his faith in antiquity and his conscience as a modernist, found the dilemma insoluble and committed suicide.

This dilemma, and the interminable quarrel that resulted between the Ancients and the Moderns, was central to the whole nineteenth century and produced its full quota of martyrs: the innovators, whether they were those first called 'Shakespearians' and then romantics, or the impressionists, were exiled from the Salons. All these pioneers were damned by the officials who had been entrusted by the establishment with the task of protecting society against any revolutionary spirit, even in the field of aesthetics.

In the romantic era, expression in the visual arts found itself completely out of joint with literary creation. The intellectual revolution had been won by the end of the eighteenth century, although it should be remembered that in order to free themselves of the shackles of classical antiquity the German and English innovators had sought for alternative precedents among the mists of northern mythology. Napoleon's favourite reading, besides his Plutarch, was provided by the poems of 'Ossian' (in fact, the contemporary Scotsman James Macpherson) which provided inspiration for another Bonapartist painter, Girodet (much to David's disgust). But the literary vogue for northern traditions at the moment of the first stirrings of romanticism still left plenty of other directions open. Jean-Jacques Rousseau, for one, was prepared to turn back as far as the 'noble savage'.

Viewed in this context, the resurgence of artistic interest in antiquity at the moment of birth of the modern world is one of the most astonishing phenomena of history. The lack of harmony between literature and the plastic arts scarcely supports Dvořák's theory of the unity of all forms of creative expression during a single era. On the contrary, such a discord would seem to lend credibility to the theories of Wölfflin and Focillon on the life of forms: if neoclassicism made a sudden appearance during the eighteenth century, it was surely because baroque in its decline called forth its opposite, despite the fact that this form was absolutely out of step with the first romantic wave which was then sweeping over minds and feelings. In addition, the neoclassical tendency was enormously encouraged by the discoveries of Pompeii and Herculaneum.

But the painters were given little chance to develop their speculations in peace and quiet. David was caught up heart and soul in the Revolution, and politics left him little time to paint. The empire offered a vast field to his imagination. When he was asked to depict the emperor distributing eagles, an exalting subject for someone so passionately attached to the idea of glory, he was not satisfied to allow the colonels bearing the standards to run

as though they were athletes: one of them even strikes a pose in imitation of Giambologna's *Mercury*. David was more at home with the *Consecration of the Emperor Napoleon I*, where he was able to give himself up entirely to his natural genius, which was bounded by his passion for antiquity on one side and his reverence for nature on the other. David's portraits, which he painted with some impatience since they distracted him from his antiquarian obsessions, display his talents at their best. With these portraits, painted with a typically French naturalness and dignity, he gave the world a final example of that beautiful traditional handling associated with the eighteenth century, and which in the nineteenth century seemed to have survived only in the crafts. He uses this traditional technique to give brilliant expression to the sense of equilibrium of man reconciled with nature and drawing from this harmony the joy of invention.

David's approach to his large, symbolic set pieces was to use the unexpected nature of the event itself to provide the impulse that would fire the spectator's imagination. Since *Le Peletier de Saint-Fargeau dying* was later destroyed by a family ashamed at having included a regicide among its ancestors, the only remaining picture in this vein is *The Death of Marat* (*pl. 190*).

Often quoted as a successful example of this revolutionary inspiration, the *Little drummer-boy Bara* does not reveal the same flair. Whatever David may have thought, the drummer-boy's nudity has nothing heroic about it, and suggests, rather, something Hellenistic, with a vague homosexual flavour which is not exactly virile; some of the pictures which Ingres was to paint later come to mind. But *The Death of Marat*, a picture of heroic simplicity, is truly the starting-point of modern painting. David undoubtedly drew all his intuitive power of expression from his republican convictions, and his later Empire compositions were false coin; *The Death of Marat* was born of harmony between man and artist, as was the *Napoleon crossing the Alps* in which he was still painting the standard-bearer of the revolution.

The painter who kept David's revolutionary spark alight was Théodore Géricault, who was not his pupil but that of another classicist, Guérin. Inspired by events, Géricault tended to consider his artistic education, which he completed by a voyage to Rome, as simply a working method rather than an end in itself. At the Restoration he had enlisted in the king's musketeers, and during the Hundred Days followed Louis XVIII on his flight. Although he soon abandoned his military career, Géricault remained in direct contact with everyday life. He

191 Théodore Géricault
(1791–1824). *The Raft of the
'Medusa'*. Paris, Louvre.

finally shook off the antiquarianism which was obsessing artists' minds and acting as a brake on their imaginations; he also managed to escape from another form of subservience to the past, the medievalism which aroused the ire of David and of the neoclassicist aesthetician Quatremère de Quincy. The example of antiquity was for Géricault a method rather than an aim. A true follower of David, he made the human body the very principle of art, the only other feature of nature which interested him at all being the horse; and that noble animal, used as a symbol of strength subdued, has always been a 'humanist' element in art.

After his return to Paris from Italy in 1817, Géricault began work on the *Raft of the 'Medusa'* (*pl. 191*), studying all the details of its composition during the course of an inquiry comparable to that of Stendhal writing *The Red and the Black*, before exhibiting the finished picture at the 1819 Salon. Although this was an entirely new kind of subject for him, he remained entirely faithful to his humanist convictions; the *Raft of the 'Medusa'* bears the same kind of relationship to David's *Horatii* as the *Laocoön* bears to the frieze of the Parthenon. Using the human body to express force, pain or death, Géricault transformed David's classicism into baroque. The conflict of rival forces provided the inspiration for his art, and he adopted subjects which would allow him to make full use of the play of muscles to demonstrate the resources of the human body. He never tired of glorifying the body, even when he painted the *Raft of the 'Medusa'*, in which, after so many preliminary studies, he still forgot that his shipwrecked mariners were supposed to be starving. His encounter in Rome with antiquity and with the work of Michelangelo had provided him with a sure knowledge of the human body. Delacroix entirely neglected this approach: for him, the body was less an anatomical organism than the clothing for a soul. Géricault also retained from classicism the feeling of those compositions constructed in bas-relief, and, in this respect again, differed from Delacroix who visualized events as occurring in a vortex.

Géricault might have provided an entirely fresh impetus to the romantic school in France had he not died tragically young. Indeed, he might well have become the greatest French painter of the first part of the century. His liberal political opinions inspired him to plan three monumental compositions, but only the *Raft of the 'Medusa'* was completed. We can only imagine how superb the *Riderless horse races, Rome* would surely have looked in the colossal dimensions he had already sketched out while in Rome. And the *Slave trade* would doubtless have

This work was conceived and painted, after much reflection, by Géricault as a veritable manifesto of modern painting.

showed the world what a painter of genius might achieve when inspired by a progressive political philosophy. The *Raft of the 'Medusa'* is a grandiose composition, marred only by the lamentable consequences of painting with bitumen, a substance with which the artist was experimenting at the time. The English painting which he studied while in London, the best existing examples of technique for painters of that era, soon cured him of this eccentricity, as can be seen in the portraits of madmen he painted at the Salpêtrière for Dr Georget (*pl. 192*). These facial studies, which constitute Géricault's final group of paintings, might have opened up a new path to painting: the careful study of human psychology, paying particular attention to morbid states, leads to a better understanding of what constitutes normality. Géricault was a precursor here, too, in the interest he took in those suffering from mental illness, but this idea of seeking the individual through the byways of tortured souls, a quest demanding absolute objectivity on the part of the artist, interested no one after his death.

All the portraits emanating from this great portrait-painting century were typical compromises between the three factors traditionally present in this branch of art: the artist, the model, and the ideal human type required by the society of the time. In this direction, Géricault continued to follow David, particularly the David who had painted his own portrait and so determined, with some cruelty, to perpetuate for posterity the details of his face made hideous by a physical deformity (*pl. 189*). Working in the seclusion of a prison cell, and thus freed of all the social constraints which he respected when confronted with an unknown model, in this self-portrait David laid bare his soul. He set out to paint all that belonged to him and to him alone, and notably his disfigurement; the ardent revolutionary expressed perfectly on canvas the wild soul which, after Thermidor, caused him to be accused of having been drunk with blood. To realize his true genius, David required a model of his own stature: Marat, Napoleon or himself. The head of Bonaparte, which he painted during the three-hour sitting which was all that the emperor ever granted any artist, radiates an intensity which makes David a genuine seer, discerning in this victorious soldier the man of the coming century.

With Géricault's death there remained two artists to represent 'great French painting', Ingres and Delacroix, and they ended up loathing each other. Ingres, despite his supremely self-confident pride, was faced with an acute dilemma: he adulated David and yet at every step he betrayed his mentor, whether it was in his drawings of Greek vases, the Gothic he eyed surreptitiously without ever daring to look it in the face, his God Raphael, even his mannerism (unless the latter tendency was natural to him, as seems more likely). Ingres finally escaped from this labyrinth of feelings, as did David himself, through portraiture, and through the nude, which is, after all, the portraiture of the body. That Ingres, to make his *Reclining odalisque*'s backbone more supple, should have added a few extra vertebrae does not alter the fact that in this picture he is in the presence of the real, whereas in his theme compositions he is merely irrelevant. This great painter, perhaps the most acute example of the contradiction facing the century, was saved from disaster by his nudes and his portraits.

Was this contradiction solved by Delacroix? The sheer volume of praise at present lavished upon this artist risks obscuring the true value of one of the most original figures in the history of art. The greatness of Delacroix is in no way diminished by the spiritual torments which he suffered: indeed, this quality of suffering makes him a singularly modern figure.

When someone lauded Delacroix to his face for being a romantic he answered: 'You are mistaken, sir, I am a pure classicist.' Delacroix's greatness lies in his having been the only artist in Europe to have discovered the plastic means appropriate to the expression of romantic man in his totality; his weakness lies, precisely, in his determination to be a classicist. A painter of even disposition, Delacroix succeeded by single-minded effort in introducing the rule of reason into his art. Despite his aspirations towards classicism, he remains the brilliant incarnation of romanticism in painting. Eager to understand and interpret all the aspects of man and nature, this born painter found nothing unworthy of his brush and depicted the dark and the light sides of life with equal ease.

Delacroix has some excuse for considering himself a classicist, in view of his services to history painting, that superior genre celebrated by the academicians of ancient times and of his own age as the only one worthy to inspire a great artist. But history, as interpreted by Delacroix, derived essentially from a romantic imagination and owed nothing to classicism: his was the Shakespearian conception whereby the past is projected in an apocalyptic process of becoming, as opposed to the process envisaged by classicism, in which emotion itself is transcended in the world of ideas.

For Delacroix, history interposed itself between his art and reality, and thus his work helped postpone that moment when his own century, the century of nature, should finally recognize its natural image. On one occasion only, Delacroix trod in the footsteps of Géricault, and of the David who painted *The Death of Marat*. His enthusiastic support of the 1830 Revolution inspired him to compose his most sublime painting, in which he truly attains the grandeur of antiquity, if not in form at least in spirit, as Géricault had done before him: *Liberty leading the People (pl. 193)*, better known as *Liberty at the barricades*, may certainly be considered an avant-garde painting, as its posthumous destiny demonstrates. Exhibited at the 1831 Salon, this work outraged bourgeois opinion and provoked mainly hostile criticism. Louis Philippe, the 'king of the barricades', whose accession to power the picture celebrates, bought it to avoid offending republican opinion. Officially, the picture was intended to decorate the Throne Room at the Tuileries, but in fact it had been acquired solely so that it could be withdrawn from circulation. The new monarchist government, despite its popular mandate, was not at all pleased by this glorification of the revolutionary spirit; first it was hidden away in the Louvre's store-rooms, then it was returned to the artist under the pretext that he wished to retouch it. With the 1848 Revolution, the painting was allowed to emerge once more from its enforced obscurity, only to prove an equal source of embarrassment to the new regime; however, Napoleon III's initially liberal attitude towards artists allowed it to be hung at the Musée du Luxembourg, where it remained until transferred to the Louvre.

Delacroix's enormous output can only be described as an unexampled product of total cultural awareness: all the myths and deeds of antiquity and the Middle Ages and modern times seem to have converged in his imagination in a kind of cult of great men, a Plutarchian ethic reinforced by Shakespeare.

To appreciate Delacroix at his true value, it is as well to accept the fact that his genius is best expressed not in his large paintings but in his smaller-scale works, those marvellous drawings and sketches endowed with life by a temperament that had not yet been cooled by the false concept of the *grande machine*, the large-scale 'masterpiece' painted for the Salon. Delacroix was so determined to impose himself as a classicist that he was fatally inclined to undertake paintings solely with a triumph at the Salon in mind. It is impossible to over-emphasize the harm done, from the eighteenth century onwards, by the aesthetic of the Salon picture, imposing on the artist, as it does, the objective of pleasing a public and a jury rather than satisfying the artist himself. It might be worth while, one day, analysing the evolution of Delacroix's

192 Théodore Géricault. Detail of *The Insane Murderer*. Ghent, Musée des Beaux-Arts.

The portraits of the insane by Géricault might have given a new direction to painting, that of the psychological study of individuals.

Salon paintings in relation to the jury system. Is the fact that his earliest pictures are the finest due simply to his youth, or also because the juries of the Restoration period showed an undoubted liberalism whereas those of the July monarchy were perhaps the stupidest of the entire century?

Dante's barque, the *Massacre at Chios*, the *Death of Sardanapalus*, *Liberty leading the People*, the *Battle of Nancy*, all the pictures in which Delacroix abandons himself to the passion of his romantic temperament, are masterpieces. But his inspiration falters whenever he becomes too conscious of being a history painter, and falls into the flabbiness of the *Entry of the Crusaders into Constantinople*, the banality of the *Sultan Abd al-Rahman* or the *Battle of Taillebourg*. It is sad to compare the impoverished realism of the latter painting with the beautiful sketch of the same theme, and to consider that the clumsily executed horses are by the same hand that could create magical hippogryphs on paper or canvas prepared for sketching.

The extent to which his imagination was inhibited by this obsession with the Salon is shown by the creative inspiration which filled him when he was left to work freely on the ceiling of the Galerie d'Apollon in the Louvre or the paintings of the Library of the Chamber of Deputies in the Palais Bourbon. The Louvre panel and the decorations in the Palais Bourbon all celebrate a theme dear to Delacroix's heart: the triumph of civilization over barbarism and intelligence over instinct. As far as the two hemicycles of the Library are concerned, it must be admitted that, as a true romantic, Delacroix was more inspired by the barbaric element. However indignant he might be at such a suggestion, the fact remains that the idyllic *Orpheus coming to bring civilization to the still savage Greeks and teach them the arts of peace* is merely a well-intentioned and somewhat spectral gathering of bodies suffering from the muscular debility which afflicted all the figures painted by Delacroix after the 1830s, whereas the *Attila followed by his barbarian hordes trampling underfoot Italy and the arts* is full of febrile excitement. The terrible Hun's charger (*pl. 194*) is surely one of the most noble animals ever depicted in the history of painting, with its leonine mane recalling that of the horse in Bernini's statue of Constantine.

The whole Library of the Palais Bourbon provides an example of a decoration entirely planned and executed by a great artist, such a rare example, in fact, that one would have to go back to Michelangelo's Sistine Chapel in order to find a parallel. Usually, themes to be illustrated were dictated by scholars or patrons. A unique aspect of Delacroix's genius is that he did not illustrate history; for him,

form emanated from the idea he had conceived, a pure impulse to which his thousands of drawings bear witness, an impulse which still animates his sketches but often becomes submerged in his large compositions. He was the most literary of painters: the breadth of his culture, his intimate feeling for the spirit of his time, the vigour of his mind, the dramas of his personal life and of his artistic vocation, the absolute integrity of his genius, the moral exigencies of his thought processes, all combine to make his work as rich a hunting ground for exegetes as is that of Goethe, with whom he has so many points in common (discussed in my paper 'Delacroix et Goethe', in *Revue des Deux Mondes*, Paris 1 June 1953).

Rather than being an 'avant-garde painter', Delacroix is the last great adherent of the doctrine, summed up in Horace's tag *ut pictura poesis*, that literature and the visual arts are subject to the same laws. This theory, which has led so many artists astray, had been condemned by Lessing in his *Laocoön* (1766); but Lessing was far ahead of his time, and his demand for laws relating specifically to the plastic arts, a demand which lies at the roots of modern art, had to wait more than a century to be acted upon; then, Wölfflin and Riegl made it the cornerstone of their approach to art history and art criticism.

In confronting the modern world, which politically she had done so much to bring into being, France discovered that the way to a new pictural language was barred by a traditionalism that the Revolution had never interrupted. In other countries not subject to the same restraints, a few pioneers invented spontaneously not only a new vision but the processes best suited to express it.

In Spanish painting, there is a great hiatus between Velázquez and Goya, which, during the eighteenth century, was filled by artists summoned from France and Italy. The Bourbons were as strange to the Iberian world as were the early Hapsburgs whose artistic policy they revived, instituting a court art which ignored Spain's profound nature; this was the same policy which had been abandoned by the Hapsburg Philip IV when he gave Velázquez a free rein. Throughout most of the eighteenth century, Spanish painting represented a kind of blend of Louis-Michel van Loo, Corrado Giaquinto and Anton Raffael Mengs. It was this banal aesthetic which Goya initially practised, notably in the sixty or so tapestry cartoons which he was commissioned to produce. His portraits, however, benefited from the lessons he received from Velázquez, and he was more at ease, refashioning the master's meditative manner in a hasty, quivering treatment. In 1793 a mysterious

193 Eugène Delacroix (1798–1863). *Liberty ieading the People*. Paris, Louvre.

Delacroix was moving towards modern painting when he painted this picture; but he later abandoned this style for a romantic approach.

194 Eugène Delacroix. Attila on horseback, detail of *Attila followed by his barbarian hordes trampling underfoot Italy and the arts*. Paris, Library of the Chamber of Deputies.

Attila's horse proves that, despite Delacroix's misguided notion that he was a classicist, his real genius as an innovator lay in romantic expression.

ailment left him deaf, but it was at this moment that his stormy love affair with the famous Duchess of Alba commenced. Now he really assumed his true character. This court painter who had been an academician since the age of twenty-eight, this sophisticated portraitist of Madrid beaux and belles suddenly became acutely aware of the troubled times in which he lived, as a fellow Spaniard, Picasso, was to become aware just over a century later.

The two separate aspects of Goya's work provide accurate reflections of the dual character of a country about to be thrust into the drama of the modern world. This was the era when Spain was still richly endowed, thanks to its possessions in the Indies, and when the love of Queen María Luisa and the feeble-mindedness of Charles IV allowed the foppish Godoy to remain absolute master of the country's destinies for a period of thirteen years: it was truly the Spain of Goya's tapestries, warm-hearted, sensual and slightly somnolent, the Spain of fops (*petimetres, petimetras*), beaux and belles (*majos, majas*), and bohemians (*manolos, manolas*). But the period of Godoy's government also saw the birth of the tragic and hallucinated Spain of *Los Caprichos* and soon the *Disasters of war*, in which violent passions and the taste for blood were aroused. Originally directed towards the invader, who was welcomed at first as a liberator, this ardour was soon turned by Spain against herself; the arrival of liberal ideas in the wake of the invader served simply to reawaken religious and absolutist fanaticism as a reaction.

From a degenerate state which had nevertheless retained a tradition of resistance, there arose an anarchic state fated to be gripped by regular convulsions. Goya successfully manœuvred his way through the various regimes which succeeded each other in Spain, becoming Joseph Bonaparte's official painter, and retaining the same post under Ferdinand VII after surviving the purge instigated by the latter. An opportunity to explore the new plastic language appropriate to his new romantic inspiration was furnished Goya by the commission in 1798 to decorate with frescoes the cupola of San Antonio de la Florida in Madrid. Although this pilgrimage church was situated in the new royal domain of La Florida, he was not called upon to produce a courtly composition: on the contrary, he was specifically free to paint what and how he wanted.

The decoration of San Antonio de la Florida, begun in 1799, is one of the high points in the history of painting (*pl. 195*). The miracle of St Anthony of Padua, which Goya depicted in a continuous band around the cupola, served the artist as a pretext to

195 Francisco Goya. Detail of *The Miracle of St Anthony of Padua*. Fresco in the cupola of San Antonio de la Florida, Madrid.

With the frescoes of San Antonio de la Florida, which he painted in 1793, Goya initiated the abbreviated treatment which was to be typical of romanticism.

196 Francisco Goya (1746–1828). *The Second of May 1808*. Madrid, Prado.

paint a popular assembly. The emphasis on popular participation in religious scenes was an ancient tradition that had been largely abandoned during the eighteenth century: Goya revived it with these frescoes. But the true originality of his undertaking lies elsewhere. Goya's audacity lies in the fact that he painted these works in the full flush of inspiration, without any preparation or preliminary sketching (one alleged sketch is a pupil's copy), and employing a summary treatment which forms the liveliest possible contrast with the neoclassical manner of his contemporary David. Thus, fresco, which had always been a mental operation demanding lengthy elaboration, was treated by Goya as a rough sketch to be improvised by the artist as he worked, not respecting even the original drawing incised in the plaster.

The year 1799, when the cupola of San Antonio was inaugurated, may be considered the real starting-point of modern painting. Goya deliberately put an end to the predominance of the statuary approach to painting which the neo-

classical aesthetic had encouraged, and created the free play of forms, lending itself to all the impulses of mind and imagination, which became the very foundation of painting from then on. This kind of handling, combining the subjective and the vital, corresponded to Goya's conviction that painting was, above all, an act of delivering a specific message, and it proved ideally suited to the expressionist fervour which was to grip the romantic artists. History soon provided Goya with subject-matter for testing out the resources of his new

handling. The Madrid rebellion against the French in 1808, and the terrible repression which followed it, engendered a few years later the famous political paintings called the *Second* and *Third of May 1808*: boldly executed, the two succinct statements transform the victims of history into tragic puppets (*pl. 196*). Here, Goya is in the same heroic vein which prompted David's *The Death of Marat* (*pl. 190*), Gros's *Battle of Eylau*, Géricault's *Raft of the 'Medusa'* (*pl. 191*), Delacroix's *Liberty leading the People* (*pl. 193*), Rude's *Marseillaise*, and, much later, Picasso's

197 Francisco Goya. Detail of *The Pilgrimage to the fountain of San Isidro*. Madrid, Prado.

Goya developed an increasingly vibrant handling to express the violence and folly of the events he was forced to witness.

The practice of watercolour painting
led Turner, very early in his career,
to use an increasingly cursory
handling which, in its turn, led him
to create increasingly allusive forms.

Guernica (*pl. 229*). This epic vein should have
provided one of the great sources of inspiration for
modern painting; for various reasons, however, it
was an approach which remained unfruitful, with
the exception of a few isolated masterpieces.

Goya went further still. For a second time in his
life, severe illness induced a change of direction in
the artist's work. At the age of seventy-three, after
almost dying, he painted what may be considered
his testament: the fourteen paintings with which he
decorated the Quinta del Sordo, a country house
which he had bought near the Manzanares. These
nightmarish visions are projected on to the canvas
by a furious brush; Bosch's monsters, with their
complex mechanisms, are children's playthings
compared with the fantastic creations which Goya
conjured from the powers of darkness. Like certain
Renaissance philosophers, Goya seems to have
derived true wisdom from the spectacle of human
folly (*pl. 197*). Even the most audacious expressionists of modern times, such as Soutine, never

surpassed this stupendous wielding of a brush which
might almost be the implement of an automatic
handwriting. Into these explosive works (painted
probably about 1820), the deaf genius, wrapped in
his dreams, concentrated as much expressive violence
as painting was capable of containing. His voice,
the last important one in Spanish painting,
delivered a supreme message which remained
ignored for a long time. What is remarkable, though,
is that this message already existed in essence within
a deep current of Spanish painting; it can be
summed up as the *vena brava* which Lafuente Ferrari
invoked with regard to Herrera. Indeed, some of
the figures in Herrera's pictures anticipate those to
be seen in the Quinta del Sordo series.

Goya's lessons went unheeded. The romantics
remained unaware of his existence, and, paradoxically, it was Manet who rescued him from
obscurity. The real source of romantic handling is
to be found in England rather than in Spain. It was,

indeed, the influence of English painting that rescued Géricault and Delacroix from the restrictive effects of David's influence. There had been nothing to suggest that the English school was destined for such greatness. Reynolds's attempt to create a new handling had produced nothing better than the meretricious and buttery technique of Lawrence. But English painters proceeded to liberate themselve from academic conventions by establishing direct contact with nature. The source of modern landscape painting, both romantic and impressionist, is to be found in England, among those late eighteenth-century artists practising drawing and watercolour who sought inspiration from the features of the countryside, with a preference for ancient Gothic buildings.

Descriptive at first, these watercolours became increasingly free, and the artist tended less to copy the structure than to catch the ever-changing caprices of the light (*pl. 198*). Turner spent a large part of his life on sketching tours through Europe, completing innumerable drawings and watercolours. By maintaining contact with nature in this way, he retained a lively sensibility which might possibly have become blunted had he abandoned himself too freely to his thoughts in the privacy of his studio. Yet Turner was not, like Bonington or Constable, a man of nature; he made himself into a man of culture, learning to write with painful slowness, and teaching himself the rudiments of mythology, ancient and even modern history. Turner was tormented by the romantic spell of the past, and in his old age, when the railway was flourishing, he typically painted the visionary picture entitled *Rain, steam and speed*. Having seen his talent recognized very early – he was only twenty-seven when he was elected a RA in 1802 – he freed himself of all restraints and became, together with Géricault, the first modern artist to be no longer dependent on commissions and to be able to approach painting as a personal adventure.

A confirmed bachelor, Turner was also a hypochondriac, and when he was not travelling through Europe shut himself up in his Chelsea studio. Here he sketched out his studies for the pictures which he peopled with the phantoms of his dreams, taken from the books he read: Ulysses, Agrippina, Admiral Tromp or Nelson. He wanted to identify himself with Claude, another self-educated man. But Claude's dreams had carried him back to a golden age in which man and nature lived reconciled; Turner, on the other hand, glimpsed a world of clashing forces in the midst of which man struggled, whirlwinds of elements, mirages of light which seemed to be visions of another planet (*pl. 199*).

Turner failed to create as free a technique in oil as in watercolour: his muddy eddies derive from Reynolds's unprofitable experiments. The honour of discovering a new manner of painting in oil fell, a generation later, to another Englishman, Constable.

Before Constable, the sensory data which informed man of the nature of the universe was solely of a visual kind. The world was a kind of pageant, ordered or natural according to the outlook of the painter but always experienced as the 'external world'; these surroundings were seen as being subject to another authority, independent of that exercised by man himself, and perceived by man only when he acknowledged its relationship with him, as providing the background, the 'theatre', of his activity.

Then at one stroke Constable plunged painting into the very substance of the world. His great

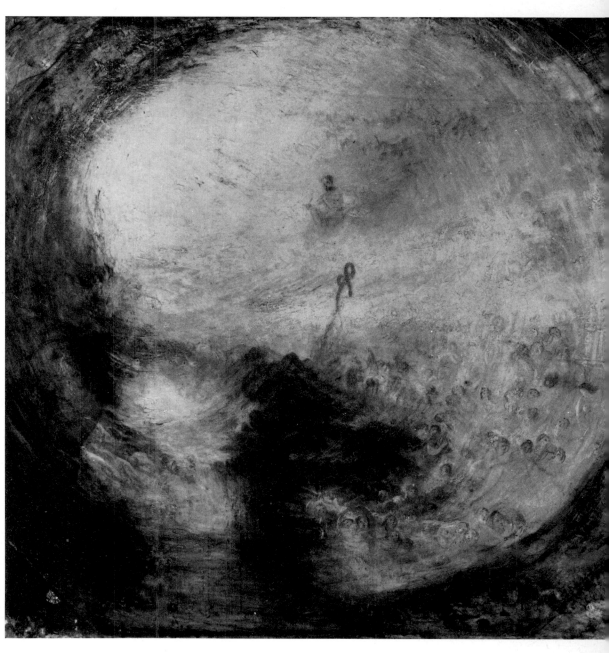

discovery was the soil. What was the soil before Constable examined its substance? Painters had shown earth as hard as a paved surface, the base upon which man lived, either as statue or ant according to the artist's view of man's place in the world. Beneath this skin, which had been smooth and unbroken with Poussin, or hard and cracked with Ruisdael, Constable discovered the earth's warm flesh. He revealed to us the mysterious universe which autumn ploughing lays bare. This son of a Suffolk miller inhaled the heady odour of the soil which the ploughshare brings to light from beneath the dusty, anonymous crust hardened by summer.

The magnificent, glutinous, glowing red substance which constitutes the earth of Constable's pictures evokes, too, all the secret treasures which the earth harbours: the stones from which we build our houses, the coal that is our source of energy, the gems with which we adorn ourselves. This is English earth, fluid as matter on the point of melting, an aquatic earth midway between water and dry soil, a damp substance that is hardly less ductile than the muddy ocean which licks its borders, under a sky heavy with thick clouds: indeed, the three elements which compose a landscape – earth, sky and water – seem here to be fused in one inseparable substance.

Others have sought infinity in space; the eternal peasant has found it in the primordial, inexhaustible soil, fathomless as the ocean. Take Constable's sketch of a *Horse jumping*, for instance (*pl. 200*): the horseman seems scarcely able to lift his rustic steed off the ground, as though it were still heavy with the original clay from which it was moulded. Constable's heavy soil shows its love by clinging, symbolizing the affinity which unites substances and human beings.

It is this thrill of universal harmony which makes the soul of romantic man vibrate like a lyre. For centuries, man fulfilled these burning aspirations in the name of God; after renouncing God, romantic man refocused his desire for the infinite upon the universe. Ruisdael had already sensed the living nature of the world, but only as a hostile, unknown force; the 'silence of infinite spaces' frightened his Pascalian soul committed to solitude. Then Constable, in a great burst of brotherly love, acknowledged everything which bound his soul to the universe, to the eternal chain of beings and things. 'Painting is only another word for feeling', he said. He inaugurated the aesthetic of feeling. His saturated pictures reveal gorged senses, a soul bursting with impatience to unburden itself completely.

No painter has expressed romantic pantheism more profoundly than Constable. Théodore Rousseau, too conscious of himself, allowed his feelings to become congealed by the cold breath of scientific positivism. Even Courbet, the man of the soil, remained the artist of a single locality, a true Frenchman who painted a particular patch of soil rather than the soil itself. Only an English painter could have been capable of expanding his soul, in a great surge of lyricism, to the dimensions of the universal.

The glory of the French artists during this first part of the nineteenth century lay in their total involvement in conflict as fighting heroes, and their first triumph. This struggle was of extreme importance for the development of art. Apart from the stimulus given to landscape painting by the English school, European art was plunged into a sort of fatalistic acceptance of the inevitable, the majority of artists remaining blissfully unaware of the volcano on which were living. In their desire to escape the grip of antiquity, German and English painters could see no other solution than to abandon themselves to an ever worse conformism, resulting from the inspiration they found in Italian painting of the early Renaissance. The Nazarener in Germany, the Pre-Raphaelites in England and the Ingrists in France all indulged in an absurd escapism which took them even further away from reality than from antiquity, reality being invariably associated, in the minds of the promoters of these movements, with the living model and nothing else. The Ingrists did at least make an effort to discard this yoke. Most of the others, though, as for example the artists of the 'Old Vienna' group, adapted a plastic formula based upon the imitation of statues to the expressive needs of realistic landscapes or scenes inspired by contemporary life. The results may not be works of

art, but they furnish a charming enough imagery tinged with a genuinely moving if superficial nostalgia.

A few men, however, dared to liberate art from history, and to give back to painting the moral and social power of expression it possessed during the Middle Ages. Millet, Daumier and Courbet, the so-called 'realists', sought inspiration in the human drama and tried to express it in terms of the harsh life which was the lot of the common people at that time. Millet exalted the tragedy of peasant life,

201 Gustave Courbet (1819–77). *The Culvert*. Besançon, Musée.

Constable and, following him, Courbet evoked the substance of the primordial earth in their paintings, and invented an appropriate technique for this purpose.

233

202 Honoré Daumier (1808–79). Detail of *The Soup*. Paris, Louvre.

In a few strokes, the violence of which conveys his revolutionary fervour, Daumier suggests the new emerging force: the people.

technique which he handled with great skill. In his best landscapes, the use of the brush is limited to the shadows; for the rest, the artist crushes the pigments, smearing them obliquely with his knife so that other, deeper layers can be glimpsed, thus obtaining a rich and sensual substance. As Constable had done thirty years previously, Courbet destroyed the homogeneity of the painting, opening the way to future experimentation far more effectively than Delacroix, whose influence on the impressionists has been exaggerated.

Courbet had shown that the instinctual approach of the self-taught artist provided one of the possible ways of breaking down the barriers which hindered the advance of painting. In his youth, he went through the normal process of studying the masterpieces in the Louvre attentively; it was later, when he began studying nature itself, that he elaborated his new means of plastic expression.

Honoré Daumier, on the other hand, was a self-taught painter pure and simple; he came to painting late, and learnt the craft without any assistance, his method being to start from scratch, without any preconceived notions. This non-intellectual approach makes many of his pictures formless, but in others, such as the *Republic nourishing her children and instructing them*, he immediately achieves monumental grandeur, thus proving that genius is often the prerogative of innocence.

This picture was a great success when it was entered, in 1848, for the competition which had been organized to choose an official effigy for the Republic, and in which nine other artists had participated. But its very success served to point up the loneliness of a man who was doubtless appreciated more for his revolutionary convictions than for his art. The jury, anxious to award the commission to Daumier, the glorious artist who had been persecuted by the July Monarchy, asked him to execute a larger-scale sketch and advanced him five hundred francs for this purpose. The artist was nonplussed by this impossible request. He had painted a picture in a burst of inspiration, and the jury's main interest in it appeared to be to extract a particular image; what had been for him a completed work, they considered to be merely a rough sketch. The misunderstanding on both sides was complete. Daumier had discovered the true process of romantic painting, which consists in the unselective projection of temperament on to the canvas, a process which Victor Hugo had discovered independently in his splendid drawings, and which Cézanne adopted instinctively in his first period, referring to it contemptuously later on as his *manière couillarde* ('pig-headed style').

while Courbet offered the city-dweller the vision of a towering humanity still close to brute existence.

Courbet may be considered the first genuinely scandalous painter of modern times. Before him, the scandal created by certain paintings related to their aesthetic content, but now it was the moral factor which caused concern. The bourgeois public was well aware of the socialist criticism implicit in these human figures, the like of which had never been seen before in painting. And indeed, Courbet made his intentions quite clear. When his *Burial at Ornans*, that painting filled with the gravity of a medieval Deposition, burst upon the 1851 Salon, it was denounced as disgusting. Courbet's gaze did not lift itself to the horizon, like Corot's, but concentrated, rather, on the humble clay of our origins; his instinct drew him towards wild animals, and in his landscapes he evoked the ages of the earth prior to the appearance of man (*pl. 201*).

To express his ideas plastically, Courbet needed an appropriate technique, and he promptly invented one himself, reviving unconsciously, and less subtly, the methods adopted by Constable. The superimposition of flat colours, applied with the palette-knife and then scratched so that the lower surfaces show through, provided Courbet's answer to traditional painting with its transparent technique and its magical effects of the shimmering of glazes in depth. Having established this very personal technique, Courbet incorporated it into a

At the time of the 1848 Revolution, these painters retained the epic style, the extreme audacity and the dramatic intensity of romanticism. Daumier, in particular, showed his deep concern with the urban poor, crushed by industrialism but still full of pride; there can be no more moving documents of human misery than *The Soup* (*pl. 202*), or the *Washerwoman* in the Louvre. The modern realists kept the sense of disenchantment of this 1848 romanticism, while abandoning its exalting form. Degas and Toulouse-Lautrec hounded this ancient human illusion, dissecting with pitiless objectivity the morals and foibles of their contemporaries.

Corot, on the contrary, traversed the first three-quarters of the nineteenth century without ever experiencing romantic anguish. His natural sociability prevailed over his desire for solitude, and in this era of eager hopes he achieved more as a painter through the love he showed his fellow human beings than most others did through their energy. The reflection of his landscapes, vibrating with latent humanity, can be seen trembling in the lost looks of his dreaming figures. He resolved the great dilemma which tormented other artists by dividing his painting into two categories, one for posterity, the other for his own delectation. The latter series began to receive the attention of the public only after he had been painting for twenty years; the first manner, though, he reserved for the Salons, and the success which greeted him there induced him to indulge in an increasing over-production which reached lamentable proportions during the second part of his career.

Corot's great virtue was that he developed an entirely personal technique in relation to nature itself, creating finished works from what painters would previously have considered nothing more than rough sketches. In Rome, his companions at first made fun of this painter who worked in the open air, but it was not long before they were imitating him. He painted only what he saw, as he saw it, but he was careful to look only at those scenes which satisfied his unavowed classicizing instinct: Rome, Tuscany, lakes, gentle countrysides and the villages of France. Yet, once these pictures have been visually absorbed, their contents go through a trance-like process of transformation which makes this classicist with his romantic treatment the true precursor of impressionism. Within this limited space, Corot's brush, working almost on a single spot, kneads and models the pigment over a small area, diluting it, sometimes picking out an accent of light through a more generous impasto, without ever allowing it to become an incrustation (*pl. 203*).

Romantic treatment of paint consists, precisely,

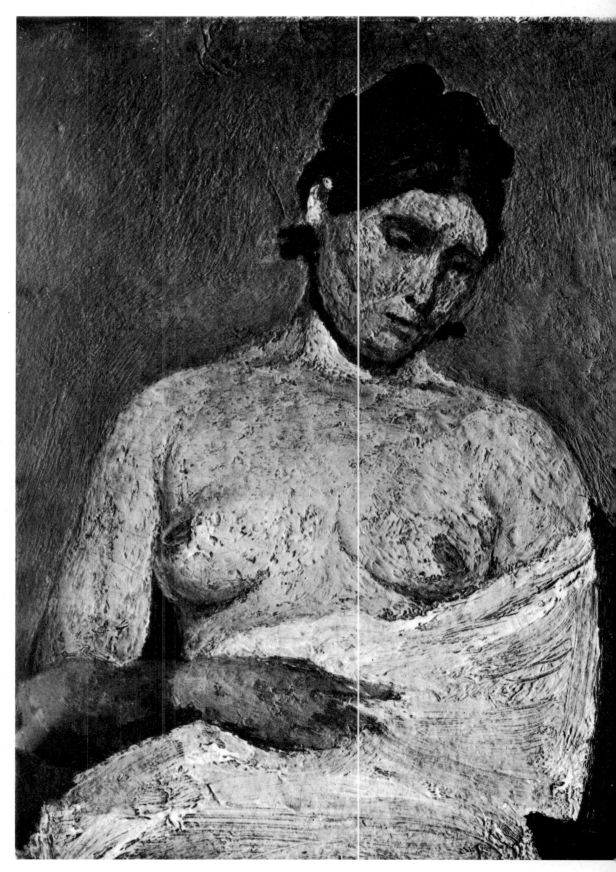

203 Camille Corot (1796–1875). *Woman with unveiled bosom.* Photograph with side lighting. Paris, collection Renan.

Corot became the master of a lively, vibrant technique, using the *demi-pâtes* traditional to French painting.

204 Pierre-Henri de Valenciennes
(1750–1816). *View of the Colosseum.*
Paris, Louvre.

A true precursor, Valenciennes,
working from nature, anticipated
Corot by half a century in
transforming a simple little
oil-sketch into a 'picture'.

of this rapid technique responding to direct or immediate impression; the English landscape school had preceded the French in this discovery. Nevertheless, it should be remembered that the true inventor of the boldly painted impression after nature was the astonishing late eighteenth-century landscape painter Pierre-Henri de Valenciennes. Valenciennes was two painters in one: indeed he introduced into landscape painting the anomaly, to which impressionism finally put an end, which consisted in the division of an artist's output into official and private sectors. He was blessed with an exquisite sensitivity which allowed him, in his oil studies, to use a brush as light and rapid as that of a watercolourist to record the most delicate nuances of light (*pl. 204*).

These rough sketches constituted the research material of a luminarist; it is surprising to find an artist of his time and nation less interested in monuments and ancient buildings than in space, and seeking out commanding viewpoints such as the Farnese Gardens on the Palatine Hill, the Borghese Gardens, or the edge of Lake Nemi, from which to capture the effect of light passing through space. His preoccupations were a good deal more extensive

than was typical of his time, exceeded Corot's, and even anticipated those of the English romantics. He made cloud studies before Constable, painted the effects of fog, rain and storm before Turner, and, more important still, studied a single site under the effects of different lights, as Monet was to do very much later.

Everything interested Valenciennes, and his innumerable drawings reveal a universal curiosity about nature which foreshadows that of Théodore Rousseau. Valenciennes may be considered a truly modern artist: for him, to see was an operation which could be accomplished only with the active assistance of the hand – seeing and recording constituted one single process. A solitary figure, he liked to wander on foot through the Mediterranean countries, admiring his beloved nature, and savouring life in the slow rhythm of walking which suited a contemplative spirit; he was, in fact, a devotee of the kind of long walking expeditions which the 'dilettantes', the disciples of Jean-Jacques Rousseau, were in the habit of making. He left the stage-coach 'to the rich ignoramuses who travel the world like so many pieces of baggage', and advised his pupils to journey by easy stages, 'on horseback if

236

205 Théodore Rousseau (1812–67). Detail of *The Plain in front of the Pyrenees*. Paris, Louvre.

Well before Seurat, Rousseau sometimes used a divisionist technique, as Vermeer had already done, to give a vibrating quality to his paint.

206 John Constable. *Dedham Church*. Brush and sepia. London, Victoria and Albert Museum.

possible, otherwise on foot like the Hermit'. Once back in his studio he was a different man, reinventing nature from his reading of Virgil and Homer. If he did consult his sketchbooks, none of the sensitive feeling of these studies is apparent in the composed landscapes with idyllic or bucolic themes which he painted in his studio and which made his reputation. Unlike Claude, who made good use of his nature studies, he was a true artist only in secret.

These precious sketches by Valenciennes remained so well hidden that they have only recently come to light. This kind of bold treatment reappeared in France around 1825 with Delacroix, his friend the English painter Richard Parkes Bonington and the innovating landscapist Paul Huet. The English example was one of the factors which helped these romantics to cut themselves loose from the classicists' descriptive and literary treatment of themes. Corot never assimilated this English influence, and his traditionally French technique of moulding paint differed radically from the broad, flowing impasto, derived from the English school and ultimately from watercolour painting, which was practised by Huet, Bonington and Delacroix.

Paradoxically, though, Théodore Rousseau's treatment was far less romantic than Corot's, at least during the period of his maturity, although he, too, had passed through a phase of bold treatment of direct impressions, during the 1830s, at the time of his travels in Normandy and the Auvergne. But the forest was to transform him completely. Under the spreading branches, in the deserts of stone of the forest of Fontainebleau, Rousseau felt that his profound solitude, his absolute isolation from humanity, brought him close to the secret of things. While at the artists' colony at Barbizon, he declared: 'This is how I would wish to live, surrounded by silence, watching for all that hums and glitters in a ray of sunshine.' Landscape, for this romantic, was the very opposite of a mood; his soul, open to the voices of nature, sought to rejoin 'the great chain of living beings'. He, too, forged a personal technique for himself, through close analysis.

For Corot, Delacroix, Bonington, Huet and the young Rousseau himself, the vision of the sky had inspired a fluid technique. When he turned his gaze earthward again, though, Rousseau sought to paint the permanent rather than the fugitive. During the second half of his career, his analytical approach resulted in an almost divisionist technique; he is the true inventor of divisionism, that of touch if not of colour. His stippling is so dense that the dots blend, but a keen eye can detect them, and it is this swarming of separate touches of paint that gives his ground surfaces, pools and foliages their intense and secret life (*pl. 205*). The development of impressionism, with its vogue for clear colours, and the decomposition of certain of his pictures due to his use of bituminous compounds, have combined to consign Rousseau to an unmerited oblivion.

During his lifetime, Rousseau was reduced to desperate circumstances through the implacable hostility of the Salon juries, whose power over artists was absolute in an era when the Salon represented the only outlet for an artist's work. It is to be hoped that the future will redress Rousseau's wrongs, by restoring this genuinely avant-garde painter to his rightful place of eminence.

207 Victor Hugo (1802–85). *Blots*. Paris, collection Jean Hugo.

Romantic painters sometimes used a blotting technique as a means of releasing their creative impatience. In his secondary role as a Sunday painter, Victor Hugo sometimes went as far as an informal abstraction which anticipates modern art.

208 Edouard Manet (1832–83).
Detail of *Olympia*. Paris, Louvre.

15 Times of boldness

The impressionists brought with them, above all, a sense of release from all sorts of complexes. They had no illusions about being Poussins or Raphaels, and did not torment themselves with the problem of rivalling the achievements of classical antiquity or the great masters of previous centuries. They simply decided to guide painting back towards the perceived image, and went to work like good craftsmen, believing in themselves without arrogance, and displaying those virtues of simplicity and common sense which had guided Fouquet, the Le Nain brothers, Chardin and Poussin.

It is scarcely necessary to recall the huge scandal which this new approach to painting provoked. The appearance of Manet's *Luncheon on the grass* (*Déjeuner sur l'herbe*) at the Salon des Refusés in 1863 was a signal for the condemnation of the whole group in the name of morality; Manet's secret triumph was that he found himself being execrated for a composition borrowed directly from that idol of the public, Raphael. The scandal which pursued the impressionists from the date of their first group exhibition in 1874 was based overtly on aesthetic objections, but in fact after the ruthless crushing of the 1871 Commune anything that failed to conform exactly to bourgeois convention was automatically considered a menace to society.

These paintings, involving nothing more than a visual reference to nature, now seem so easy to assimilate that the original hostility towards them must appear incomprehensible to us today. But we tend to forget that the act of seeing with one's own eyes is an exceedingly rare and difficult achievement; most people, once they have grown up, no longer perceive reality as anything more than a system of references to ideas. And no public was more encumbered with ideas than that of the 1860s, burdened as it was with the twin heritages of classicism and romanticism. By daring to look at nature with an innocent eye, the impressionists showed the greatest audacity, and such an attitude was inevitably labelled subversive by their contemporaries. Worst of all, Courbet had gone so far as to claim a socialist significance for all aesthetic ideas inspired by nature.

The sun of impressionism rose from behind the dark clouds of romanticism. The impressionists have been reproached for creating a dehumanized art, but why should joy be considered a less natural feeling in the human heart than sadness? Manet celebrated the enchantment of worldly appearances. Monet, in love with light, sacrificed everything to it, going to the limit of plastic means in his desire to complete the exploration of light in space begun two centuries previously by Claude. And the exuberant Renoir, who was entirely exempt from romantic passion, fashioned an earthly paradise in which humanity could live in pagan innocence.

The year 1863 saw not only the public exhibition of Manet's *Luncheon on the grass* but also the death of Delacroix: a symbolic juxtaposition of birth and decease. Manet's purpose was to rediscover painting's true path, by clearing away all the tangled undergrowth of ideas that threatened to swallow it up. Realizing that his imagination was sluggish, and being disinclined to visualize any universe more extensive than that which could be comfortably contained within the dimensions of a canvas, Manet had the good sense to limit his ambitions to rediscovering the meaning of painting in the act of painting. It is this factor which accounts for his systematic tendency to base his work – even those compositions inspired by a contemporary event – upon some precedent borrowed from one of the old masters. Rather than claiming equality with the masters, as Delacroix did, he sought to capture their secret. The process of painting became all the easier for him because of his freedom from the necessity to invent; he created an entirely new handling, clean and precise, built up, in the French manner, with a minimum of transparency, through the interplay of heavily and lightly impasted paint, worked in calm and flowing strokes of the brush applied evenly and broadly (*pl. 208*). This technique distinguished him from the 'temperamental painting' practised at that time by Daumier, and by the young Cézanne who was sowing his wild oats of romanticism before setting out on the impressionist path.

By rescuing painting from literature and returning it to an explanation of its own resources, Manet prepared the way for Monet to create a new art starting out from art's fundamental premise, nature. To find a precedent for such an attitude, one would have to go back to the Gothic artists, who also rejected the logical outcome of entrenched forms and created new ones derived from a process of reasoning and observation. It needed the simple courage of these two men to topple the idols which had reigned in the West for four centuries, and this without any theory, manifesto or declaration of faith to bolster them – just a brush in the hand, working like those master craftsmen who built their cathedrals with trowel and chisel.

Monet was unquestionably the bolder of the two artists. While Manet prudently sought justification for his experiments in the work of the masters, Monet simply left his studio and became the first artist for centuries to dare look at the world without preconceived notions (*pl. 209*). The tragic aftermath of the 1870 War, reflected in the Salon's reactionary policy, turned Monet into a landscape painter. Previously, he had dreamed of showing modern man, life-size, in natural surroundings, thus following the path opened up by Courbet in his *Burial at Ornans*, *Stonebreakers* and *Bonjour, Monsieur Courbet*. Encouraged by the 1866 Salon, Monet undertook to paint a nature study as large in size as Courbet's *The Artist's Studio*. This composition, which he completed at Barbizon while staying at the inn there, depicted a group of men and women picnicking under the trees on a glorious summer Sunday; it was envisaged as a reply to Manet, who had arranged his art students and unclothed models in front of a theatrical setting. Dire poverty obliged Monet to leave this enormous canvas with the innkeeper, as security for unpaid bills. No doubt the huge picture would have been refused by the Salon; in any case, he subsequently cut it into sections, and today only two fragments survive (*pls 210–11*).

I have shown elsewhere (in my *Impressionist Paintings in the Louvre*, London and New York 1958) how this incident broke Monet's career, imposing upon him the more modest dimensions of easel painting, and scaling his ambition down to a delicate analysis of visual phenomena which resulted in his serial studies. Although modern art owes its whole inspiration to the stoicism of these painters, who preferred to suffer hardship rather than make concessions, officialdom succeeded nevertheless in stifling Monet's and Gauguin's first impulse towards large-scale painting. The exhibition wall space which had been given over to Delacroix in the first half of the century was reserved for Puvis de Chavannes in the second half.

The technique developed by Monet was, like that of Courbet, born of a rejection of transparent painting (*pl. 212*). Instead of superimposing layers of colours in glazes, as the masters had done, Monet juxtaposed them in brief touches, the resulting 'optical mixture' being designed to produce an effect of chromatic richness analogous to that of transparent painting. Seurat was to rationalize this process, but in the hands of Monet it retained all its pristine vivacity, the freshness of the 'impression'. Renoir, on the other hand, continued to use the transparent handling he had learned in studying Rubens, Fragonard and Delacroix at the Louvre, and attained a virtuosity in this technique comparable to their own. As for Degas, his technique during his first period was influenced mainly by the judicious and precise handling of the sixteenth-century French and seventeenth-century Dutch portrait painters, as well as by Ingres. Furnished with such excellent descriptive methods, he felt able to tackle the most unusual subjects, particularly those nudes represented, so very unacademically, at various stages of their toilet. Degas's boldness as a painter encompassed all the processes which we now associate with the cinema, from close-ups to panoramic views, and so, for him too, the basic source of discovery in painting was the pure visual fact (*pl. 213*). He made use of a camera to help him in his researches, but handled it like a reporter at a time when photographers were still doing their best to produce imitations of paintings.

If Renoir owes a debt to Delacroix (a debt which he acknowledges in his 1872 *Parisian women dressed as Algerians*), Degas a debt to Ingres, and Manet to the Spanish school, it becomes evident that the boldest of them all, the one who dared measure himself against nature without any intermediary, was Monet. It was from Monet's researches, rather than from Manet's, that the future of painting flowed. His continual process of evolution, within the context of his experimentation, brought him back, towards the end of his life, to his youthful dreams of large-scale painting, only this time they were to express light, and light alone. Never satisfied with the results, frequently destroying or mutilating his canvases, Monet went on from one audacity to another, often disconcerting his friends, until his series of huge *Water-lilies* (*Nymphéas*), painted from 1916 onwards, made him the precursor of abstract expressionism (*pl. 264*).

For Seurat and Gauguin, the door was wide open. Seurat wanted to give a scientific basis to the breaking-down of the tone-scale which Monet had practised instinctively. Gauguin, on the other hand, felt a strong urge to return to the intrinsic order of classic art, where form was governed by idea; only, he chose to replace classical mythology with the

209 Claude Monet (1840–1926). *Snow effect, region of Honfleur.* Paris, collection Société Guerlain.

mythology of the Polynesian civilization. His romantic life, which has made him the very symbol of the *peintre maudit*, has masked the true nature of his art.

Van Gogh, in his turn, worshipped the idol of the sun in place of Monet's idol of light, symbolizing the fire devouring his soul by a solar furnace which turned his world into a burning mass. Van Gogh appears almost as the sworn enemy of Monet, destroying the fragile world of appearances which the latter had created. His originality lies, above all, in his handling, consisting of great sweeps of pure colour (*pls 214–15*). This handling deteriorated

during his Auvers period, losing its suppleness and becoming mechanical and atomized, the strokes breaking into small licks. It may well have been because he felt his talent declining that he put an end to his life.

Van Gogh instilled new vigour into the tradition of expressionist painting and opened the way to the excesses of the fauves. In his letters to his brother Theo he continuously emphasized his romantic affiliations. In a letter to Theo dated August 1888, for example, he wrote: 'You know, whatever this sacrosanct impressionism may be, all the same I wish I could paint things that the previous generation,

Monet was the first to look at nature with an absolutely innocent eye, free of all convention or formalism.

243

◄ 210 Claude Monet. Detail of *Luncheon on the grass* (surviving fragment). Paris, Louvre.

211 Claude Monet. Sketch for *Luncheon on the grass*. Moscow, Pushkin Museum.

In 1865, Monet was bold enough to paint a picture thirty feet square, entirely from nature. Poverty, and the incomprehension of the public, forced him to cut up this outstandingly important work, as the disappointed Rembrandt had had to do, two centuries earlier, with his *Conspiracy of Julius Civilis*.

212 Claude Monet. Detail of *Madame Gaudibert*. Paris, Louvre.

Monet invented a supple handling which he improvised to suit the particular object to be painted.

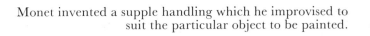

213 Edgar Degas (1834–1917).
*The Ballet Scene from Meyerbeer's
'Roberto il Diavolo'*. London,
Victoria and Albert Museum.

So intense is his curiosity that, in his
researches into previously
unrecorded aspects of reality, Degas
anticipates cinematic techniques.

247

◀ 214 Vincent van Gogh (1853–90). *Cornfield and cypress trees*. London, Tate Gallery.

215 Vincent van Gogh. *Self-portrait*. Photograph with side lighting. Paris, Louvre.

Van Gogh's contact with impressionism brought to the surface his instinctive northern feeling for expressionism, and he may thus be held to have opened the way to the excesses of the fauves.

250

216 Adolphe Monticelli (1824–86). *Under the trees by the water's edge.* Collection Alfred Lambert.

217 Adolphe Monticelli. *The White Jug.* Paris, Louvre.

The Marseillais painter Monticelli, an astonishing precursor, invented a free technique which proved as revelatory to van Gogh as impressionism.

218 Paul Cézanne (1839–1906). *The Repentant Magdalen*. Paris, Louvre.

The artist who wished to base painting on visual data started out as a visionary, and in this early phase Cézanne was certainly the most passionate exponent of 'temperamental' painting.

Delacroix, Millet, Rousseau, Diaz, Monticelli, Isabey, Decamps, Dupré, Jongkind, Ziem, Israëls, Meunier, a heap of others, Corot, Jacques, etc., could understand. . . .' Van Gogh's attachment to the romantics was slightly confused, some of his preferences being literary and others artistic: the ex-missionary at Borinage admired Millet's socialism, while in the case of Delacroix he appreciated the 'suggestive' colour.

But there is a particular painter who marks the transition between the very different styles of Delacroix and van Gogh. This painter is Adolphe Monticelli, an underestimated figure who lived near Marseilles and remained aloof from all the groups and schools of the time. This obscure link between the romantic Delacroix and van Gogh was nevertheless an important one. Coming from romanticism, Monticelli transformed the style of the 1830 school into a painting of temperament, more thoughtful than was at first apparent, and based upon an intelligent exploration of the museums. Emerging from his first manner, with its earthy pigments, van Gogh's first instinct, on arriving in Paris and being introduced to impressionism, was to throw away his palette altogether. What changed his mind and made him determine to continue painting was his discovery of Monticelli, examples of whose work he had been able to see when Theo had taken him to visit a fellow art dealer, Delarebeyrette, who had been selling Monticelli's paintings for many years.

The influence exercised by Monticelli over van Gogh is attested by the frequency with which the latter mentions the Marseillais artist in his letters to Theo. Describing to his brother some spectacle of nature – a setting sun, a cypress swaying in the wind – or else discussing one of his own compositions, van Gogh often takes Monticelli as a reference point. Writing in 1888 he describes his paintings in these terms: 'The studies now are really done with a single coat of thick enamel paint. The touch is not much divided and the tones are often broken, and altogether I am involuntarily obliged to lay it on thick in Monticelli's way.' And he goes so far as to add: 'Sometimes I think I really am a continuation of that man, only I have not yet done the figures of lovers as he did.' Monticelli's genius appeared to van Gogh to be so close to his own spirit that at Saint-Rémy, at the moment when he was discussing quite lucidly his fear of losing his reason, van Gogh quoted Monticelli as an example of a painter who had died insane. Indeed, van Gogh's admiration was so great that when in 1890 Albert Aurier published a laudatory article about him in the *Mercure de France*, he reproached the critic in the following

terms: 'What I wanted to say was that all the good things you say about me should really be applied to Monticelli to whom I owe so much.'

The work van Gogh completed in Paris shows him divided between two tendencies. In some of his paintings, particularly the landscapes, he went as far as adopting divisionist technique in his desire to make use of the analytical vision of impressionism. In his flower pieces, on the other hand, he gives himself up entirely to the unrestricted joy of painting, and in these still-lifes the influence of Monticelli's flower pieces is unmistakable.

Who, then, was Monticelli, this painter who played such an important role in developing van Gogh's artistic self-awareness? Obscured during his lifetime by his independent stance and his provincial environment, his reputation suffered, after his death, from the absurd legends about him concocted by writers such as Gustave Coquiot. Although Monticelli's habits were certainly no more eccentric than those of Cézanne, he became the symbol of the dauber, the bohemian hawking his pictures around café *terrasses*, a slightly ridiculous figure always in and out of love, fond of the bottle, claiming to be a marquis descended from an imaginary dukedom of Spoleto.

Once the layers of legend have been peeled away, however, one finds an honourable painter, *déclassé*, a simple man and amiable companion, passionately devoted to his art, never exposed to the financial difficulties from which the impressionists suffered. His noble lineage becomes reduced to a family of artisans from Turin (including two gilders) whose origins can be traced back to the seventeenth century. An ancestor came to Marseilles in 1767 to get married; he was the great-grandfather of Adolphe-Joseph-Thomas Monticelli. This love-child, before being legitimized by his parents' belated marriage, passed his early childhood under conditions of secrecy, in the shadow of the ruined monastery of Ganagobie, in the harsh heat of Haute Provence, with the stars, cicadas and goats his only teachers.

Monticelli's genius was slow to mature. He took a long time to find his true path, hesitating between his admiration for various artists living and dead, Watteau, Delacroix, Diaz de la Peña, and his fellow Marseillais Gustave Ricard. He may also have been influenced by the painter Joseph Guichard, a pupil of Delacroix, whom he knew before 1863 in Lyons. Ricard's painting, a sort of glossy academicism, almost deflected him from his true vocation. Diaz de la Peña was a more wholesome influence: this Spanish adherent of the Barbizon school painted at two levels, landscapes from nature and small-scale compositions featuring nudes which he

219 Achille Emperaire (1829–98). *Studies of nude women.* Drawing. Paris, Louvre.

The nudes of Achille Emperaire almost certainly influenced Cézanne, who was friendly with Emperaire during his youth in Aix and was himself timid about painting from the nude female model.

dashed off in a free style and for which there was a ready market. Monticelli, who during 1856 was briefly Diaz's neighbour, imitated his painting so faithfully that a Lyons newspaper commented: 'M. Monticelli is continuing at Marseilles his sparkling pastiches of Diaz. . . .' Diaz's encouragement of Monticelli's attempts at this kind of genre painting was perhaps misplaced, since the results were comparatively weak; on the other hand, Diaz took him with him to Fontainebleau to paint from nature, encouraging him by his own example to abandon Ricard's oleaginous tones, and teaching him the marvels of colour sustained by the muted tones of the warm shadows. In Monticelli's work of the second period, during the decade from 1860 to 1870, his genius can be seen slowly emerging; the paintings are still conventional in terms of subject and arrangement, but a sense of concealed power can already be felt.

In 1871, Monticelli escaped from the horrors of war-stricken Paris and walked all the way to Marseilles. He was forty-seven, and never returned to the capital. The last fifteen years of his life were by far the most fruitful, and he spent them all in the southern port, dividing his activities, like a true romantic, between imaginative works painted in his studio and studies from nature – landscapes, flower pieces, portraits and picturesque scenes. A victim hitherto of the inferiority complex of a provincial in Paris, his imagination suddenly blossomed. Leaving the museums happily behind him, and cured of his oppressive veneration for the 'masters' of his time, he no longer sought to rival one hero or another: at last he became himself. It was none too soon; his return to Marseilles was providential.

As though determined to compensate for an overlong repression of his instincts, Monticelli, having at last discovered his true destiny, proceeded to produce a huge body of work during the next fifteen years. He worked with a passionate enthusiasm foreshadowing van Gogh's ardour, accumulating more than eight hundred pictures in less than ten years. Recording feverishly the scenes suggested to him by his own imagination or by nature, Monticelli dashed his colours on to small walnut or mahogany panels, using brushes whose bristles he had cut off half-way down to make them stiffer (contrary to general supposition, he very seldom used a palette-knife). Although he occasionally succumbed, especially in his last years, to the facility which is the hazard of all artists of 'temperament', this pictorial laxity conquered him only when his imagination became overheated in the solitude of his studio. The challenge of reality provoked magnificently inspired triumphs: still-lifes (*pl. 217*) of a rich splendour which leave those of Willem Kalf and Jan Davidsz. de Heem far behind, landscapes (*pl. 216*) depicting a golden age such as Renoir was to conceive later on when he, too, first experienced the Provençal sunshine, portraits with glowing features anticipating those of van Gogh and Soutine.

From what source did Monticelli derive his romantic instinct? What allowed him, when freed from the stifling atmosphere of Paris, to paint with a freedom never previously attempted? His art has sometimes been explained by his Provençal background, as though this region, whose imaginative and verbal fluency has been celebrated by Alphonse Daudet, should naturally produce painters of temperament. This assumption is perhaps not so far from the truth, for Monticelli is not an isolated figure. There exists in Provence a tendency towards the free artistic expression of temperament which has produced a number of painters of exceptional ability.

It is evident that the methods of painting of Daumier, and of the Cézanne of his 'black' phase, are akin to that of Monticelli. The three styles are characterized by a complete absence of aesthetic tradition, by a freedom of invention limited but also abetted by technical ignorance, and lastly by a recourse to the exaggerated impasto which is the typical approach of self-taught painters ignorant of the complex procedures involved in the expert use of transparent paint. This kind of exaggeration is the reaction of an untrained artistic temperament exasperated by the problem of expressing what masters of technique such as Frans Hals or Velázquez could say in a few diaphanous glazes. Monticelli was so prodigal with his impasto that his paintings sometimes resemble bas-reliefs: in the astonishing *Fortune-tellers*, for example, the pigment rises to craggy ridges almost an inch thick!

220 Paul Cézanne. *Woman with a coffee-pot*. Paris, Louvre.

After starting out as a libertarian romantic and traversing the disciplines of impressionism, Cézanne restored the grandeur of classicism in a modern form.

221 Paul Cézanne. *The Montagne Sainte-Victoire seen from the Bibémus quarry.* Baltimore, Museum of Art.

During the course of his long contemplation of this mountain, Cézanne passed gradually from classicism to the anxious painting of his final years.

During the nineteenth century, transparent painting reigned supreme in Paris, as much with the classicizing painters as with the romantics, and after a moment of hesitation (Manet, Monet) the impressionists too adopted this well-tried process (Degas, Renoir). But in Lyons and Marseilles, the only two important French centres of artistic activity outside Paris, a more or less evenly spread impasto was the technique in general use, by the most conservative of academics as well as by experimental artists such as Monticelli. In Lyons, in particular, a thick muddy technique has been practised religiously by all its artists from the romantics onwards: not only Guichard, Seignemartin, Ravier, Carrand and Vernay, but even Puvis de Chavannes himself, who retained from his Lyonnais origins this consistent, brownish treatment. In our own days, the tradition has been continued by Charmy, Couty and the extraordinary Bouche, who spent his life developing a handling with the colour and consistency of a cow-pat.

The Provençals, on the other hand, are blessed with an instinct for the baroque which has allowed them to indulge in all the freedoms of a technique in the service of the imaginary. Daumier, Monticelli and Cézanne all rejected formal texture of any kind and lashed their canvases with those great weals of colour which were already to be seen in certain paintings by Fragonard, that virtuoso who ran the gamut of feeling from Rembrandt to Rubens and from Ruisdael to Guardi.

Had Cézanne died at the age of thirty he would have belonged not to impressionism but to Provençal painting. The violence of a passionate temperament liberated itself in those first paintings, executed clumsily and brutally with a palette-knife in a sombre impasto gashed with whites and streaked with flashes of colour. The young artist visualized this dark frenzy as a demonstration of energy, and it was this phase of his painting which he referred to, coarsely, later on as his *manière couillarde*. He thought of himself then as a revolutionary, and his art made no demands on the perceived object. Obsessed by erotic dreams, he painted fantastic compositions seething with human larvae, monstrous embraces, scenes of assassination, murder and rape. On the rare occasions when he introduced nature into these compositions, it was in a twisted, tortured form corresponding to his violent instincts.

Cézanne's *Red roofs* of 1870 already contains the essential ingredients of Vlaminck, and his still-lifes of the 'black' phase have the emotional concentration of the *bodegones* of Velázquez and Zurbarán. The paintings of the youthful Cézanne are black flowers of romanticism; like those of Monticelli and Daumier they derive from the continuing tradition of southern romanticism, permeated with the idea of darkness, and leading from Tintoretto to Goya by way of Strozzi, Crespi, Francesco del Cairo, Carbone, the enigmatic Monsù Desiderio, Cavallini, Salvator Rosa, Magnasco and Jacques Gamelin. However, the Cézanne of the first manner, drawing upon the ancestral resources of baroque feeling, was also preparing himself for the future. It has been said that when this great painter, perhaps the greatest painter of the century, found his true destiny he sowed the seeds of the future of art at the same time. Certainly, if the composer of the *Bathers* (*Grandes baigneuses*) reaches out his hand to the cubists, the author of so many frenzied inventions in paint points the way to fauve expressionism. And a picture such as the *Repentant Magdalen* (*pl. 218*) embraces not only El Greco and Daumier, but premonitions of Rouault, and even the contortions of Lorjou! This inspired artist was so possessed by the demon of painting that he contained within himself its past, present and future. He himself was conscious of this future. In 1896 he wrote to Joachim Gasquet: 'Perhaps I arrived too early. I was the painter of your generation rather than my own.'

According to Cézanne's letters to Zola, and the recollections of a few of the artist's friends who were his drinking companions during that period, the circle of art students and budding poets in Aix-en-Provence was in a constant fever of anti-conformist ideas and subversive projects. As evidence of this embryonic romantic school in Aix, with Cézanne as leader, there remain the few paintings and, more important, the beautiful drawings of that strange artist Achille Emperaire, a dwarf with the face of a musketeer, of whom Cézanne has left us a touching portrait which has the harsh grandeur of Velázquez's clowns. The subject-matter and technique of Emperaire's pictures relate them to those which Monticelli was painting, with greater talent, during the same period. The drawings, on the other hand, especially the nudes with their plump outlines (*pl. 219*), evoke the graphic quality, impatient, cursive and baroque, of Cézanne's manner at that same time.

The very extent of this pictorial licence gives some idea of the degree of restraint Cézanne had to impose upon himself to conquer his 'temperament'. It is characteristic of youth to assume that the uninhibited display of instincts represents the most genuine expression of individuality. But instinct is the undifferentiated voice of the human species; personality is born from mastered passion. The discipline that Cézanne had lacked during his artistic apprenticeship he acquired, with Pissarro's help, in impressionism, to which he submitted with surprising docility considering his impetuous nature. Re-educated by Pissarro, the most theory-minded of the open-air painters, Cézanne learned to see nature and to base his imagination upon nature, investigating with the other members of the school the shared results of their researches into light and optical truth.

The Suicide's House (*La Maison du pendu*), painted at Auvers-sur-Oise in 1873, represented the point of no return for Cézanne. The pigment was still heavy, and like roughcast in texture, but the blazing colour had the brilliance of enamel. At that juncture, he was still fascinated by unctuous, granular pigment, to which the urgency of his brushstrokes communicated a living, breathing quality. Liberated from the black tones of his first period, but still retaining his sense of the baroque, Cézanne's momentary hesitation between these two aspects of himself produced a few paintings evocative of Fragonard, such as the exquisite second version of the *Modern Olympia* (Louvre).

Two or three years later, though, Cézanne deliberately entered his classic period, renouncing the eloquence of pigment and touch, and trusting to the skilful arrangement of forms and colours to reveal to him the secret of harmony. Reversing his technique, he painted from now on only in thin applications of pigment, following watercolour technique, and practised a strict economy of means (*pl. 220*). However, although Cézanne, in his still-lifes, landscapes, portraits and figure-compositions such as the *Card players*, devoted himself thenceforward to the patient elaboration of a new classicism, nevertheless certain *Bathers* and the vestiges of eroticism in a few subjects revealed that although his deep emotions had been largely repressed they were still seething under the surface.

Doubtless it is this only partially neutralized baroque urge which explains so many peculiarities and apparent *gaucheries* in Cézanne's art: those carefully constructed compositions which come tumbling down like a house of cards, those tottering vases, those fruit-dishes spilling their contents, those wobbly armchairs bringing down in their collapse the people who are sitting in them. All these defeats must be seen as reasons for the despair which constantly nagged at Cézanne, as symptoms of the ceaseless inner battle between his classical intentions and his baroque temperament.

'Contour evades me,' he once said. Contour provides the classical definition of the object, but the baroque painter deliberately breaks the object's texture in order to allow the pigment to live and breathe; Cézanne always had difficulty in imposing upon himself a classical restraint of surface and volume. Another thing that evaded him was a sense of the vertical and horizontal; he was constantly haunted by obliqueness, the famous diagonal of baroque compositions. To exorcise this temptation, he took care to impose upon most of his pictures an imaginary graph composed of the two Cartesian co-ordinates, making a tree, the rim of a basin, a bottle or the edge of a table substitute for an axis.

In the last ten years of his life, his baroque instincts rose to the surface once more. He had no need, though, to return to the unnecessary excesses of his romantic technique, for he was now able to draw, with astonishing economy, upon the rich resources of thirty years of unremitting effort: *The Montagne Sainte-Victoire* (*pl. 221*) shaken by earth tremors, the *Château noir* devoured by flames resembling the flamboyant tracery of Gothic churches, *Bathers* (*pl. 222*) who already encompass the art of Rouault and Picasso.

The word impressionism, coined by a critic to describe Monet's picture *Impression: sunrise* which had been shown at the group's first exhibition in 1874, corresponded quite well, in fact, to the new tendency's intentions at that time. All these painters, Monet, Sisley, Pissarro and Renoir, had let themselves be carried away by lyricism and by the discovery of light; Degas had not yet revealed his 'cruel streak'; Cézanne had renounced the 'black' romanticism of his youth and was learning open-air painting under the tuition of Pissarro. But the power of the new ferment was such that impressionism not only rapidly outgrew its original objectives but through a process of natural evolution began to assume a contrary position.

Impressionism as a movement, like the Renaissance, embodied very diverse tendencies and favoured the recognition and encouragement of individual geniuses, thus providing fruitful conditions for every possible audacity. This was, indeed, the first time in the history of painting that artists had been able to create in complete freedom, having deliberately liberated themselves from all social and aesthetic restraints, at the cost, for some of them, of tragic poverty. The space of forty years witnessed the birth of experiments as different as those of Seurat and Gauguin, culminating in the searching analytical studies which Degas made, around 1880, of movement and space. The creation in 1884 of the Salon des Indépendants, the first Salon without a jury, took this liberalization a stage further by allowing self-taught artists to show in public for the first time. As the records of these Salons show, such artists were not slow to respond to this new

222 Paul Cézanne. *Bathers (Les Grandes Baigneuses)*. London, National Gallery.

The whole of modern art is heralded in this key picture which contains both Rouault and the Picasso of *Les Demoiselles d'Avignon*.

opportunity, although the only one with genius was Henri Rousseau, the 'Douanier', whose worth was recognized immediately by the symbolists, as it was later to be by Alfred Jarry and by the cubists. The other self-taught painters sank into oblivion, although their work serves today to reinforce the stock of fake Rousseaus in circulation. Rousseau's rehabilitation of the instinctual approach to painting gave the initial impetus to a whole branch of modern painting: the naïves (*pl. 223*).

Having run its course between two wars, the Franco-Prussian War and the First World War, during that period known rightly or wrongly as the '*Belle Epoque*', impressionism has come to seem a symbol of a joyous, carefree attitude to life. But the lyricism of Monet, Gauguin and Seurat should not blind us to the pessimistic tendency apparent in Degas's cruel analysis of human weaknesses (*pl. 224*) and in van Gogh's despair. Toulouse-Lautrec preferred to conceal his profound pessimism, derived perhaps from his Languedoc origins, beneath the frivolous mask of Paris at play; but the light-hearted air is deceptive, for these paintings are immediate precursors of the anguished compositions of Picasso's 'blue' and 'rose' periods. Lautrec is the bridge between the era that ended with the *Belle Epoque* and the era of totalitarianism (*pl. 225*).

The man of genius in the nineteenth century was a prophet who used the past as evidence in predicting the future; but the present remained deaf to his voice. That disdainful philosopher Delacroix closed his mind to the ignorant masses, preferring the spiritual company of the great men of previous ages, and his contemporaries all behaved in the same way, consciously or unconsciously. In the middle of this world of the blind and the deaf the Louvre alone stood as a sanctuary for the most revolutionary artists of the century, for Courbet, Manet and Cézanne. It is a curious paradox that a century so fertile in discoveries should have remained so solidly entrenched behind tradition. The culture amassed like treasure over the ages by the French had culminated in this great outburst of invention; and the nineteenth-century artist behaved like the profligate heir to some huge fortune, spending it with such extravagant liberality that he left nothing at all for his descendants of the following century.

One might almost say that the artists of the nineteenth-century French school decided to assume responsibility for the entire evolution of French painting in order to enrich it with new values. For example, David, the primitive of the school, re-created the sharp line, flat tints and rounded volumes of Fouquet, and shared his quality of objectivity. It

was logical that the new French painting, like that of previous ages, should have rooted itself in the autochthonous tradition of sculpted form: David sought in antiquity the artistic continuity which Fouquet inherited naturally from the stone carvers of the cathedrals. There is no difficulty in detecting in Ingres, on the other hand, the effeminate mannerism and nervous arabesque of the French Renaissance. Ingres himself doubtless sensed this affinity when he transformed Jean Goujon's *Nymph* into his own *Source*.

It was left to the painters of 1830 to rediscover the gravity of the seventeenth century. Corot was, of course, a direct descendant of Poussin and Claude, but on the whole the art of the romantics, however impassioned it may have been, possessed the loftiness of ideas of the age of Louis XIV. Delacroix aspired to the universality of the great masters. In his cabin in the village of Barbizon, surrounded by sky, rock and water, Théodore Rousseau, the new Pascal, remained sunk in the anxious contemplation of the infinite and its awesome implications: the art of this romantic became so overwhelmed by intellectual considerations that it finally exhausted itself in dry stylization. In the nineteenth as in the seventeenth century, the greatness of man in the simplicity of his elemental powers was a central preoccupation of the artist's imagination, and Millet, Courbet and Daumier continued in the same path as the three Le Nain brothers.

Impressionism succeeded romanticism just as the eighteenth century rebelled against the seventeenth. The pleasures of existence were recorded for the world by artists who for the first three-quarters of their careers scarcely experienced those pleasures. The disillusioned lucidity of Degas cut through this joyous celebration, and his black hues cast a shadow over all the glowing light; but this implacable observer of human nature fulfilled the same essential role in relation to impressionism as did La Tour in relation to the century of Voltaire.

Instead of working themselves to death at their canvases like the romantics, the impressionists rediscovered the sketch as the basic inspiration of French art. Renoir inherited Fragonard's lightness of touch, but enriched it with Rubens. His paintings throb with pulsing blood and sap and the colour of flowers; his plump nymphs succeed in putting to flight the black angels of romanticism, nocturnal birds scared away by the bright daylight of impressionism.

Thus the great century of French painting drew to a close, not in a spirit of devotion to its own achievements but in a fresh burst of faith and desire. The ignorant masses were at last conditioned to

admire work that had formerly been considered audacious; but four generations had not succeeded in quenching the vital force of the French school. Young artists were to arise who would subject these men, the authors of so many masterpieces, to a ruthless criticism aimed at rediscovering in them, in its pure state, the pitiless fever of creation. These young artists, having toppled the old idol of nature that Jean-Jacques Rousseau had erected for the French to worship, launched themselves deliriously into abstract speculation, glittering fields of thought as black and icy as interstellar space.

223 Henri Rousseau (le Douanier) (1844–1910). *The Dream*. New York, Museum of Modern Art.

During the period when symbolism was flourishing in French literature, Rousseau opened the way to the dream painting and naïve painting of the twentieth century.

◀ 224 Edgar Degas. *The Rape*. Philadelphia, collection MacIlhenny.

225 Henri de Toulouse-Lautrec (1864–1901). *At the foot of the scaffold*. Collection Dr Doris Neuerburg.

The trenchant art of Degas and Lautrec often reflects the cruel and cynical atmosphere of the realist novels of the time.

263

16 Revolt into conformism

'If one really thinks about it, all one really has is one's self,' said Picasso to Edouard Tériade in 1932. This individualistic declaration of faith had already been formulated twenty years previously, in a more philosophical context, by the German critic Wilhelm Worringer whose *Formprobleme der Gotik* (*Form in Gothic*, London 1927) extolled the faculty of exacerbation of the ego which he attributed to northern artists. Contemporary art springs, essentially, from a strong urge for rebellion resulting from the creative individual's acute awareness of his alienation from his environment.

The total lack of understanding shown by society towards the artist for three-quarters of a century was bound to lead to a crisis; the impressionists succeeded in postponing it only by seeking to establish with nature the communication refused them by their fellow men. In this quest for himself the artist is a discoverer who must first of all create a means of externalizing his ego, or what in Vasari's time would have been called a *maniera*. The hundreds of original painters which this libertarian attitude has helped to proliferate in every country are perfectly entitled to invoke avant-garde principles: but only a few of them can be described as precursors.

It is usual to situate the starting-point of contemporary art between the years 1905 and 1910, but even the earlier date is twenty years too late. It was in 1885, in fact, that the first open protest was made against an art of representation. This protest, in the sense of liberation of the instinct of subjectivity, expressed itself in the violence of the deformations imposed by the artist upon nature, which, after being ardently wooed for so long, now came in for rough treatment. This subversive campaign was initiated by northerners: the Dutchman van Gogh, who had learned from impressionism the eloquence of colour; the Belgian James Ensor who lived like a hermit in Ostend, in a nightmare world of phantoms wearing death's-head masks (*pl. 228*); the Norwegian Edvard Munch, whose flamboyant approach to form brings him so close to van Gogh, as well as relating him to *art nouveau* (*pl. 226*).

The work of the Swiss painter Ferdinand Hodler is typical of the state of crisis that had arisen in art.

A style might have developed out of the quest for expression apparent in a painting such as the *Student* (Zurich), inspired by Holbein and Dürer, had the artist not come up against the obstacle of Swiss Calvinism. And no doubt Hodler's attachment to his social milieu also played its part in imposing the straitjacket of academicism on his budding expressionism, which survived only in occasional landscapes. A Frenchman, Gustave Moreau, suffered from an even more marked discrepancy between the official aspect of his art and the private side represented by informal sketches; these last have been claimed as the first examples of fauvism, although that honour might more appropriately be reserved for the sculptor Jean-Baptiste Carpeaux's rare paintings, which anticipate Rouault.

Toulouse-Lautrec would figure among these pre-expressionist painters were it not for the fact that the elegance of his line brings an indefinably aristocratic aura to the street-walkers who were his models and the victims of his wit. And Gauguin's drawings have no expressionist significance, although occasionally an expressionist feeling tinges certain paintings, such as the *Devil's words* (1892).

It is possible for a mental illness to accelerate the process of liberation from aesthetic and moral constraints by contributing to the hypertrophy of a tragically alienated ego. This was the case with van Gogh, and, under totally different circumstances, with Edvard Munch. Van Gogh's art is a paroxysm of joy transformed into heartbreak, but if his soul is consumed, it is in the burning rays of the sun, like that of Mirèio, the heroine of Mistral's epic poem. Munch, on the other hand, incapacitated by his phobias, ended up a recluse on his own estates at Ekely, among his four houses and forty-three studios, painting hospital scenes, burials, and the old Germanic theme of women embracing skeletons. Like van Gogh, he was obsessed by his own face, which he painted many times; he, too, underwent clinical treatment (in 1908) for a nervous disorder; he, too, feared the contact of women.

The principal events generally considered to have opened the way to modern art are the 1905 Salon d'Automne, where the painters called *les fauves* ('the wild beasts') by Louis Vauxcelles showed as a

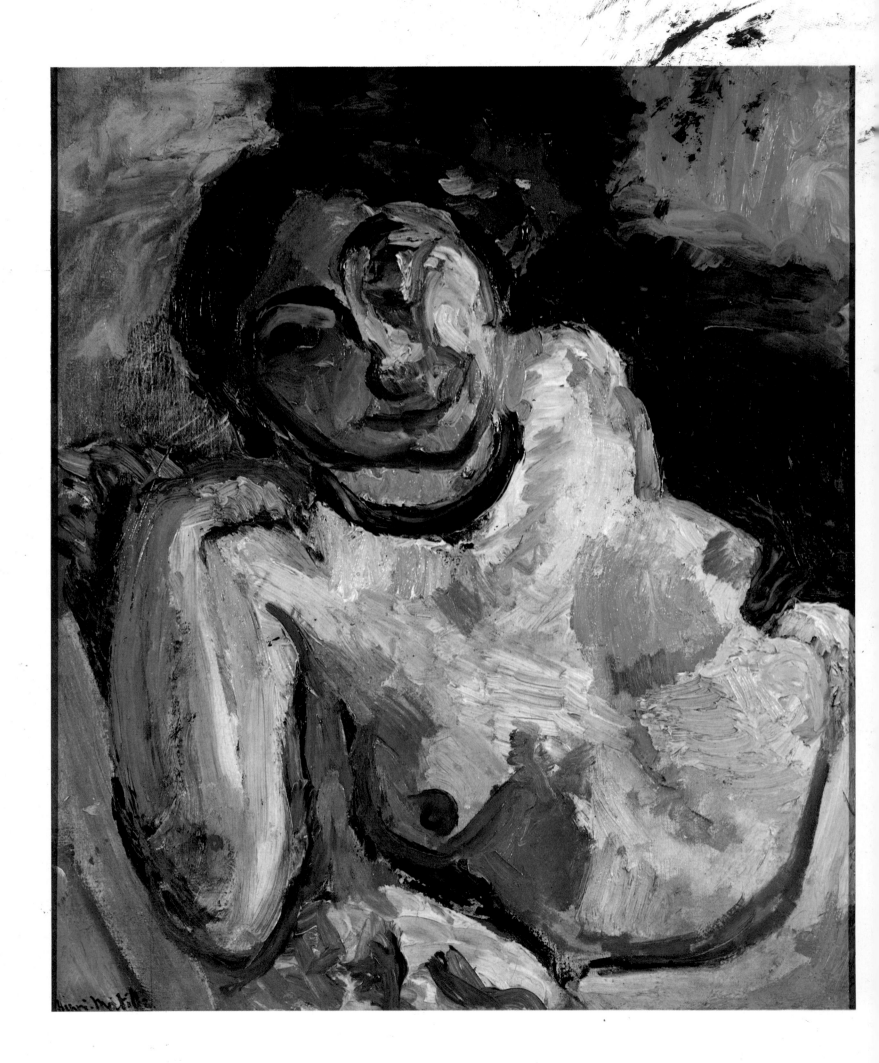

227 Henri Matisse (1869–1954). *The Gypsy (La Gitane).* Saint-Tropez, Musée de l'Annonciade. Exhibited at the Salon d'Automne of 1905, this picture was a violent protest against all the traditions of painting, those of classicism as well as those of impressionism.

group; the 1908 Salon d'Automne which included pictures by Picasso and Braque labelled 'cubist' following a remark by Matisse; the foundation of the group called *Die Brücke* ('the bridge') in Dresden in 1905; and that of the group called *Der blaue Reiter* ('the blue horseman') in Munich in 1911. But the real point of rupture may be sought more accurately

in the 1892 exhibition by Munch of forty-five pictures at the Association of Berlin Painters, since the controversy provoked by his style resulted in the closing of the show after a few days and the break-up of the group of artists which had invited him. His supporters immediately founded in Berlin the Free Association of Artists, and the same year organized the aptly named 'Sezession' group in Munich. Resistance to modern ideas was even greater in Germany than in France, which had had half a century's experience of the polemics aroused by scandals in the world of art. In Germany, nationalistic

228 James Ensor (1860–1949). *Skeletons fighting over a herring.* Brussels, collection Benedict Goldschmidt.

Distant progeny of those of Hieronymus Bosch, the monsters of James Ensor raise a violent protest against rationalism as well as against naturalism.

229 Pablo Picasso (b. 1881). *Guernica*. New York, Museum of Modern Art (on loan from the artist).

Picasso performs the mutation of plastic cubism into an
expressionist language, to execute what is surely the most
tragic work in the whole history of painting.

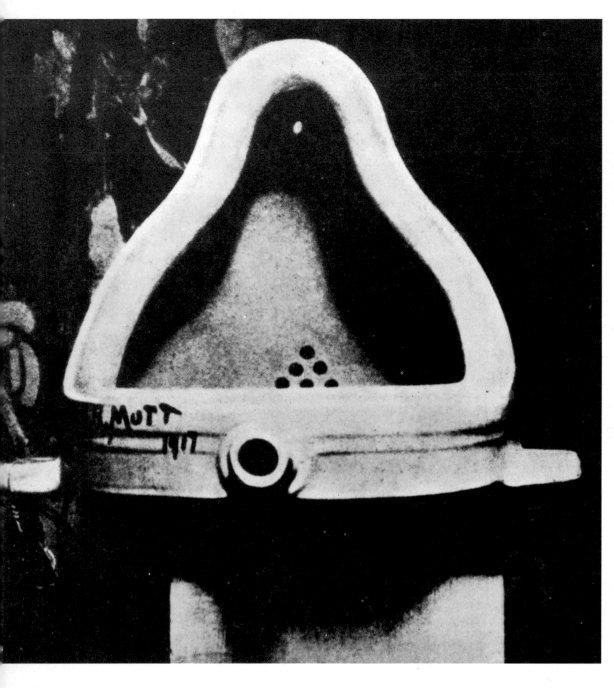

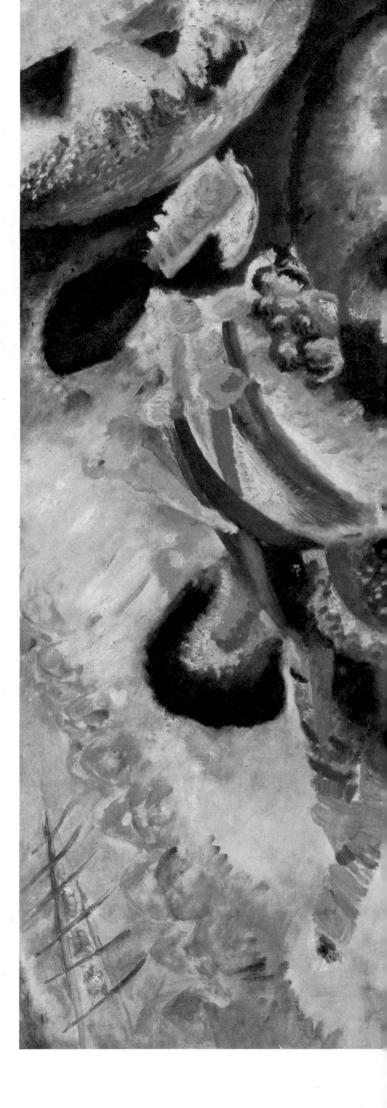

230 Marcel Duchamp (1887–1968). *Fountain*. Signed 'R. Mutt' and submitted to the 1917 exhibition of the Society of Independent Artists in New York.

Dada broke deliberately with the traditional concept of the work of art.

factors also played a part, since the Parisian artists invited to exhibit by their colleagues in Munich were widely considered to be tainted by a degeneracy from which it was necessary to preserve virtuous Germany at all costs.

Fauvism and cubism, the two great sources of contemporary art, may be said to have sprung from two separate dramas: the tragic drama of van Gogh, desperate at his inability to force a way of painting, derived from impressionism, beyond certain experimental limits; and the silent drama of Cézanne seeking, gropingly, to rediscover appearances, to re-create the texture of forms broken by Monet.

The so-called 'fauve' movement, pioneered by Matisse, Marquet, Rouault and Vlaminck, was an instinctive revolt against the fidelity to appearances

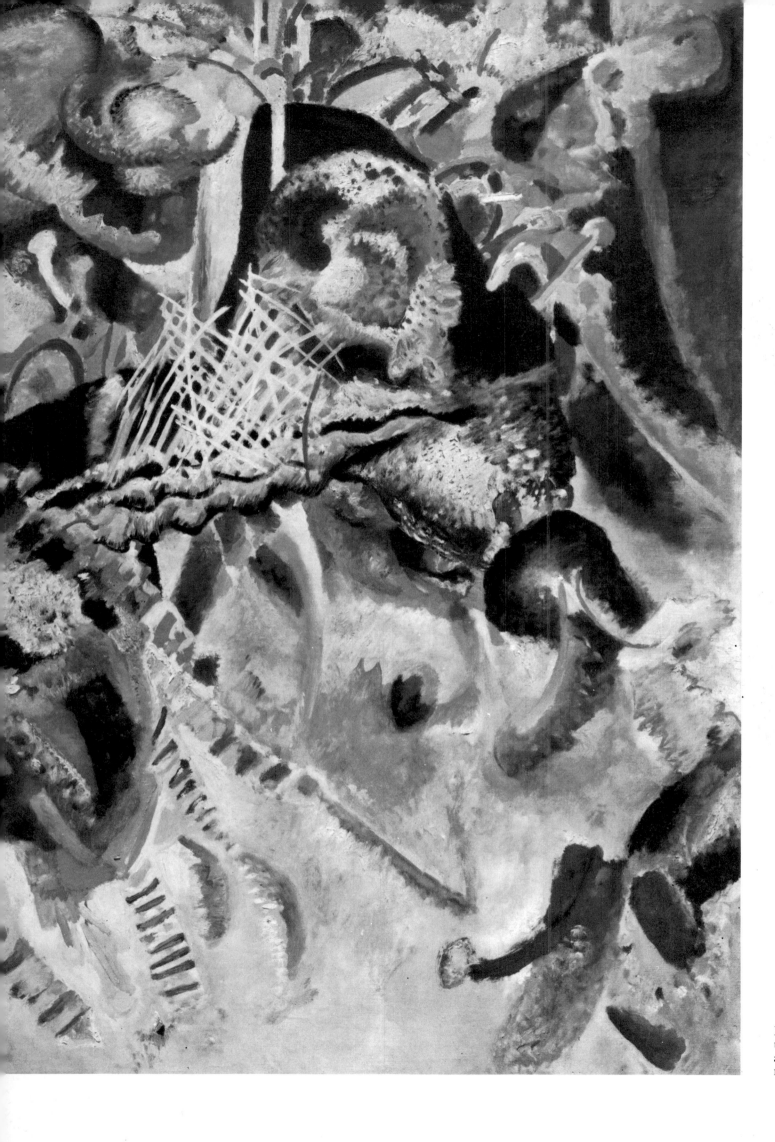

231 Wassily Kandinsky (1866–1944). *Grosse Fuge*. New York, Solomon R. Guggenheim Museum.

Kandinsky's first works are closer to the origins of abstract painting than are cubist pictures, which are the result of analysis of the object.

which was the principle of impressionism. This liberation, whereby colour was promoted to being a means of expression in its own right, permitted its adherents, united briefly in what has wrongly been called a 'school', to explore completely incompatible objectives and styles; it provided the means for Matisse (*pl. 227*) to develop the intellectualism of an art which was to be its own justification, for Marquet and Dufy to express their desire to revert to the representation of the external world, for Vlaminck to project his own particular temperament, for Rouault to formulate a Christian lamentation upon the miseries of the world (*pl. 237*). The fauvist liberation of colour also provided the basis for the kind of expressionism practised a few years later by the growing colony of Slav painters in Paris.

The cubism of Georges Braque and Pablo Picasso was a stricter discipline, although it drew upon sources as varied as recently discovered African carvings and the last works of Cézanne who died obsessed with cones, cylinders and cubes. Cubism was more methodical than fauvism in its attack upon appearances, breaking them up and then reconstituting them according to the principles of a geometry whose laws no longer demanded anything beyond the definition of a painted form in terms of a given surface. The resulting destruction of traditional space represented the culmination of a process already set in motion in 1895 by the movement calling itself 'Les Nabis', founded by Paul Sérusier and including among its adepts Pierre Bonnard, who spent his life attempting an impossible reconciliation between depthlessness and the impressionist mirage of appearances.

These factors all helped to create a new aesthetic climate, in which painting became a self-contained language, a willing instrument in the hands of the artist who, after having distorted appearances, ended by abolishing them.

Until 1910 the creation of modern painting in Paris remained largely the prerogative of French artists; Picasso was a major exception. However, the prestige which France gained from the glorious achievements of her nineteenth-century masters, crowned by the triumph of impressionism, brought a wealth of artistic talent flooding into Paris from all parts of the world, and especially the Slav countries. This phenomenon can be compared only to the attraction exercised by Rome in the years around 1600. It was as though artists had decided they could only express themselves in the free atmosphere of Paris. This influx of artists, escaping from their own countries' traditional attitudes in order to discover themselves in Paris, created a limitless range of expression for the new art whose language had been invented by the masters of 1910.

Invented by a Frenchman and a Spaniard, cubism soon became enriched by variations brought by the Pole Marcoussis, the Spaniard Juan Gris, the Frenchmen Albert Gleizes, Jean Metzinger, Roger de la Fresnaye, Jacques Villon, Fernand Léger; another recruit, Robert Delaunay, went beyond cubism by eventually banishing appearances of all kinds, including distortions, from his compositions, in favour of pure colour variations (*pl. 233*).

In the second decade of the century cubism, having consolidated its conquests, became a language supple enough to allow Braque to develop the aesthetic of the object-picture which he had first explored between 1905 and 1910 (*pl. 232*); and supple enough, too, to allow Picasso, in the third decade, to employ the breaking-up of forms to express in *Guernica* (*pl. 229*), and in the 'slaughtered figures' which followed, the horrors of war and genocide.

The Slav group in Paris, headed by Chagall, Soutine, Kisling and Pascin, employed the language of colour in the context of an expressionism filled with an atavistic anguish, a tendency which the Italian Modigliani transformed into the more subtle tonality of a melancholic art.

Rather than denying appearances, cubism used them selectively and freely, for plastic or expressive purposes. The movement which was to lead to the complete renunciation of all forms emanating from the external world was contained, in embryo, in Worringer's 1908 thesis *Abstraktion und Einfühlung* (*Abstraction and Empathy*, London 1953), and fully explained in Wassily Kandinsky's 1912 work *Über das Geistige in der Kunst* (*Concerning the Spiritual in Art*, New York 1947). Unlike cubism, which was entirely empirical, this new movement was therefore endowed with a theoretical basis; but, perhaps because the newly formulated ideas were too far ahead of the times, its proponents were not able at the time to emulate the cubists by setting up a group. Non-figurative painting asserted itself gradually during the first three decades of the century, represented initially by isolated artists such as Kandinsky (*pl. 231*) in Germany, Delaunay (*pl. 233*) in France, Mondrian (*pl. 234*) and van Doesburg in Holland; after the Second World War, non-figurative art blossomed in a variety of styles and theories, ranging from a formal or geometric abstraction to informal approaches characterized in general as abstract expressionism.

If these movements renounced nature as the source of inspiration for art, they did not renounce the work of art as an object in its own right; on the contrary, this objective quality was enhanced by

232 Georges Braque (1882–1963).
Violin and jug. Basle, Kunstmuseum.

During their cubist period, Braque
and Picasso elaborated an
egocentric art in which the object
is exploited as a source of formal
variations on a given surface.

233 Robert Delaunay (1885–1941). ▶
Circular forms: sun and moon.
Zurich, Kunsthaus.

274

the complete break with any external reality outside the artist's own temperament. It remained to the artist to reject the work of art as an autonomous object and, by corollary, to reject art as a human activity consisting of 'fashioning' such objects.

The man to undertake this act of negation was a genuine precursor, Marcel Duchamp, one of the pioneers of dadaism and the only contemporary figure in the world of art to have remained unshakably faithful to an attitude of refusal. He had already affirmed this refusal in 1912, with his selection of 'readymades', manufactured objects of

no special significance and as far removed as possible from the idea of a work of art. The most notorious of these readymades is undoubtedly the urinal which he signed 'R. Mutt' and submitted to the 1917 exhibition of the Society of Independent Artists in New York. This initiative gave rise to innumerable variations and imitations. The 'object with a symbolic function' of surrealism may be considered a descendant, although the artificial significance attributed to such objects by their creators makes them the opposite of Duchamp's readymades whose true meaning is precisely their

234 Piet Mondrian (1872–1944). *Composition in blue, grey and red.* Otterlo, Kröller-Müller Museum.

In Germany with Kandinsky, in France with Delaunay, and in Holland with Mondrian, the year 1912 saw a simultaneous break away from all those aspects of appearances which had not already been demolished by cubism. Delaunay was already exploring the art of pure colour variations in 1912, forty years before it began to be practised on a wide scale.

235 Yves Tanguy (1900–55). *Landscape*. Paris, Musée National d'Art Moderne.

Yves Tanguy is among those artists who have recorded most authentically the upsurge of unconscious forces liberated by surrealism.

desperate attempt to grasp at its source the power of negation of contemporary art was doomed to failure because it lacked the shock-effect of surprise and originality.

Throughout the nineteenth century the spirit of rebellion was fed by a literature of which Sade was the initiator: de Vigny, Dostoievsky, Lautréamont, Nietzsche and Rimbaud all played a part, in their different ways, in establishing a radical tradition of refusal. But the painters of the time ignored the message. Once the revolutionary fervour had subsided, the romantics became good bourgeois citizens once more, following the lead of their standard-bearer Delacroix. The first real rebel of French painting was Courbet, who refused the imperial government's offer of the Legion of Honour and desired his art to become a means of expressing social demands. The impressionists, however, never allowed this spirit of rebellion to enter into their artistic calculations. Even when, like Pissarro or Monet, they were personally sympathetic to such ideas they failed to heed Zola's appeal to join his campaign of socialist action; it may well have been this disappointment that caused the novelist to repudiate the impressionists towards the end of his life.

Nothing could have been less subversive than this most revolutionary of all movements in painting; never had such bold innovators been so entirely lacking in the will to revolt. The impressionists made no critical assessment of the achievements of their artistic predecessors. They simply worked on instinctively, in the light of their own discoveries, without realizing that the new universe they were entering was cutting them off from a social environment determined to view them solely as rebels. However keenly they felt the state of separation imposed upon them by society, they remained convinced that it was nothing more than a misunderstanding. And they avoided a feeling of isolation by remaining in close communion with nature, as well as by preserving an atmosphere of solidarity among themselves based upon the encouragement of a small group of art lovers who had faith in them. Some of the impressionists, including Degas, Cézanne and Monet, remained deeply embittered by the treatment they had received in their youth; Monet, for example, by now at the height of his glory and the friend of Clemenceau, repeated Courbet's gesture and refused the Legion of Honour. But this resentfulness was never reflected in any way in their art. It is this purity of intention which gave impressionism its unique character and allowed its influence to penetrate

meaninglessness. The origins of surrealist imagery, with its appeal to the subconscious, as manifested in dream states, should be traced back rather to the paintings which Giorgio de Chirico executed in Paris between 1911 and 1917.

By making the simple gesture of destroying the traditional subject-object relationship, Duchamp anticipated the critical nihilism of existentialism. The so-called neo-dada movement which flourished fitfully in America and Europe during the 1960s may perhaps signify a more or less conscious desire to reassert this nihilistic philosophy, but this

even an age, our own, which has witnessed the negation of all such principles.

Rebellion finally broke out with the advent of Gauguin, but it was in some ways a gratuitous rebellion affecting the man rather than the painter; Gauguin as an artist tended – apart from his imagery – to renew ties with certain classical traditions which the impressionists had set aside. Van Gogh, too, was a rebel, but in the spirit of moral dedication of a prophet such as Nietzsche's Zarathustra: no one could have been less nihilistic than this man whose heart was filled with a missionary sense of love.

It has been left to our contemporaries to raise a barrier of total opposition to all their predecessors: the art of Picasso, Matisse, Rouault, Kirchner and Nolde is based upon a spirit of contradiction, a determination to destroy the artistic capital accumulated by Western civilization. Their attitude may be compared to that of the first marxists, whose revolt against the role of capital led them to envisage the establishment of a new society not based on the accumulation of wealth: an ideal which industrial society, founded as it is on production, forced the successors of these same revolutionaries to betray in their actions.

The anarchistic position of avant-garde painters at the beginning of the century was summed up by their rallying cry: 'Burn the museums!' This impulsive attitude found expression in brutal distortions or caricatures of the human figure and of nature, thus transgressing both the sacrosanct elements of Western art which had been handed down through the centuries and which were now given an added richness by the impressionists. This rebellious instinct gradually transformed itself into a revolutionary consciousness designed to constitute a new order.

Matisse established his rigorously formal system on the basis of the wholesale destruction of values which had been achieved by fauvism. As for Picasso, it is reasonable to believe that the violence of his rebellion was tempered by the prudence of Braque who encouraged him, towards the end of his 'negro' period, to join him in setting up the experimental laboratory from which cubism was to emerge. But Picasso was incapable of remaining imprisoned in a discipline for any length of time. After a few years he reasserted his freedom, demonstrating with the monstrous figures of his 'neo-classical' period that he had abandoned the efforts of his cubist period to achieve a 'synthetic' effect deriving from a meticulously developed analysis of form.

Throughout his career, Picasso has never ceased to rebel against everything, and against himself,

condemning himself to repeated adventures and misadventures, a few classically orientated drawings providing his sole relief. His instinct for rebellion has been strengthened by the tragic events which succeeded each other in Europe. The Spanish Civil War, and then the Second World War, seemed to justify in turn his own savage slaughter of the human form. This is not to say that he has become unmindful of the forms of the past: on the contrary, everything, from Greek vases and Chinese scrolls to the paintings of Velázquez, Cranach and Manet feeds his hunger for destruction. For Picasso, painting is an act of transgression,

236 Ernst Ludwig Kirchner (1880–1938). *Seated woman.* Minneapolis, Institute of Arts.

In the twentieth century, German painting roused itself from a long lethargy and found fresh inspiration in its deep-seated indigenous inclination towards expressionism.

a transgression of reality as much as of art. Inscrutable in his purpose, he has become the very symbol of our modern era and remains its quintessential rebel.

Braque is Picasso's antithesis. His career developed in a straight line. Towards the end of his life, rich in experience and in full mastery of his creative powers, he allowed the musician to take over from the geometrician, and indulged in the pleasures of harmony. In the pictures painted between 1938 and 1948, every possible musical approach is brought into play: counterpoint, direct or inverse mimicry, augmentation, diminution, stretto, the opposition of subject and answer, a delicate choice of timbre, a subtle knowledge of the harmonic resonance of tones. In turn austere and gracious, bold yet prudent, always discreet, a Cartesian spirit leaving nothing to chance yet possessing a sensibility as delicate as that of Corot, Braque is the most French of all the painters of this century.

With the twentieth century, the notion of an avant-garde in painting conforms more closely to the etymological and military sense of this phrase. Artistic creation remains an adventurous exploration of virgin territories, and the painter a kind of pioneer; but in contrast to the nineteenth century, this situation has become positively beneficial for him. Contemporary artists have met with far less resistance, in their campaign to destroy all the traditional values in painting, than the impressionists encountered in setting off a final firework display of that naturalism which represented the ethical basis of bourgeois society. It is an irony of fate that the nineteenth-century bourgeoisie failed to recognize this fact, and remained blinded by an academic aesthetic which it saw as one of the forces of inertia to be used as a bulwark against anything that seemed to threaten the established order.

The fauvists and cubists were more fortunate than the impressionists. Even at the beginning they could count on the support of a number of dealers, and they gradually attracted a following which seemed to grow in proportion to the subversive content of their art. Indeed, whenever passions seemed to be dying down, the artists hastily whipped up fresh antagonisms even if it meant picking a quarrel with themselves. Audacity became the stimulus of an artistic creativity which came increasingly to resemble an industrial output and which, like any industrialist, found itself forced to go on producing fresh types and models in order to attract customers and ensure a constant sales turnover. The very notion of audacity has been turned inside out, in the end, to produce a situation where-by the 'avant-garde' has become a real conformism, and a vital necessity to the artist.

The concept of the creator is becoming increasingly confused with that of the inventor. This process, expanding as the century progressed, has now reached a point where a painter's work is launched by exactly the same publicity methods as a commercial product. It seems that our industrial civilization attaches the notion of value automatically to anything that is *new*. Indeed, there are Americans, collectors and museum curators, citizens of a country which indisputably constitutes the 'avant-garde' of technical progress, who take this relationship so much for granted that after paying enormous sums for historic works of art they have these precious objects restored, at the risk of causing irreparable damage, solely because a brand-new appearance is considered an indispensable aspect of the prestige which the works have acquired.

An artist in the public eye needs an annual exhibition in just the same way that a department store or fashion house depends upon regular displays and sales offers; the artist has become the pampered slave of a production-line, forced to produce a never-ending series of novelties for the delectation of his public. In some ways he has reverted to the days when every minor prince or great lord included a painter among his retinue, to amuse the court with fanciful inventions. In other ways he is not unlike the artist-magician in primitive cultures, whose creations are heavy with the power of mystery.

The painter of today has renounced the solitude of genius, in which the work of art took shape in a painstaking dialogue with the inner self, that lonely creative process adopted by the romantics and by some of the greatest painters in history, such as Tintoretto and Rembrandt. He is more akin to those Florentine craftsmen or Swiss watchmakers who work in their own shop-windows, in full view of the public. Exhibitionism has become a professional obligation. Profiting from the aura of heroism which has surrounded the artist since the impressionists, and from the revolutionary prestige acquired by his elders at the beginning of the century, the contemporary painter has become, whether he wants to or not, one of those products of the consumer society which are manufactured by publicity and called 'stars'. He is faced with the choice of being a 'celebrity' or being nothing at all. A 'promising young painter' has a biography before he even has a life, and the future is assured of being fully informed about the least doings of some ephemeral favourite, whereas the life story of a Théodore Rousseau or a Giorgione was allowed to sink into irredeemable oblivion.

237 Georges Rouault (1871–1958).
The Prostitute. Watercolour. Paris,
Musée National d'Art Moderne.

Setting out the principles of French
expressionism, and transcending
Lautrec's disillusioned art, Rouault
evokes the misery of prostitutes at
the moment when Maillol is exalting
in sculpture the beauty of the
human body.

17 Beyond the avant-garde

Artistic movements originating in Europe have generally taken a certain time to achieve an echo in North America. After the outbreak of the Second World War, however, the process of assimilation became accelerated with the arrival in America of a number of European artists, many of whom made their homes there, some adopting American nationality. In addition, over the last twenty-five years, America has for the first time in its history witnessed the birth of indigenous forms of art.

Abstract expression emerged in New York in 1943, more or less under the influence of the surrealists Max Ernst, Joan Miró, Yves Tanguy (*pl. 235*), André Masson and Matta. This new tendency differed radically from the abstract movement in art which received its initial impetus in France at about the same time and reached its zenith during the decade following the end of the war, in the work of Le Moal, Manessier (*pl. 241*), Bazaine, Singier, Vieira da Silva, de Staël and Piaubert. The Parisian artists, whether they proceeded from a natural impression, progressively reduced from the real until it represents little more than the translation of a perceptual stimulus, or by-passed this reductive process to confront abstraction directly, all tended to 'stylize' in the traditional manner (which was still that of cubism, inherited from Cézanne); and the end result was in either case a 'form' resulting from patient elaboration. However, the American abstract expressionists, Arshile Gorky (*pl. 238*), Franz Kline (*pl. 246*), Willem de Kooning (*pl. 245*), Clyfford Still (*pl. 247*), Jackson Pollock (*pls 239, 265*), Philip Guston, Robert Motherwell (*pl. 248*), invoking the principle of automatic handwriting extolled by the surrealists, claimed to operate under the effect of immediate inspiration, in a sort of hypnotic state.

Pollock's trance, as he squirted paint from full tubes, or even from syringes, on to canvases stretched on the ground, may be compared to the dance of a witch-doctor. The American critic Harold Rosenberg, thinking particularly of Pollock, has called this manner of painting 'action painting'. Michel Seuphor has likened de Kooning's relationship with his own paintings to an all-in wrestling match; and it is doubtless more than chance which

has led the French painter Georges Mathieu, whose work is closely related to abstract impressionism, to name a number of his paintings after battles.

Immediately after the war, an analogous movement came into being in France, existing side by side with abstract art properly so called: this movement asserted its independence of the speculative tendencies of other kinds of European abstract art, calling itself '*abstraction lyrique*'. Among its adherents were Atlan, Hartung (*pl. 249*), Wols, Soulages (*pl. 242*) and Mario Prassinos.

From 1935 onwards the American west coast painter Mark Tobey, who during his travels in Asia had studied the function of ideograms as 'abstract' elements in Japanese painting, found inspiration in Japanese calligraphy for a series of gouaches entitled 'white writings' (*pl. 243*). After the war the Frenchman Henri Michaux gave a particular expressive value to the same technique (*pl. 244*); indeed, Western non-figurative painters have found Oriental calligraphy to be a far more authentic historical precedent for their work than the frequently invoked eighth-century Anglo-Irish miniatures. Georges Mathieu, renouncing relief and shading in favour of blob and line, transposed calligraphy on to a monumental scale, completing enormous canvases in record time (*pl. 240*). Claiming to have added the dimension of speed to the artistic gesture, Mathieu explained that speed was the essential factor of improvisation. Improvisation, in its turn, was to be considered the true value of an art which rejected the composed in favour of the instantaneous and set out to be 'an exploration of the psycho-sensorial world active for the first time at a pure ontological level' which would thus restore to the pictural 'event' the 'primitive potentiality of the sign', freed of all the representational and illustrative irrelevances attendant on the 'spiritual ossification' of Greek art and Renaissance humanism.

The gestural aspect of the creative act now assumed such significance that it turned into a public performance. Mathieu, for example, began painting in public, as though he were a musician giving a recital of improvisations. For many artists, the act of painting began to seem more important than the painting itself. A great deal of thought was

239 (overleaf) Jackson Pollock
(1912–56). *Painting*. Paris, collection
Paul Facchetti.

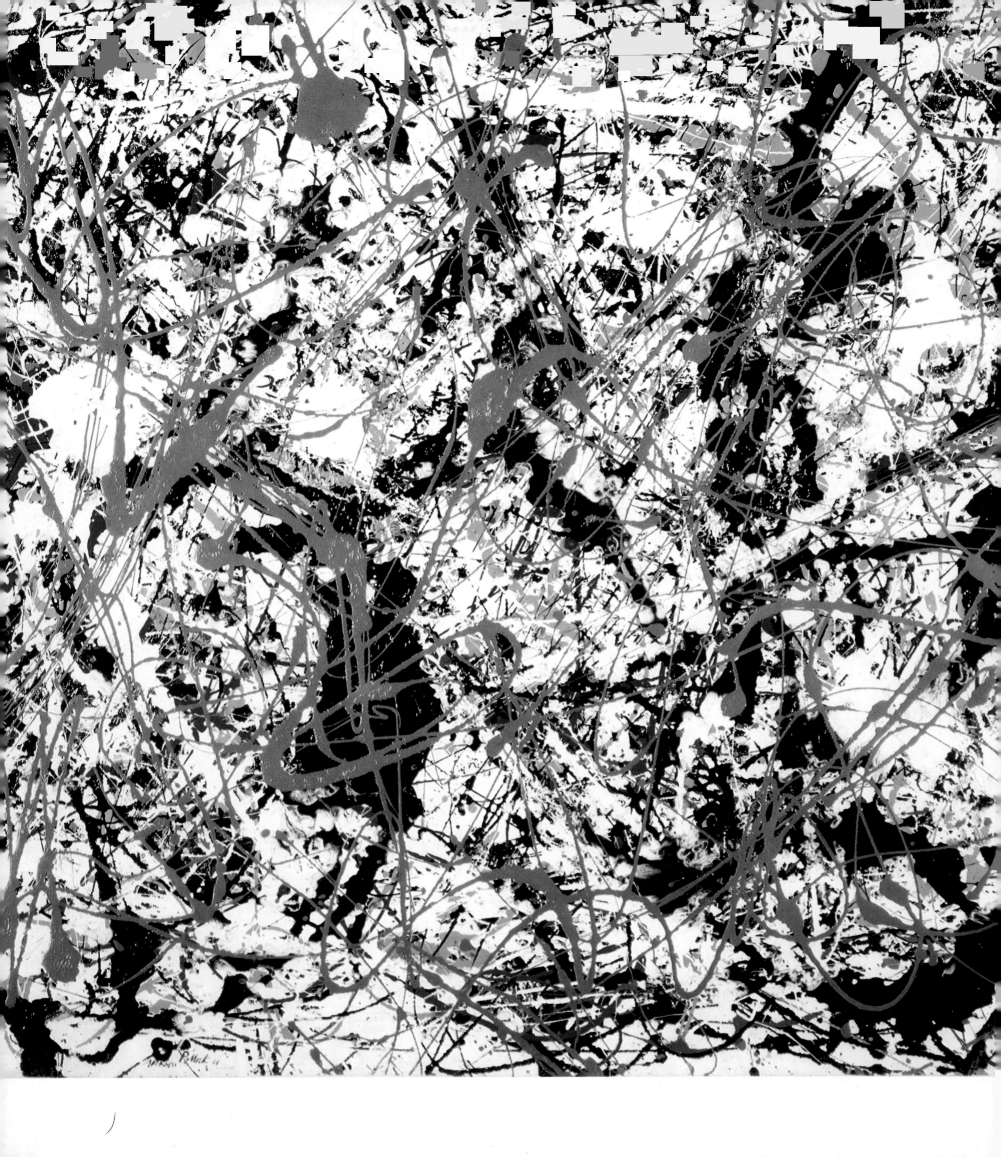

given to the ways in which colours could be projected on to the chosen bases, the criterion being the unusual nature of the method. One member of what was called the *Nouveau Réaliste* group, Yves Klein, made a naked woman press herself against a canvas after she had been smeared with paint. Another riddled his canvases with bullets from an automatic rifle. An ingenious artist had the idea of calcining the surfaces of his paintings by means of a blow-lamp. Yet another exhibited fragments of advertisements torn from billboards and hoardings. A final example of such 'inspiration' is so-called Art-Scotch, which consists in tearing off, with the aid of a length of cellophane adhesive tape, long narrow strips of the printed surface of pages of books

240 Georges Mathieu (b. 1922). *Mathieu from Alsace goes to the convent at Ramsay.* London, collection Anthony Denney.

Jackson Pollock's post-war drip paintings are, in a sense, an application to painting of the surrealist principle of automatism. The pattern produced by the 'drip' technique conveys a sense of restless movement in a number of close, parallel planes covering the entire surface of the picture. In the work of Mathieu, who arrived at his rapid, improvisatory technique independently of Pollock, single flamboyant shapes stand out against a uniform background.

241 Alfred Manessier (b. 1911).
The Night. New York, collection
Mr and Mrs Otto Preminger.

or newspapers 'to obtain a writing which possesses a new affective dimension when arranged on a flat surface'.

This artistic production was accompanied by a chorus of literary and critical speculation. John Dewey's *Art as Experience* (1934) had as great an influence on the development of the post-war art scene in America as did Kandinsky's *Über das Geistige in der Kunst* in Europe at the same time (an English translation of Kandinsky's book appeared in 1947, and a French translation in 1949). Meanwhile, in his determination to 'deconsecrate'

Aristotle and to exorcize the 'abject' Descartes, Mathieu invoked successively the names of Heraclitus, Empedocles, Plotinus, St Augustine, Gregory of Tours, St John of the Cross, Meister Eckhart, the doctrines of Zen Buddhism, Taoism, Ch'an Buddhism and the mystical revelations of Ibn Al'Arabi.

Artists and critics began to invoke the support of science. In 1946, in my book *Crépuscule des images*, I suggested that the new forms invented by modern art might correspond secretly to the most recent conceptions in physics. This idea caught on, and artists began exploring feverishly the writings of

242 Pierre Soulages (b. 1919).
Painting. Munich, Moderne Galerie
Otto Stangl.

Manessier's work includes an
element of stylized reality, whereas
Soulages, like the other members of
the *'abstraction lyrique'* movement,
lays claim to the same freedom of
inspiration which is inherent in
abstract expressionism.

285

243 Mark Tobey (b. 1890).
Tropicalism. Gstaad, Galerie
Saqqârah.

244 Henri Michaux (b. 1899). *Gouache*. Paris, Galerie Le
Point Cardinal.

Tobey and Michaux both use Oriental calligraphy as a
source for their remarkably expressive forms. Tobey's
all-over patterns link him clearly to abstract expressionism;
Michaux, too, recalls Pollock in his deliberate exploitation
of 'heightened' states of consciousness.

various philosophers and scholars. Heisenberg,
Bohr and Planck became objects of discussion in
artists' studios. Deductions from science were considered admissible, however, only in so far as they
served the artists' purposes. Thus, certain theories
of the physicist Louis de Broglie, the mathematician
Bourbaki and even Einstein himself, were rejected
as deriving from a conformist mental attitude 'still
under the sway of Aristotelian superstition'. A
logician, Stéphan Lupasco, the author of a theory
of contradictory propositions, has exercised a certain
influence on the practitioners of so-called *art
informel* among the Paris-based abstract painters,
and has himself written a book on the subject
(*Science et art abstrait*, 1963).

245 Willem de Kooning (b. 1904). *Gotham News*. Buffalo, N.Y., Albright-Knox Art Gallery.

No sooner has a new fashion in painting appeared on the scene than the critics pounce anxiously on its message, as though they were Roman augurs consulting the entrails of a bird. Artists, following Kandinsky's example, have abandoned brush for pen and launched into print to explain their intentions; books by practising artists, such as Michel Seuphor's *L'Art abstrait* and Georges Mathieu's *Au-delà du tachisme*, give vivid expression to the mental climate in which large numbers of modern painters work.

I suggest that, in trying deliberately to cut painting loose both from nature as celebrated by the impressionists and from the new directions proposed by the pre-First-World-War movements, these artists who claim to have discovered an affinity with philosophers and scientists risk condemning painting to the most dreadful of all servitudes, that of being an illustrative process.

There is no disputing that an intimate relationship exists between ways of thinking and feeling and artistic creativity in any one era. What is new is that today the artists themselves emphasize connections which previously were unconscious, and which have been revealed in our times thanks only to the perspicacity of modern historians of art. Thus, the great Gothic cathedrals stood for seven centuries before Erwin Panofsky made the discovery that their structure presents profound affinities with those of scholastic philosophy; and it was not until

De Kooning uses the technique of abstract expressionism in an aggressively energetic approach to figure or landscape; in his hands, action painting cuts its links with surrealism, mysticism and introspection.

246 Franz Kline (1911–62). *Meryon*. London, Tate Gallery.

247 Clyfford Still (b. 1904). *1948–D*. New York, collection William Rubin.

three centuries after Galileo had expounded his cosmographic system that analogies were drawn, again by Panofsky, between it and certain aspects of baroque art. Similarly, it goes without saying that the Byzantine artists would have been surprised to learn from André Grabar that their vision of the world was comparable to that of Plotinus; and Picasso and Braque were doubtless unaware of the new physics which was transcending the world of appearances at the very moment that they were destroying traditional space in their paintings.

But it would seem that, for the last twenty years, artists, deprived of the authority of nature, have felt the need to appeal to an alternative system of reference, thus reimposing upon painting another

form of that literary servitude from which it had been rescued, after a heroic struggle, by Manet, and from which all the schools of painting up to fauvism and cubism had subsequently kept it free. A picture by Mathieu can arouse feelings of pleasure at its rhythmic grace, and one by Pollock may give one a voluptuous impression of opulent matter analogous to the creations of the German rococo stucco-workers (*pls 239–40*); however, wholly unjustified claims are made on their behalf. Even if one bears in mind that there exists an essential relationship between this painted non-figurative world and the world of modern science, it is fallacious to invoke the element of the 'irrational' in modern science as an analogy for so-called 'lyrical abstraction'; in science the arid path of the irrational possesses a logic of its own to which no creative frenzy can ever supply a short cut. The working methods of scientific research can be compared more accurately with the attitude of Picasso and Braque, between 1907 and 1910, as they achieved the cubist reduction of reality to abstraction through a patient pro-gramme of analysis and synthesis.

It is equally false to argue, as some have done, that abstract art in some way brings us closer to the discovery of a universe situated beyond our senses.

248 Robert Motherwell (b. 1915). *Jour la Maison, Nuit la Rue*. Idaho, collection Mr and Mrs William Janss.

Kline's massive gestures and Still's blazing expanses of colour typify 'gestural' and 'chromatic' abstraction respectively, two major and contrasting currents within abstract expressionism. The paintings of Motherwell represent a self-conscious, rhetorical use of the abstract gesture.

289

To compare the attitude of an abstract painter with that of an ecstatic mystic is sheer delusion; God is not to be found in a spasm at the tip of a paintbrush. For a painter to imagine that he can simply tear himself away in a trance from the world of representation, cross the threshold of the normal consciousness, and, like some St John of the Cross or Meister Eckhart, attain a state of pure being, is to forget the long path of asceticism that the saint needs to travel in order to detach himself from the world of appearances and attain the summit of awareness.

The notion of painting as a means of transcending the rational and the conscious so as to attain the hidden sources of human experience has inevitably led some artists to paint under the direct prompting of the unconscious. Although the surrealists had advocated this process, they had not achieved it; in the last analysis their dreams are waking dreams. In the last decade, however, a number of artists have deliberately induced in themselves mental states similar to psychosis either through the complex disciplines of Zen or yoga or by taking hallucinogenic drugs such as the peyote-derived mescalin, and LSD (lysergic acid diethylamide). Aldous Huxley, in *The Doors of Perception* (1950), had described the experiments he had conducted while under the influence of mescalin, but the artist who pioneered this kind of investigation was Henri Michaux, who, in 1957, painted the visions which resulted from his use of mescalin. Experiments with LSD, formerly carried out on a wide scale in American hospitals but subsequently banned by the government, are still frequently made in private, by artists and others.

It must be said that the artistic results of these visions are rather disappointing and are unlikely to surprise those already acquainted with the art produced by mental patients. Ever since the end of the last century, when Dr Hans Prinzhorn first argued the therapeutic effect of artistic expression on the mentally disturbed, psychiatric hospitals have made increasing use of drawing and painting materials for this purpose. The resulting works are scientifically valuable on two levels: they provide diagnostic indication of the progress of a patient undergoing specific treatment; and they furnish information about certain mechanisms of artistic creation.

It is noticeable that those artists who paint under the influence of hallucinogenic drugs employ many of the same symbols (egg, phallus, ovule, flame) and procedures as the insane, and that the paintings can often be classified in a similar way according to personality types. A practised eye can detect, by studying their work, whether such artists tend to be paranoid, manic-depressive or schizoid. Schizoid tendencies predominate, thus supporting the hypothesis that a latent schizophrenia frequently underlies the artistic psyche. The best paintings by the artificially hallucinated present the same features as the drawings executed by schizophrenics: a world closed in on itself, consisting of an endless repetition of the same patterns, and an attempt to hold fast the disintegrating personality through a rigorous symmetry and a lapidary colour scheme which together give the painting a kaleidoscopic appearance.

The observed effects of hallucinogenic drugs on normal personalities suggest that schizophrenia is almost certainly due to a chemical disturbance of the cell-structure, since analogous effects can be produced by introducing a chemical substance into the body. Paintings so produced attain a quality rarely present in the work of the insane, except when

◄ 249 Hans Hartung (b. 1904). *T. 56–21*. Paris, private collection.

250 Ben Nicholson (b. 1894). *Still-life (off green)*. London, private collection.

Nicholson and Hartung provide examples of the two fundamental tendencies within abstract art: 'formal' or geometrical, and 'informal' or gestural.

the latter are already endowed with artistic talent (a fact sometimes revealed by the shock of the illness itself), but tend to be less original than those created by artists in a normal state of health.

Paintings which are based on the sensations induced by drugs have been christened 'psychedelic art', and have exercised an important influence on fashion and the decorative arts (*pls 251–2*). Psychedelic art has in fact provided the essential ingredients of 'environmental art', which consists in placing the spectator in an atmosphere bringing together music, movement and the plastic arts in a single public manifestation.

The tendency towards large-scale painting which can be seen in the work of abstract expressionists in particular, can be traced back to Fernand Léger, and no doubt expresses the same desire to shatter the restrictive space of easel-painting and reach out towards a dynamic space. Painting, in this last decade, has gone one step further and freed itself from the flat surface, bending it, dislocating it and distributing it through the three dimensions of real space. A New York artist, Allen Atwell, for instance, has painted a 'psychedelic temple' in his studio, spreading over the walls and ceiling the coloured projections of his drug-induced visions; the spectator is no longer situated in front of the work of art, but within it, thus fulfilling an ambition which the Italian futurists had already formulated in 1910 (*pl. 253*).

In environmental art, painting itself has become no more than a single element in an interplay of light ('op art', 'lumia art'), movement (kinetic art), and music or electronic sound patterns, which confronts the spectator with a total audio-visual experience. The spectator himself is often called

251 Isaac Abrams (b. 1939). *Here it comes*. Zurich, Galerie Bischofberger.

252 Paul Ortloff (b. 1942). *Exhalation*. Halcott Center, N Y., collection the artist.

253 Allen Atwell (b. 1925). *Zurich Mandala*. Zurich, Galerie Bischofberger.

The paintings, in hard acrylic colours, of so-called psychedelic artists are an attempt to reproduce some of the perceptual distortions (and consequently, perhaps, some of the sense of heightened awareness) which result from the use of hallucinogenic drugs such as LSD. Strident and claustrophobic in effect, they bear a strong resemblance to the paintings of schizophrenic patients.

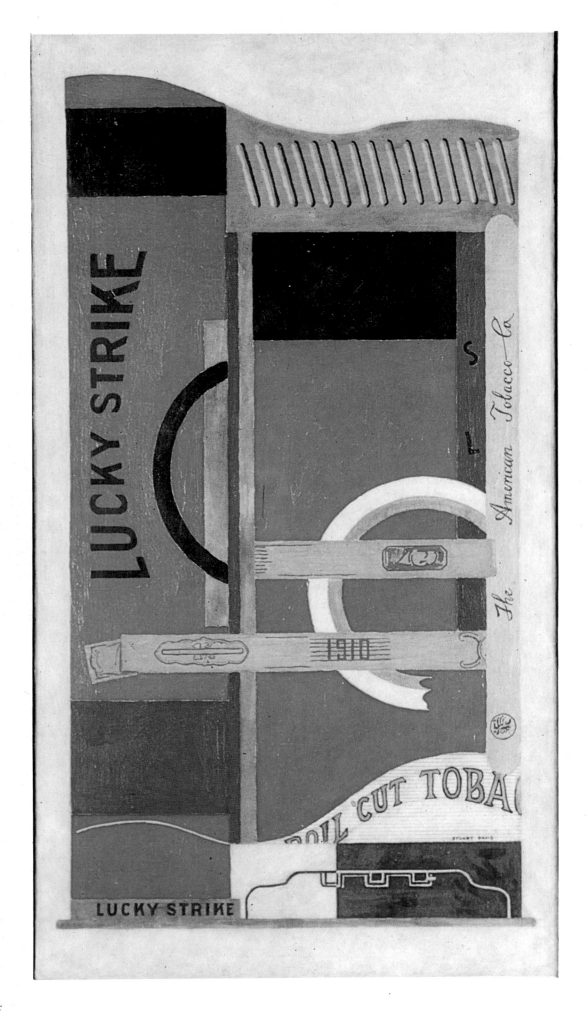

upon to participate in the development of this multi-faceted art, when the involvement of actors or dancers and the use of theatre or night club as a background convert this into an 'event'. This aspect of 'environmental art' recalls the ideal of the 'total work of art' (*Gesamtkunstwerk*) to which many German artists aspired in the rococo era.

Thus the spectator finds himself reintegrated, almost forcibly, in an art which for fifty years had seemed to be nothing more than the result of the speculations of schools, cliques and studio groups. This desire to come close to the 'public', in the widest sense of the word, was the main factor which led to a revival of figurative imagery, and, in particular, to pop art, a movement which had its origins in England. In the mid 1950s, the English critic Lawrence Alloway coined the term 'pop' which was subsequently applied to artists such as Eduardo Paolozzi (*pl. 257*), Richard Hamilton, Peter Blake, Richard Smith (*pl. 263*), R.B.Kitaj and their followers. From the early 1960s, pop art began to flourish independently in New York and California, the artists initiating this movement in New York being Andy Warhol (*pl. 256*), Roy Lichtenstein (*pl. 255*), Tom Wesselmann (*pl. 261*), James Rosenquist (*pl. 262*) and Claes Oldenburg (*pl. 259*). The principle of pop art is to present perfectly identifiable images of the external world as interpreted by the mass media (display advertising, photography, comic strips), or even to use the objects themselves, following the example set by Marcel Duchamp from 1915 onwards and repeated more recently in some of the work of the painter Jean Dubuffet (*pl. 258*), whose concept of *art brut* led him in one case to exhibit a slab of asphalt as a work of art.

The figurative simplification of pop art derives from Léger, from Herbin, from Ozenfant and Le Corbusier's purism, and from the literary imagery of certain surrealists such as René Magritte. Pop artists prefer, whenever possible, to work with industrial materials and substances. Thus, while abstract art appeals to the inner life, pop art plunges the spectator into the setting which assails him daily in the workshop and the street. The possibilities of pop are manifold. Most of the artists involved practise a literal realism, though some have adopted a geometrical formalization which brings them close to the abstract. Pop art is infinitely adaptable: it may be symbolic or dramatic, metaphysical or down-to-earth, and so becomes a natural element of environmental art.

Are the artist's avowed intentions sufficient on their own to confer aesthetic value on forms borrowed from the mass media and from *Kitsch*, both

254 (opposite) Stuart Davis (1894–1964). *Lucky Strike*. New York, Museum of Modern Art, gift of the American Tobacco Co. Inc.

255 Roy Lichtenstein (b. 1923). *Woman with flowered hat*. New York, private collection.

Davis's cubist treatment of a cigarette pack (1921) and Lichtenstein's bravura marriage of comic strip and Picasso (1963) show art in direct confrontation with mass culture. This relationship is the source of pop art.

256 Andy Warhol (b. 1930). *Four Campbell's soup cans*. New York, Museum of Modern Art (upper right), collection Mr and Mrs Leo Castelli (others).

257 Eduardo Paolozzi (b. 1924). ▶ *Work sheet collage*.

of which, visually, are mere by-products of modern art? Pop art is vulnerable to criticism on the grounds that, although it may have been launched with the intention of re-establishing the 'sociability' of art, it has ended up as a renunciation of art itself.

Periodic international festivals – all modelled on the oldest of their number, the Venice Biennale –

seek to persuade the public that the whole fabric of art has been refurbished during the more or less brief interval since the previous exhibition. These events are exactly comparable to those fairs at which the world's industrialists compare their wares, with the added attraction that they offer substantial prizes. At these gatherings, artists of various

Warhol once took a leaf from Duchamp's book by signing real soup cans as works of art; in these paintings of soup cans, the artist's role extends beyond mere 'choice' to the introduction of arbitrary distortions of colour and scale. Warhol's work is characterized by a taste for mechanical repetition and for utterly banal iconography. By contrast, Paolozzi's collage of slightly esoteric printed matter is a celebration, without apparent irony, of the ramifications of 'print culture'.

258 Jean Dubuffet (b. 1901). *Danse brune*. London, collection Anthony Diamond.

Dubuffet, a painter whom the surrealists have recognized as a kindred spirit, has made a special study of what he calls *art brut*, 'crude art': graffiti, paintings by mental patients, found objects such as pieces of stone or masonry. In a sense, his own work is 'crude art', with its earthy textures and its primeval directness of expression; this example is a banana-skin collage on papier mâché.

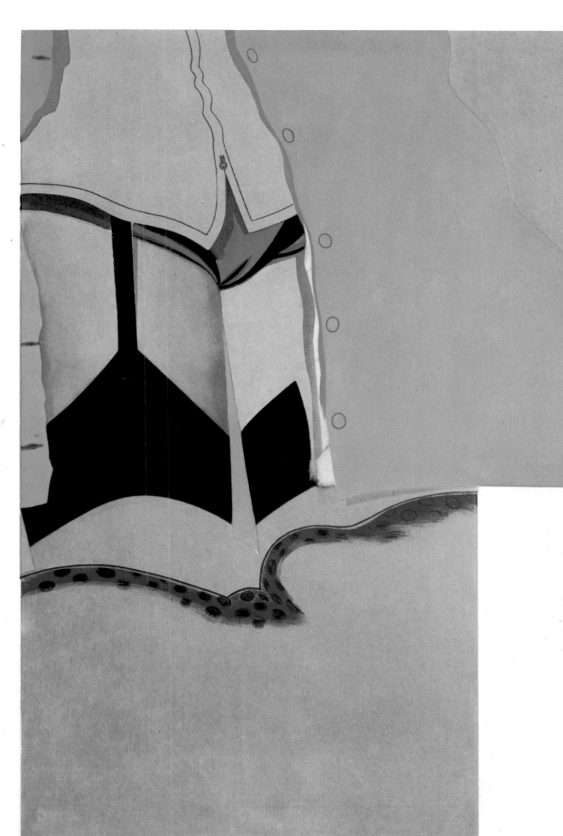

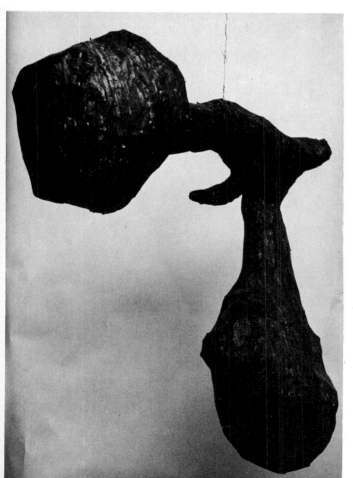

◀ 259 Claes Oldenburg (b. 1929). *Empire Papa Ray Gun*. New York, collection the artist.

260 Allen Jones (b. 1937). *Green Dress*. Zurich, collection Bruno Bischofberger.

Oldenburg, like the dadaists, is hostile to the word 'art'. In this case an object has been created by what might seem the most logically anti-artistic technique of all: fire. Jones belongs to a different pop tradition: he uses imagery from advertising art in teasingly ambiguous patterns which come close to pure abstraction.

261 Tom Wesselmann (b. 1931). *Still Life No 33*. New York, courtesy Sidney Janis Gallery.

nationalities can indulge in the ecumenical pleasures of a shared pictorial language, often deriving therefrom the illusion that art has been objectified in the manner of a science.

Museums of modern art, after observing all these artistic innovations uneasily for a long time, have now transformed themselves into something like experimental laboratories, accumulating works indiscriminately as material for analysis, testing them – so to speak – as they come off the assembly line. The world of art has come to resemble a single gigantic and complex organism, and in the process

262 James Rosenquist (b. 1933). *1,2,3, and Out*. New York, private collection.

263 Richard Smith (b. 1931). *Tailspan*. London, Tate Gallery. Wesselmann's gigantic billboards, and Rosenquist's juxtapositions of *trompe-l'œil* elements from commercial art, are obviously transpositions of reality; but there are also abstract paintings which employ a variant of the same glossy, 'post-painterly' idiom.

264 Claude Monet (1840–1926).
Detail of *Ile aux Fleurs*. New York,
Metropolitan Museum of Art,
Bequest of Julia W. Emmons.

265 Jackson Pollock (1912–56).
Detail of *One 1950*. New York,
Museum of Modern Art.

It is not Pollock's comparatively
crude 'drip' technique, nor his use of
lacquer and aluminium paint, that
marks him off from the tradition to
which Monet belongs: in fact, the
texture of his paintings is
magnificently opulent. The
distinction lies in the attempt made
by Pollock, and other
twentieth-century abstract painters,
to replace the artistic representation
of reality, with its indirect appeal to
profound levels of the consciousness,
by a direct frontal attack on the
depths of the human psyche.

301

its creative products have become more and more remote and self-sufficient in relation to the social environment; this has happened at the very moment when, paradoxically, society is being urged to applaud their ingenuity. The pursuit of originality at all costs, which has become the basic motivating factor of contemporary art, has been interpreted by its admirers as a manifestation of individualism, bringing with it a feeling of having escaped the grip of 'mass culture'. But the opposite is perhaps the truth: in fact the dissemination of abstract expressionism, encouraging huge numbers of artists all over the world to try their hands at 'action painting', constitutes an authentic mass phenomenon.

Condemned to originality, the modern artist must retain the attention of a blasé public by constantly changing the media with which he works, and thus creating a new art form each time. The resulting proliferation of 'arts' has reached a point at which it seems that there are as many movements, groups and manifestos as there are artists, and that each artist thinks up a new theory at least once a year. Apart from the basic post-war movements such as abstract expressionism (*art informel, art autre, tachisme*), *art brut*, New Figuration, *Nouveau Réalisme* (New Realism), geometrical abstraction, post-painterly abstraction (pure colour-field abstraction), and so on, there are the various offshoots of abstract expressionism, pop art, geometrical abstraction and neo-surrealism: minimal art (primary structures), lumia art, neo-dada, assemblage, funk art, *affichage* (*décollage*), junk culture, nuclear art, *Mecanismo*, Eventstructures, etc., etc.

Sometimes the work of art itself is renounced. Certain artists create works intended to become obsolescent or to be destroyed, or amuse themselves by re-creating their gadgets at each exhibition for the delectation of the spectator, like circus jugglers or strongmen at sideshows. Painting, this realm of the eternal, has been brought forcibly 'up to date' to a point where it has become no more than a province of the ephemeral world.

An art devoid of all outside references, refusing all imagery except that provided by the most wretchedly banal themes, is deemed to offer a substitute for transcendence; nonsense is considered to be full of sense, and the insignificant is hailed as the supreme significance; non-painting is identified with the principle of non-being, but a non-being which, paradoxically, never ceases to thrust up from its depths an unmanageable proliferation of being.

Like those mutants, in some theories of evolution, fated to live only long enough to help the species accomplish a new phase, painters are chained to the invention of fashions and unusual processes in order to escape from painting itself. Creation has become synonymous with innovation, and each innovation forces the artist to take one further step along the path which separates him, ineluctably, from an external world which for thousands of years had been the source of his inspiration even when he had sought to withdraw from it.

An obsession with the absolute has gradually eliminated from the work of art everything which is not intrinsically part of it, everything outside the process of painting itself which can contribute to its realization: subject, imitation, expression, idea. This mountaineering on the high and icy peaks of the human spirit may be intoxicating, but any attempt to attain pure essence in a work of art runs the risk of depriving it of existence altogether. For pure being is inaccessible: to become manifest, it must always blend with existence. The aim of art must surely be, in Etienne Gilson's words, to 'reconcile being with what appears to be', to 'cause being and its appearance to coincide'.

Biographical notes

Fourteenth century

BARNA DA SIENA (active *c.* 1350/6), is said by Vasari to have died in 1381 as a result of a fall from a scaffolding in the Collegiata at San Gimignano, where he was finishing a great cycle of frescoes illustrative of the *Life of Christ*. His style shows him to have been a follower of Duccio, Simone Martini and Ambrogio Lorenzetti.

CIONE, Nardo di (active 1343; d. Florence 1365/6), was one of the three brothers of Andrea Orcagna, the Florentine painter, sculptor and architect who directed a busy workshop in which Nardo and his brothers Jacopo (also a painter) and Matteo (a sculptor) worked. Although Nardo's reputation was long eclipsed by Andrea's fame, modern criticism has tended to endorse the judgment of Vasari who considered Nardo a greater painter than his younger brother Andrea. Ghiberti's attribution to Nardo of the frescoes in the Strozzi Chapel of Santa Maria Novella in Florence (*Last Judgment*, *Paradise* and *Inferno*) have made it possible to reappraise his work and distinguish it from that of Andrea. The frescoes of the *Passion* in the Bastari Chapel of the Badia Church in Florence, long thought, on the authority of Vasari, to be by Buonamico Buffalmacco, have now finally been attributed to Nardo di Cione.

GIOTTO, real name Ambrogio di Bondone (b. Colle nr Vespignano *c.* 1266; d. Florence 1337): the diminutive form Giotto was doubtless derived from Angiolo. He is supposed to have worked briefly in Cimabue's workshop. About 1290 he received a commission to design a crucifix for Santa Maria Novella, Florence. In *c.* 1296–7 he was summoned to Assisi to paint the frescoes of the *Life of Christ* and *Allegory of St Francis* in the Upper Church of San Francesco, although his authorship is denied by some critics on stylistic grounds. About 1298, he was commissioned by Cardinal Stefaneschi to design in mosaic the *Navicella* (*Christ saving St Peter from the waves*) for the atrium in Old St Peter's, in celebration of the jubilee proclaimed in Rome in 1300, but although this still survives, frequent restoration has left little of the original. In 1304–6 he painted the frescoes of the *Life and Passion of Christ* in the Arena Chapel, Padua. From about 1311 onwards, Giotto was a wealthy man (he bought estates in Mugello) and appears to have remained from then on mostly in Florence where, after 1317, he painted the frescoes of the Bardi and Peruzzi chapels in Santa Croce. However, in 1329–33 he worked in Naples for Robert of Anjou. In 1334 he was appointed to succeed Arnolfo di Cambio as chief architect of Florence Cathedral, and designed the campanile, of which only the base was completed in his lifetime.

LORENZETTI, Ambrogio (active 1319–47), was a Sienese painter, brother of Pietro Lorenzetti and probably the younger of the two. It is possible that both died in the plague that ravaged Siena in 1348. First mentioned in 1319, he was probably his brother's pupil. He worked in Florence between 1332 and 1335.

His most important works, and those in which he shows the greatest originality, are the frescoes of the *Allegory of Good and Bad Government* in the Palazzo Pubblico of Siena, painted in 1337–9.

Fifteenth century

ANGELICO, FRA, real name Guido di Pietro (b. Vicchio di Mugello probably *c.* 1400; d. Rome 1455), was known in religion as Fra Giovanni da Fiesole. He is first mentioned as a painter in 1417–18, while still a layman, and must have entered the Dominican Monastery in Fiesole soon afterwards. The pictures of his first period show him working as a miniaturist, in the tradition of Dom Lorenzo Monaco and Gentile da Fabriano. On the other hand, the *Linaiuoli Madonna* (Florence, San Marco), commissioned in 1433, gives evidence of an entirely modern preoccupation with volume and perspective. Between 1439 and 1445 he supervised a workshop in decorating with frescoes the convent of San Marco which Cosimo dei Medici had ordered Michelozzi to build for the Dominican Order in Florence. In 1447 he began a series of frescoes of the *Last Judgment* for the San Brizio Chapel in Orvieto Cathedral which was later finished by Signorelli. His last work, the frescoes of *St Stephen* and *St Lawrence* in the chapel of Nicholas V in the Vatican, is permeated with Roman atmosphere. He returned to Fiesole as prior at the end of 1451. The problem of distinguishing between his own contribution and the work of his pupils in his very extensive output is often extremely difficult to resolve.

ANTONELLO DA MESSINA (b. Messina *c.* 1430; d. there 1479), seems to have been the pupil of the court painter Colantonio in Naples. He is known to have been living in Messina in 1456, then to have gone to Calabria, and to have returned once more to Messina where he remained until 1465; there is a gap in the records between 1465 and 1473. He paid a visit to Venice in 1475, demonstrating there his proficiency in the new method of oil-painting which he must have learnt from some Flemish painter. In 1476 Duke Galeazzo Sforza invited him to come to Milan, but it is not known whether he undertook this journey or not, since he is recorded as being in Messina in September 1476. Having become infirm, he made his will on 14 February 1479; he died before the 25th of the same month. His work consists of religious pictures and portraits, but only a small proportion of these has survived.

BALDOVINETTI, Alesso (b. Florence, *c.* 1426; d. there, 1499), may have worked briefly in the workshop of the engraver and goldsmith Maso Finiguerra; he also collaborated with Fra Angelico. His inquisitive mind led him to undertake technical experiments – mixing distemper, fresco and oil – which have damaged his works, a trait which he shared with Leonardo. All that remains of his fresco representing the *Nativity* in

the atrium of Santissima Annunziata in Florence (1463) is the huge-scale cartoon, showing a landscape of greater dimensions than appears in any previous known fresco.

BELLINI, Giovanni, known as Giambellino (b. Venice *c.* 1430; d. there 1516), was the most celebrated representative of a family of Venetian artists. He was the natural son and pupil of Jacopo Bellini; his brother Gentile was also a painter, and his half-sister Nicolosia married Mantegna in 1454. He and Gentile stayed in Padua 1458–60, at the moment when Mantegna had just completed his frescoes for the Eremitani. Between 1470 and 1480 his art developed a personal character, reaching its peak with the large altarpiece of San Giobbe (*c.* 1485) and the small altarpiece of the church of the Frari (1488). As the sixteenth century approached, his style broadened; in 1514 he painted a *Feast of the gods* which he left unfinished, and which his pupil Titian reworked. His reputation was great, and his workshop much frequented. The school of art he created was rich in talent and survived for a long time in and around Venice. Giorgione was his pupil, and appears to have exercised some influence on him.

BOSCH, Hieronymus (b. *c.* 1450; d. 's Hertogenbosch 1516), was a member of an artist family that came from Aix-la-Chapelle (Aachen), whence his alternative name of Hieronymus (or Jerome) van Aeken. He spent his whole life in 's Hertogenbosch, and may even have been born there. Between 1480 and 1512 he is mentioned several times in the records of the Confraternity of Our Lady of 's Hertogenbosch. In 1504 Philip the Fair of Burgundy commissioned a *Last Judgment* from him.

CASTAGNO, Andrea del (b. San Martino a Corella 1423; d. Florence 1457), started life as a shepherd boy. He is known to have been working in Florence about 1440, and to have arrived two years later, in July or August, in Venice where he painted a series of frescoes in the vaults of the San Tarasio Chapel in San Zaccaria. In 1444 he was enrolled in the guild of *medici e speciali*. He died of the plague at the early age of thirty-four.

EYCK, Jan van (b. probably Maaseyck *c.* 1390; d. Bruges 1441), probably came from the region of Maastricht. From 1422 to 1425 he was working for Count John of Holland at The Hague, and in 1425 entered the service of Philip the Good, Duke of Burgundy, as court painter and '*varlet de chambre*'. He probably accompanied the duke to Aragon in 1426; in 1428 he led an embassy to Portugal to negotiate on the duke's behalf for the hand of the Infanta Isabella, and to paint her portrait. He was back in the Netherlands by the end of 1429, established in Bruges before 1431, and married in 1434. His reputation was enormous in his own lifetime, and Duke Philip, who was godfather to one of his children, held him in high esteem. A meticulous craftsman, he left few pictures. His principal work is the *Adoration of the Lamb* in Saint-Bavon, Ghent, which he completed in 1426; the question of the authorship of this polyptych is confused, in view of the problematical contribution by a brother, Hubert van Eyck, about whom little is known, but to whom some works are attributed which may in fact be by the youthful Jan.

FOUQUET, Jehan (b. Tours *c.* 1420; d. ?Tours by 1481), was the major French painter of the fifteenth century. Little is known of his early life, but his art was admired in Rome, and at some time between 1443 and the end of 1446 he painted two portraits of Pope Eugenius IV. While in Rome, Fouquet met Filarete, who speaks of him and his 'living likenesses' in his treatise on architecture. He was back in Tours probably by 1448, and in 1461 he collaborated in the preparations for the entry of the newly crowned Louis XI into Tours. In 1470, after the foundation of the Order of St Michael, he is recorded as having been paid for fashioning certain pictures for the use of this order. In 1475 he received the official title of 'King's Painter', and he died between 1477 and 1481. Fouquet was at his greatest as an illustrator of books, including the *Hours of Etienne Chevalier* (Chantilly). Apart from such miniatures, several panel portraits, some drawings and a self-portrait in enamelled copper are attributed to him.

KONRAD VON SOEST (active early fifteenth century), was the most distinguished painter of the Westphalian school, active in Dortmund from 1394, in which year he is recorded as having married. His principal work, the *Crucifixion* polyptych in the parish church at Niederwildungen, appears to be dated 1404.

MANTEGNA, Andrea (b. Isola di Carturo, between Vicenza and Padua, 1431; d. Mantua 1506), was the pupil and adoptive son of Francesco Squarcione, who is credited, perhaps over-generously, with a reform in painting comprising the imitation of the antique, the expression of relief through the study of perspective, and incisive precision of line. However, Mantegna left Squarcione at the age of seventeen, and it was no doubt through studying Donatello's sculpture in Padua that his own genius was first revealed to him. That same year, 1448, he started working with other artists on frescoes depicting the *Legends of St James and St Christopher* for the Ovetari Chapel in the Eremitani Church at Padua, which he completed alone soon after 1457; they were destroyed during the Second World War, though two sections moved to Venice remain. In 1454 he married Nicolosia, daughter of Jacopo Bellini. Between 1457 and 1459 he painted a large altarpiece for the church of San Zeno at Verona, the upper half of which has remained in this church, while the predella has been dispersed between the Louvre and the Musée des Beaux-Arts, Tours. He moved to Mantua in 1460 at the invitation of Lodovico Gonzaga, became his court painter, built a house for himself in that city and remained in the service of the Gonzagas for the rest of his life. Between 1468 and 1474 he painted the frescoes of the Camera degli Sposi in the Castello di Corte; and between 1485 and 1492 he painted a series of tempera cartoons representing the *Triumph of Caesar* (Hampton Court, Royal Collection). The frescoes he executed in 1490 for Innocent VIII's private chapel in the Belvedere at Rome have been destroyed. He completed a great number of pictures, mostly religious, during the long period

between 1468 and his death. The great *Our Lady of Victory* (*Madonna della Vittoria*), commissioned by Francesco Gonzaga to commemorate the Battle of Fornova, was completed in 1496; it is now in the Louvre. The *Parnassus* (1947) and the *Virtue triumphant over Vice* (1501–2) which he painted for the boudoir of Isabella d'Este show the belated influence of his brother-in-law Giovanni Bellini; they, too, are in the Louvre.

MASACCIO, real name Tommaso di Ser Giovanni di Guidi (b. Castello San Giovanni nr Florence 1401; d. ?Rome 1428), was the son of a lawyer. He was a pupil of Masolino, whose influence can be seen in his earliest paintings such as the *Madonna with St Anne* (between 1420 and 1424, Uffizi). His 1426 Pisa polyptych, of which the central *Madonna and Child* is now in London (National Gallery), shows a change of direction. A friend of the sculptors Ghiberti and Donatello, he sought to represent the mass and volume of objects in the round, as in the *Crucifixion* (Naples). In 1427 he worked on the cycle of frescoes in the Brancacci Chapel of Santa Maria del Carmine in Florence, which had been left unfinished by Masolino on his departure for Hungary; the *Expulsion of Adam and Eve from Paradise* and the series devoted to the Life of St Peter are definitely by his hand. His early death prevented him from completing this cycle of frescoes, which was finally terminated by Filippino Lippi half a century later.

PIERO DELLA FRANCESCA *or* DE' FRANCESCHI (b. Borgo San Sepolcro 1410/20; d. there 1492), is first recorded in 1439, when he was in Florence as assistant to Domenico Veneziano. In 1442 he was back in Borgo, serving as a town councillor; in 1445 he began work on a polyptych of the Madonna for the Compagnia della Misericordia in Borgo, in which the influence of Sassetta may be detected. Piero executed commissions for the courts of eastern Italy, and those of Ferrara, Rimini, Urbino and Bologna. Between 1452 and 1459 he painted his most important work, the fresco cycle in the choir of San Francesco at Arezzo, depicting the *Legend of the True Cross*. The frescoes which Piero painted for the Vatican in 1459 have vanished. He wrote two theoretical treatises, *De prospectiva pingendi* and *De quinque corporibus regularibus*, the last appearing after his death, its authorship ascribed incorrectly to his pupil, the geometrician Luca Paccoli. Piero was blind in his last years.

PIERO DI COSIMO (b. Florence 1462; d. there 1521), was the son of a goldsmith, Lorenzo di Chimenti, but adopted as his patronymic the name of Cosimo Rosselli, whose pupil he was and whom he assisted on his frescoes on the Sistine Chapel of the Vatican (1481–2). In his later years he became a recluse, entirely taken up by the study of nature and mythology. He blended various influences indiscriminately in his art, and was less concerned to be stylistically original than to achieve surprise through unusual imagery. Many of his pictures evoke the irrational and bizarre world of occultism.

PISANELLO, Antonio (b. Verona, 1397; d. ?Pisa, *c.* 1455), was probably the pupil of Stefano da Verona.

In 1431 he completed a series of frescoes commenced by Gentile da Fabriano for the Lateran Basilica. His gifts as a medallist and as a painter of portraits and animal studies made him much in demand by the princely courts of Italy, and he worked in Ferrara, Mantua, Rimini, Milan, Naples and Rome. There is no further mention of his activities after 1449, when he was in Naples; he seems to have been still alive in 1455, though certainly not in 1456. Only a very few of his paintings have survived, but important collections exist of his drawings (Louvre) and medals (London, Victoria and Albert Museum).

QUARTON, Enguerrand (b. Laon *c.* 1410; d. ?Avignon 1466 or later), was a native of Picardy, mentioned as working in Avignon from 1444 onwards. In 1452 he painted, in collaboration with Pierre Villatte, the *Virgin of Mercy* now in Chantilly (Musée Condé). In 1453 he signed a contract for a *Coronation of the Virgin* which was intended for the chapel of the Carthusian Monastery at Villeneuve-lès-Avignon and is now in the Hospice there. The Avignon *Pietà* derives directly from his style, although it is not possible to attribute it to him with any certainty.

TURA, Cosimo *or* Cosmè (b. Ferrara *c.* 1430; d. there 1495), was the official painter at the court of the Este in Ferrara under two successive dukes; he carried out for them numerous portraits and frescoes, designed decorative schemes and pageants, and executed large polyptychs which have now all been dispersed. He absorbed and blended northern influences (Rogier van der Weyden) and those of the school of Padua (Mantegna).

UCCELLO, real name Bolo di Dono (b. Florence 1397; d. there 1475), was called 'Uccello' perhaps because he loved birds or at some time painted them. His career as a painter seems to have started fairly late; at first he practised the minor arts, as a goldsmith, mosaic-worker and inlayer. He is first recorded, at the age of ten, as a *garzone* in the workshop where Ghiberti's First Baptistry Doors were being made. He was friendly with Donatello, and it is not surprising, therefore, that he should have sought to express volume in his paintings. In 1425 he went to Venice and worked on mosaics in St Mark's for about five years. In 1436 he gave a demonstration of his knowledge of perspective with his fresco painting, in imitation of an equestrian statue, of the English soldier of fortune Sir John Hawkwood, in Florence Cathedral. During the same period he painted scenes of the *Preachers in the Wilderness* in the cloister of San Miniato, and scenes of the *Creation* in the Chiostro Verde of Santa Maria Novella. Between 1443 and 1445 he executed two cartoons for stained-glass windows for the cathedral, painted some frescoes in Prato, and in 1445 was summoned to Padua by Donatello. On his return to Florence, probably that same year, he painted the astonishing *Deluge* in the Chiostro Verde of Santa Maria Novella. His most celebrated work is probably the *Rout of San Romano*, an episode in the war between the Florentines and the Sienese, which he depicted in three large panels for the Medici (Uffizi, Louvre and National Gallery). His last documented work is the predella for an altarpiece which he painted between 1465 and 1468 for the Confraternity of the Corpus Domini at Urbino (the *Story of the Holy Sacrament*, Galleria Nazionale delle Marche, Urbino). He appears to have given up painting in his old age. His preoccupation with perspective also found expression in a number of drawings which are exercises in the application of relief.

WEYDEN, Rogier van der (b. Tournai *c.* 1399; d. Brussels 1464), was also known as Rogier de la Pasture. He was a pupil of Robert Campin in Tournai, and became official painter to the city of Brussels in 1436. His life is well documented, and the details of a number of his commissions are known, though none of these correspond exactly to surviving works identified as being by his hand. It would seem, though, that the Escorial *Descent from the Cross* (Madrid, Prado) was commissioned by the Guild of Crossbowmen of Louvain, while the *Seven Sacraments* (Antwerp) was painted for Jean Chevrot, Bishop of Tournai between 1437 and 1460.

WITZ, Konrad (b. *c.* 1400; d. ?Basle *c.* 1447), was the son of Hans Witz, a goldsmith and itinerant painter who worked for the dukes of Brittany and Burgundy. Father and son arrived in Constance in 1412, and then settled in Tottweil, Upper Rhine, the seat of the Imperial Court of Justice. In 1431 Konrad went to Basle, attracted by the Church Council which convened there that year, and in 1434 painted there the large Altarpiece of the Redemption (*Heilspiegelaltar*), parts of which are now missing; most of the remaining panels are now in the Kunstmuseum, Basle. He was in Geneva in 1444; the museum in that city possesses the two wings (one signed and dated) of a small polyptych which he painted for the episcopal chapel of the Bishop of Geneva.

Sixteenth century

ALTDORFER, Albrecht (b. Regensburg (Ratisbon) *c.* 1480; d. there 1538), was the son of the painter Ulrich Altdorfer who had been granted the freedom of the city of Ratisbon in 1478. His earliest known paintings are dated 1507. Drawings dated 1511, showing views of the banks of the Danube, provide evidence of a journey to Upper Austria, during which he is presumed to have met the painter Michael Pacher. In 1518 he painted a large altarpiece for Sankt Florian Monastery, near Linz. In 1529 William IV of Bavaria commissioned from him *Alexander's victory* (*Battle of Issus*), now in Munich. Towards the end of his life he became a councillor and the city architect of Ratisbon.

ARCIMBOLDO, Giuseppe (b. Milan 1527; d. there 1593), came from a noble family. In 1562 he entered the service of the Emperor Ferdinand I and spent twenty-six years in Prague as court painter to the Hapsburgs, becoming one of the favourites of Maximilian II and, more especially, of Rudolph II, for whom he was artistic adviser and organizer of princely entertainments. In the field of music, he distinguished himself by the invention of a colorimetric method of musical transcription. In 1587 he retired to Milan, and was created a Count Palatine by Rudolph II in 1591.

BASSANO, Jacopo, real name Jacopo da Ponte (b. Bassano 1510/18; d. there 1592), was the most distinguished member of a family of Venetian painters who worked in Bassano. The earliest mention of his activities is in 1530. In 1534 he became a pupil of Bonifazio de' Pitati in Venice, but his works show successive waves of influence, including that of Titian, Pordenone, Parmigianino and, later, Tintoretto. His painting evolved in the direction of naturalism and an increasingly free treatment.

BRUEGEL, Pieter I (b. *c.* 1525; d. Brussels 1569), took his name from a village which has yet to be identified precisely. The influence of Hieronymus Bosch visible in his first works has led to the theory that he may have been brought up in 's Hertogenbosch. He became pupil assistant of his future father-in-law Pieter Coeck at Antwerp, and on the death of the latter in 1550 entered the workshop of Hieronymus Coeck. He became a master in the Antwerp Guild in 1551; immediately after this he went to Italy, visiting Rome and Naples and travelling as far south as Sicily. Returning to Antwerp in 1553, he began to make drawings for a number of engravers working for Hieronymus Coeck. In 1563 he married Maria Coeck, the daughter of his first master, and moved to Brussels. His works, the best collection of which is in Vienna, all show a meticulous care and attention to detail. His earlier paintings were signed Brueghel, but in 1557 he changed his signature to Bruegel, the spelling generally adopted today.

CAMBIASO, Luca (b. Moneglia nr Genoa 1527; d. Madrid 1585), was a precocious artist who at the age of fifteen was already assisting his father, a Genoese painter, in painting frescoes for the decoration of a palace. He became acquainted with Roman art before 1557, when he was once again in Genoa, working with his father as a fresco painter and sculptor. About 1560, the influence of Correggio and Parmigianino becomes apparent in his work, following a visit to Emilia; he made further journeys to Rome and Florence which allowed him to study the mannerist art being produced in those two centres at that time. His reputation was such that in 1583 he was summoned by Philip II to finish a series of frescoes in the Escorial begun by Castello. Cambiaso never saw his native country again.

CAMPI, Antonio (b. Cremona *c.* 1514; d. there 1587 or after 1591), belonged to a Cremonese family of painters which included his father Giulio, his brother Vincenzo and his cousin Bernardino. Antonio's first known work is dated 1546. He worked in Milan and Cremona. A refined and erudite personality, he published works of history, was a cosmographer, architect and sculptor.

CONINXLOO, Gillis van (b. Antwerp 1554; d. Amsterdam 1607), was, like Pieter Bruegel, a pupil of Pieter Coeck. A landscape painter and engraver, Coninxloo travelled widely in France and Germany as well as his native Flanders before settling in Amsterdam in 1595. He was the first Flemish painter to incorporate wooded scenes into his landscapes, thus inspiring his pupil Hercules Seghers.

CORREGGIO, real name Antonio Allegri (b. Correggio *c.* 1489; d. Parma 1534), probably got his artistic education in Mantua; his first work authenticated by a document, the *Madonna of St Francis* (1514-15, Dresden), shows local influences. But the inspiration for new heights of imagination and audacity seems to have been provided by a visit to Rome, which must have taken place about 1517 and would have revealed to him the work of Raphael and Michelangelo. He worked mostly in Parma: in about 1518 he painted frescoes of mythological allegories in the Camera di San Paolo in the convent there; in 1520 he decorated the cupola of San Giovanni Evangelista with the *Vision of St John at Patmos*; in 1526–30 he decorated the cupola of the Cathedral with the *Assumption of the Virgin*. During this time he painted both religious and mythological pictures, whose sensuous charm continued to captivate other artists until the eighteenth century.

DEUTSCH, Nikolaus Manuel (b. Berne 1484; d. there 1530), became a member of the Grand Council of the city of Berne in 1510, and accompanied Albert de Stein on his military expeditions into Italy, in the capacity of *secrétaire de camp*, in 1516 and again in 1522. His artistic career was somewhat hampered by his energetic political and diplomatic activities, and his passionate advocacy of the Reformation.

DOSSI, Dosso (b. Ferrara *c.* 1479; d. there 1543), is first recorded in Mantua in 1512. His real name was Giovanni Luteri. His art was formed in the romantic atmosphere of Ferrara, but it developed after contact with Roman art and, especially, Venetian art, the influence of Giorgione and Titian being particularly strong. In fact, Dossi collaborated with Titian in painting one of the pictures intended for the decoration of the *camerini d'oro* at Ferrara. Dossi was also profoundly steeped in the romantic atmosphere of the poetry of Ariosto, and his mythological compositions were heavy with symbolism.

DÜRER, Albrecht (b. Nuremberg, 1471; d. there, 1528), was the son of a Hungarian goldsmith who had settled in Nuremberg; from 1486 to 1490 he studied painting under Michael Wolgemut, and quickly showed a precocious genius for drawing. To complete his training, he travelled between 1490 and 1494, visiting Basle, Strasbourg and then Colmar where he had intended to seek instruction in the studio of Martin Schongauer, who had just died. In 1494 he returned to Nuremberg and married, and in the autumn of that year travelled to Venice, where he became acquainted with the art of Bellini and Mantegna. On his return to Nuremberg in 1495 he opened a painting and engraving workshop which quickly became famous throughout northern Europe. His engravings met with such success that attempts were made to counterfeit them, and it was no doubt with the aim of putting a stop to this activity that he went to Venice at the end of 1505. While there he painted several works, including the *Madonna of the rose garlands* (Prague), which were strongly influenced by the art of Giovanni Bellini, whom he greatly admired, and Mantegna. He then went on to Bologna, to study the art of perspective. His success in Venice was so great that the Seigniory tried vainly to persuade him to stay there. He left Italy reluctantly at the beginning of 1517, to go home to Nuremberg. His subsequent painting was profoundly affected by this journey, which had had the effect of leading him away from the Gothic and towards an Italianate classicism (*Four Apostles*, 1526, Munich). Like Leonardo, he composed various theoretical treatises, most of which are lost. He made several copper engravings, all difficult to interpret, bearing witness to his chief preoccupations: Christian (the *Knight, Death and the Devil*, 1513), humanist (*St Jerome in his cell*, 1514), and philosophical (*Melencolia*, 1514). Fleeing the plague which was raging in Nuremberg in 1520, he made a journey to the Netherlands where he was received with great honour, and fêted by his fellow artists Quentin Massys, Joachim Patinir, Bernard van Orley and Lucas van Leyden. During this voyage he felt the first signs of the illness to which he was to succumb, probably a liver disorder.

GIORGIONE, real name Giorgio Barbarelli (b. Castelfranco 1476/8; d. Venice 1510), was not called Giorgione until after his death. The one thing really certain about his life is his death of the plague, in the autumn of 1510 at Venice, at the age of about thirty-four. In 1506 he shared a studio in Venice with Vincenzo Catena. In 1507/8 he was working in the doge's palace, and in 1508 he was painting frescoes on the outside of the Fondaco dei Tedeschi, the headquarters of the German merchants in Venice.

GIOVANNI DA UDINE (b. Udine 1497; d. Rome 1561 or 1564), was a printer, painter, stucco-worker and architect. He is mentioned as working in Rome between 1513 and 1516. In 1517 he did the stucco decoration of the Vatican Loggie, under Raphael's supervision. After a visit to Florence he returned to Udine in 1523, but was back in Rome almost immediately in response to a summons from Clement VII to execute further decorations. After the Sack of Rome in 1527 he returned to Udine once again, and thereafter worked mostly in the regions of Venice and Friuli, though paying several visits to Rome to carry out commissions there.

GRAF, Urs (b. Solothurn *c.* 1485; d. ?Basle 1527/8), was the son of a goldsmith, and was himself a goldsmith, painter, artist in stained glass, graphic artist and engraver. He led an active life, participating in the political campaigns in Basle, and became notorious for his brawls, banishment, imprisonment, and mistreatment of his wife. He fought as a mercenary in the battles of Marignan and La Bicoque.

GRECO, EL, real name Domenikos Theotokopoulos (b. Crete 1541; d. Toledo 1614), was a Spanish painter by association, though of Greek origin. He went to Venice on leaving his native Crete, at some time between 1560 and 1570, and while there was much influenced by Titian, Jacopo Bassano and Tintoretto. He arrived in Rome in 1570 with an introduction to Cardinal Farnese, and appears to have stayed there until 1575. Some recent critics have attributed to him a whole semi-Byzantine youthful *œuvre*, but this fails to match the pictures of the Italian period which are known to be by his hand. He went to Spain in 1576, settling in Toledo the following year. He soon received major commissions, including the High Altar for Santo Domingo el Antiguo (1577–9) and the *Disrobing of Christ* (*El Espolio*) for the Cathedral. A son was born to him in 1578. In 1581 Philip II commissioned the *Martyrdom of St Maurice and the Theban Legion* for the Escorial, but the finished picture pleased neither the king nor the monastery. El Greco had to abandon the ambition of becoming court painter, and he passed the rest of his life far from court, in Toledo, where an archaic society had preserved a traditionalist outlook. In 1586 he painted the *Burial of Count Orgaz* for the church of San Tomé. His ecstatic and passionate style became heightened with time. In order to keep pace with the many religious commissions he received, he was obliged to make several replicas of some of the most popular pious images; he organized a workshop for this purpose, which raises questions of attribution.

GRÜNEWALD, Matthias, real name Mathis Nithart (b. ?Würzburg before 1480; d. Halle 1528), was wrongly called 'Matthias Grünewald' as a result of an error committed by the seventeenth-century painter-historian Joachim Sandrart, and has recently been identified as Mathis Nithart (or Neithardt) who later substituted the name Gothart and was a native of Aschaffenburg in Lower Franconia. From 1508 to 1514 he was court painter to the Archbishop-Elector of Mainz, and then to Cardinal Albrecht, Elector of Mainz. His master work, the altarpiece for the monastery of Isenheim in Alsace (it is now at Colmar), was painted between 1512 and 1515. After the Peasants' Rising of 1525 he lost his post at court and took refuge, first in Frankfurt and then in 1527 in Halle where he died. He was sympathetic to the ideas of the Reformation.

HUBER, Wolf (b. Feldkirch, Vorarlberg, *c.* 1490; d. Passau 1553), became court painter to the Prince Bishop of Passau. He is mainly noted for his drawings and woodcuts, and only a small number of his paintings survive.

LEONARDO DA VINCI (b. Vinci nr Empoli 1452; d. Château de Cloux nr Amboise 1519), learnt the art of painting in the studio of Andrea del Verrocchio in Florence. From 1482 to 1499 he lived in Milan, where he painted the fresco of the *Last Supper* in the refectory of Santa Maria delle Grazie, and worked on a project for a bronze equestrian monument to Francesco Sforza. Leonardo left Milan shortly after the entry of the French troops in 1499, returning to Florence in 1500 and remaining there until 1504. But in 1506 he went back to Milan once again, at the request of the French government. A stay in Rome between 1513 and 1516 proved unsatisfactory, since the pope made no use of his talents. He then accepted Francis I's invitation to France in 1517, spending his last years in the small château of Cloux, near the royal residence of Amboise on the Loire.

LOTTO, Lorenzo (b. Venice *c.* 1480; d. Loreto 1556), was noted both for his religious paintings and his portraits. His origins are unknown, though the suggestion that his forebears were seafaring folk has been put forward as an explanation for the restlessness which led him to spend his life moving from one town to another in Lombardy and the Marches. It is not known whether he was married and, if so, whether he had any children. He died alone and poor, although he had received lucrative commissions throughout his life. An account book which he kept from 1538 (when he was in Ancona) onwards has survived and provides us with certain details about his life; these suggest that he was a troubled and difficult character, but deeply religious. He travelled constantly between 1503 and 1512, then based himself in Bergamo from 1513 to about 1526; it was here that he produced some of his most beautiful altarpieces, though he continued, during these years, to travel through the Marches as well as paying visits to Venice and Rome. In an unsuccessful attempt to raise funds, while in Ancona in 1552, he held a lottery for his paintings. The last two years of his life were spent in the Santa Casa Monastery at Loreto, where he became a lay brother.

MICHELANGELO Buonarroti (b. Caprese nr Arezzo 1475; d. Rome 1564), was apprenticed to the painter Domenico Ghirlandaio in 1488, but remained in his workshop for only a very short time. He learnt the art of sculpture in the School set up by Lorenzo 'Il Magnifico' in the Medici gardens, where the collection of classical sculpture was under the supervision of Bertoldo, the pupil of Donatello. It was at this time that, according to tradition, his nose was broken in a fracas with a fellow pupil, Torrigiano. Between 1490 and 1492 he stayed with Lorenzo in his palace on the via Larga. He fled the revolutionary upheavals in Florence in 1492, but returned after a year to find the city sadly changed by the stern preaching of Savonarola. He was back in Rome between 1496 and 1501, when he returned to Florence yet again, remaining there this time until 1505. The only easel-painting that he is definitely known to have completed before undertaking the decoration of the Sistine Chapel is the *Holy Family* (or *Doni tondo*) executed in 1503 for his patron Angelo Doni (Uffizi), although the *Virgin and Child, St John and Angels* (London, National Gallery) may possibly have been a work of about his twentieth year. The cartoons he made for the never-completed fresco of the *Battle of Cascina* have been lost. Pope Julius II summoned him to Rome to design a fitting tomb for him, but soon diverted him from this task by commissioning him to paint the ceiling of the Sistine Chapel (1508–12). Michelangelo returned to Florence on several occasions to execute various works of architecture and sculpture (the Biblioteca Laurenziana, the Medici Chapel in San Lorenzo). In 1527, after the Sack of Rome, he placed himself at the disposal of the Florentine republic, at war against the pope and his allies, as military engineer. Paul III required him to paint the altar wall of the Sistine Chapel with the *Last Judgment* (1536–41). His last work in painting was the decoration of the Pauline Chapel with frescoes of the *Conversion of St Paul* and the *Crucifixion of St Peter*.

PONTORMO, real name Jacopo Carucci (b. Pontormo 1494; d. Florence 1556), worked under Andrea del Sarto about 1512, and was the true creator of Florentine mannerism, a tendency which can first be detected in his work in 1517. Between 1522 and 1525 he painted an important cycle of frescoes depicting scenes from the Passion in the Certosa of Galluzzo. He appears to have been highly neurotic; he lived a solitary existence and kept an obsessive Diary.

PORDENONE, real name Giovanni Antonio de' Sacchis (b. Pordenone *c*. 1484; d. Ferrara 1539), was named after his birthplace in the province of Friuli which was at that time under the influence of Venice. He seems to have discovered Giorgione very early (*Madonna*, 1516, Susegana), and may have gone to Rome *c*. 1515–16. In 1521 he painted a series of frescoes depicting scenes from the Passion in Cremona Cathedral, taking over a commission withdrawn from Romanino. He also painted frescoes in San Rocco, Venice.

RAPHAEL, real name Raffaello Sanzio (b. Urbino 1483; d. Rome 1520), was the son of a painter at the court of Urbino, Giovanni Santi. After the death of his father he was apprenticed to the painter Timoteo Viti at Perugia, and subsequently entered the workshop of Perugino there, collaborating with the latter in the Cambio. Perugino's influence on him was so great that during this first period it is sometimes difficult to distinguish between the work of the two artists. Raphael's personal style emerges fully in 1504, in the *Betrothal of the Virgin* (*Lo Sposalizio*), his first signed and dated work. At the end of this year he went to Florence, where he discovered the work of Leonardo; his art now went through a transitional stage of classicism, expressed in a series of Madonnas such as the *Madonna del Granduca* (Pitti). Towards the end of 1508 Julius II summoned him to Rome and commissioned him to decorate the Stanza della Segnatura with a series of frescoes which he completed in 1511. In the last decade of his short life he was overwhelmed with work and had a large team of assistants working for him under the supervision of his favourite pupil Giulio Romano: continuing his decorative scheme in the Vatican, Raphael painted the Stanza d'Eliodoro, the Stanza dell' Incendio, the Sala di Costantino, and the Loggie. For his chief patron, the banker Agostino Chigi, he decorated the Farnesina with a fresco of *Galatea* (1514), and painted the *History of Psyche* (1518) for the garden loggia of the palace. Among innumerable other tasks he assumed the responsibility of succeeding Bramante as architect of the new St Peter's. During this period, Raphael also painted a number of easel pictures, including the *Sistine Madonna* (Dresden, Gemäldegalerie), and designed a series of cartoons for a tapestry of scenes from the lives of St Peter and St

Paul (London, Victoria and Albert Museum). He died at the age of thirty-seven, at the height of his glory.

ROMANINO, IL, real name Girolamo di Romano (b. Brescia *c*. 1484; d. there after 1562), formed his art under the influence of Giorgione, Titian and the German etchers. In 1519 he was commissioned to execute a series of frescoes, depicting scenes from the Passion, for Cremona Cathedral. He painted mythological scenes in the Castello del Buonconsiglio at Trent.

ROSSO, Giovanni Battista, also known as Rosso Fiorentino (b. Florence 1494; d. Paris 1540), worked under Andrea del Sarto and was one of the founders of Florentine mannerism. The most important work from his Italian period is the 1522 *Descent from the Cross* (Volterra). He went to Rome about 1524 and fled after the sack of the city in 1527, wandering around Italy until 1530 when he went to Venice. That same year he left for France at the invitation of Francis I, and took over the direction of the decoration of the palace of Fontainebleau. According to Vasari he committed suicide; he is known, in any case, to have had a neurotic temperament.

SAVOLDO, Giovanni Girolamo (b. Brescia *c*. 1480; d. ?Venice after 1548), was registered as a painter in Florence in 1508, but is recorded as living in Venice by a document of 1521, the same year that he married a Florentine woman. He may have worked in Milan *c*. 1529/35. His small output consists mainly of easel-paintings, and he seems to have had little liking for large-scale religious commissions.

TINTORETTO, real name Jacopo Robusti (b. Venice 1518; d. there 1594), acquired his familiar name from his father's occupation as a dyer (*tintore*). He may have been a pupil of Titian for a very short time, and was probably associated with Schiavone and Paris Bordone. His earliest dated work is of 1545. In that or the following year he visited Rome for the first and only time, the rest of his life being spent entirely in Venice. Here he was constantly overwhelmed with commissions, which he executed with extraordinary rapidity, with the help of a huge workshop and the use of numerous assistants. He worked for the State, the Confraternities, the churches and private patrons, and was also much in demand from outside the city. His 1548 *St Mark rescuing the slave* (Venice, Accademia) made his reputation, and he was already famous when in 1564 he won the competition for the redecoration of the Scuola di San Rocco and so assured himself permanent success. He eventually decorated the entire building, completing the scheme in 1588. He was the most prolific painter of the whole Italian school. The *Paradise* which he and his workshop were commissioned to paint for the Sala del Maggiore Consiglio in the doge's palace in 1588 is the largest work in the history of Western painting before modern times.

TITIAN, real name Tiziano Vecellio (b. Pieve di Cadore 1485/90; d. Venice 1576), learnt the art of painting in the workshop of Giovanni Bellini. With Bellini's death in 1516 Titian became the most

important Venetian master, Giorgione having died in 1510. He rapidly rose to fame, and enjoyed the esteem of the rulers of Europe. At the end of 1529 or the beginning of 1530 he was introduced to Charles V in Bologna and painted his portrait; in 1533 the Emperor rewarded him by making him a Count Palatine and a Knight of the Golden Spur. In 1546 he was created an honorary citizen of Rome. In June 1548 he went to Augsburg, where he painted several portraits, returning to Venice at the end of October; on a second visit to Augsburg in 1550 he painted Prince Philip, who was to become Philip II of Spain, and for whom he executed a number of works. In 1551 he returned to Venice, where he lived and worked for the rest of his long and glorious life.

Seventeenth century

BAROCCI. Federico (b. Urbino *c*. 1535; d. there 1612), went to Rome in the mid 1550s, and became acquainted with the work of the mannerists there. In 1556 he was in Urbino, but returned to Rome soon afterwards. During this second visit to Rome he claimed that an attempt had been made to poison him by colleagues jealous of his success; it is certainly true that for the rest of his life he was crippled by ill health, suffering great pain and forced, at one point, to give up painting entirely for four years. His *Deposition*, commissioned in 1576 for Perugia Cathedral, shows continued mannerist influence. He returned to Urbino, probably in 1570, and remained there for the rest of his life. Between 1575 and 1579 he painted the large altarpiece the *Madonna of the People* (*Madonna del Popolo*) for the parish church of Arezzo; this picture (which is now in the Uffizi) is his personal declaration of emancipation from mannerism. Although he was essentially a painter of religious themes, he completed a few portraits during his last years.

CARAVAGGIO, real name Michelangelo Merisi (b. Caravaggio 1573; d. Porto Ercole 1610), was the son of a mason in a village near Milan, and was apprenticed for four years to Simone Peterzano. At the age of about sixteen, in 1588 or 1589, he went to Rome and entered the workshop of the Cavaliere d'Arpino, painting the accessories and still-lifes in the latter's pictures. In 1590 he shared the commission for the Contarelli Chapel of San Luigi dei Francesi with his master, but finally completed the work alone, executing a *St Matthew and the Angel* (replacing an original version rejected as indecorous), together with the *Calling* and *Martyrdom* of the saint. These pictures, which appear to have been completed after 1600, embody the transformation of his art from the picturesque to the dramatic. In 1606 his *Death of the Virgin*, painted for Santa Maria del Popolo, was refused by the church's clergy, but the picture was promptly bought by Duke Vincenzo Gonzaga, on the advice of Rubens; in answer to public demand, the work was put on display for a week before being removed from Rome. Between 1605 and 1607 the police dossiers were filled with reports of his adventures: in 1606 he actually killed a man during a brawl, was wounded himself, and forced to flee from Rome, seeking refuge first of all in the Sabini Mountains and then, in 1607, in Naples. In 1608 he was summoned to Malta by the Grand Master of the Order of St John, but was soon imprisoned for assault; he escaped to Sicily, and stayed briefly first at Syracuse and then at Messina, painting pictures but still pursued by agents of the Order. Back in Naples in 1609 he was seriously wounded in a brawl and his death was generally reported. He had to flee once again, and left Naples by boat for Porto Ercole, a Spanish enclave on the Tuscan coast. Here he was imprisoned by mistake and found, on his release, that the boat had sailed without him, taking his baggage with it. He died of malaria at Porto Ercole on 31 July 1610.

CARREÑO DE MIRANDA, Juan (b. Avila 1614; d. Madrid 1685), worked under the direction of Velázquez at the Alcazar, and also formed his style by studying the Flemish and Venetian paintings in the royal collection. In 1669 he was appointed court painter to Charles II, and he later became official portrait-painter of the king's second wife, Maria Anna of Neuburg. He is chiefly known as a portraitist, but he was not happy following the style set by Velázquez, and his finest pictures are those with religious themes.

CLAUDE LORRAIN, real name Claude Gellée (b. Chamagne, Lorraine, 1600; d. Rome 1682), arrived in Rome at the age of about thirteen, and became servant-assistant to the landscape-painter Agostini Tassi. In 1625 he returned to Nancy, where he worked briefly as an assistant to Claude Dernet, but by the beginning of 1627 he was back in Rome for good. He led a tranquil life there, associating most closely with northern artists but also highly esteemed by Roman patrons of the arts. The earliest work known by him is dated 1635. He kept a reference book, which he called the *Liber veritatis* (London, British Museum), in which he made drawings of his paintings to guard against copying and forgery. He made innumerable life studies, paintings as well as drawings, but none of these have survived. All his paintings were executed in his studio.

DESIDERIO, MONSÙ (seventeenth century), is a name concealing a French origin (Monsù=Monsieur), and covers two distinct groups of works. The first group consists of some panoramic views of Naples by Didier Barra, an artist of Lorraine, who settled in Naples about 1617 and in 1647 signed a picture Desiderius Barra of Metz. The other group, which is both more extensive and more interesting, depicts fantastic architecture: the author of these *capricci* has been identified as François de Nomé, also from Lorraine, born in Metz in 1593, who went to Rome in 1602 and to Naples in 1610.

ELSHEIMER, Adam (b. Frankfurt-on-Main 1578; d. Rome 1610), left his home town about 1598 to work in Venice, then went to Rome in 1600. He remained there for ten years, producing small pictures invariably painted on copper. He introduced a Caravaggesque inspiration into landscape-painting.

GENTILESCHI, Artemisia (b. Rome 1597; d. Naples after 1651), was the daughter of Orazio Gentileschi, and the pupil of her father and of Agostino Tassi. In 1621 she left Rome with her father for Florence; she later lived in Rome and Naples, and joined her father in London during 1638-9. She was back in Naples by 1640 and continued working there for the rest of her life. Her own style, applying itself often to themes of violence and even of cruelty, gradually evolved from the Caravaggesque style of her father.

HALS, Frans (b. Antwerp c. 1585; d. Haarlem 1666), was the son of a draper who established himself in Haarlem soon after Frans's birth. Hals learned painting in the studio of Karel van Mander. He was in touch with Rubens, visiting him in Antwerp and possibly being visited by Rubens in return. His first important works are the group portraits, especially the *Officers of St George's Company of Archers* (1616), the *Officers of St Adrian's Company of Archers* (1622), and a 1627 version of the *St George's Company* (all at the Frans Halsmuseum, Haarlem). His late works include the great 1664 groups depicting the *Governors* and *Women Governors* of the Old People's Almshouse in Haarlem. Almost his whole life was spent in Haarlem; despite his great success as a painter he lived in constant financial difficulties.

HERRERA, Francisco, surnamed El Viejo (the Elder) (b. Seville 1576; d. Madrid after 1657), may have been the pupil of Francisco Pacheco in Seville. We have very little information about the career of this painter of frescoes and history pictures, etcher and medallist. He established himself in Madrid in 1640, and was still alive on 5 September 1657, the date on which he drew up his will before a commissioner. His first known works date from 1610 and 1617, and he achieved mastery of technique in 1629, in the pictures he was commissioned to paint for the altar of the college of San Bonaventura at Seville; for some reason he was replaced by Zurbarán when the commission was only partly completed.

LA TOUR, Georges de (b. Vic-sur-Seille, Lorraine, 1593; d. Lunéville 1652), may or may not have visited Rome, but his work suggests acquaintance with that of Terbrugghen and Honthorst, and although nothing is known of his training he was certainly influenced by Caravaggio and the Utrecht school. He was established in Lunéville by 1618, and in 1620 was certified as a master painter. He worked for Duke Charles IV of Lorraine, and he is referred to on two occasions as 'painter in ordinary' to the King of France. The pious imagery he created had a great success, and his paintings were much copied, as well as giving rise to numerous pastiches and imitations.

MAFFEI, Francesco (active Vicenza 1620; d. Padua 1660), formed as an artist by the great sixteenth-century Venetians, may be considered the true local Venetian painter of the seventeenth century, at a time when the Venetian school was composed mainly of artists from other parts of the country. He worked in Vicenza, Padua, Venice, Brescia and Rovigo. His first known work is dated 1626.

MAZZONI, Sebastiano (b. Florence c. 1611; d. Venice 1678), is supposed to have left Florence after composing some satirical verses which made him enemies. It is not known just when he arrived in Venice, although it was before 1648. He died as a result of a fall from a ladder.

POZZO, Andrea (b. Trent 1642; d. Vienna 1709), worked first of all in Trent, then in Como and in Milan, and in 1665 became a Jesuit lay-brother. In 1679 he created an astonishing *trompe-l'œil* decoration for the central cupola of the church of San Francesco Saverio in Mondovi (Piedmont). Brought to Rome in 1681 by Padre Oliva, the general of the Order, he designed altars for the Order's churches. Between 1691 and 1694 he painted his masterpiece, the ceiling of the nave of San Ignazio in Rome. In 1702 he was summoned to Vienna by the Emperor Leopold, to whom he dedicated his treatise on perspective, *Prospettiva de' pittori e architetti . . .* , published in Rome between 1693 and 1700. In Vienna he supervised the reconstruction of the Jesuitenkirche, and painted ceilings in the Liechtenstein Palace. A school grew up around him in central Europe, partly as a result of his direct influence and partly through the impact of his treatise on perspective, which was translated into German, French, Dutch and English.

REMBRANDT Harmenszoon van Rijn (b. Leyden 1606; d. Amsterdam 1669), was the fourth son of a prosperous miller. After about a year at Leyden University he was apprenticed for three years to a Leyden painter, Jan van Swanenburgh, then spent some six months in Amsterdam under Pieter Lastman. On returning to Leyden in 1625 he set up a workshop in company with Jan Lievens. At the end of 1631 or early in 1632 he moved to Amsterdam, and it was doubtless the success of his *Anatomy lesson of Professor Tulp* (1632, The Hague, Mauritshuis), commissioned by the Amsterdam Guild of Surgeons, that encouraged him to remain in that city. In 1634 he married Saskia van Uylenburgh, and the next few years formed the most prosperous and brilliant period of his life, during which he bought a mansion and built up a fine collection of art. But in the same year, 1642, that he painted the great group portrait, the *Company of Captain Frans Banning Cocq*, Saskia died, leaving him with a son, Titus. After 1642 Rembrandt's fortunes declined, and his bankruptcy, as a result of various unwise speculations, followed in 1656. Meanwhile he was living with Hendrickje Stoffels, but was never able to marry her because of the conditions laid down in Saskia's will, so exposing himself to persecution by the Calvinist church session. During these years his art developed in the direction of greater introspection. In 1662, his immense *Conspiracy of Julius Civilis*, commissioned for Amsterdam Town Hall, was refused by the municipal council. His work continued to become more intimate in tone and deeper in emotional content, and his many self-portraits showed an increasing power of anguished self-analysis. His death was made more lonely by the fact that he had lost Hendrickje in 1663 and his son Titus in 1668.

RUBENS, Sir Peter Paul (b. Siegen, Westphalia, 1577; d. Antwerp 1640), studied art at Antwerp under Tobias Verhaecht, Adam van Noort and Otto van Veen, and in 1598 was elected to the Painters' Guild of St Luke. Going to Italy he worked from 1600 to 1608 as court painter to Vincenzo Gonzaga, Duke of Mantua, and in 1603 went to Spain on the duke's behalf; during these years he also worked in Venice, Rome, Florence and Genoa on various commissions from churches and from the duke. He returned to Antwerp in 1608; in 1609 he was appointed court painter to the Spanish governors of the Netherlands, the Archduke Albert and the Infanta Isabella, and that same year he married Isabella Brandt. The triptych of the *Raising of the Cross*, painted for Antwerp Cathedral in 1610, assured his reputation, and he followed this with the equally important *Descent from the Cross*, painted in 1611–14, also for Antwerp Cathedral. From this point onwards he received so many commissions that he depended upon the collaboration of pupils and assistants, themselves eminent painters such as Jordaens, Snyders, Paul de Vos and Lucas van Uden. The young van Dyck joined his studio about 1617 and assisted Rubens in 1620 in the decoration of the Jesuit Carolus-Borromeuskerk in Antwerp (the ceiling paintings were all destroyed by fire in 1718). Between 1622 and 1624 he executed the twenty-one large compositions of the *Life of Marie de Médicis* for the Palais du Luxembourg (now in the Louvre). He became the confidential adviser of the Archduchess Isabella, who entrusted him with various diplomatic missions which took him to Spain, where he met Velázquez (1628–9), and to England (1629–30). At the age of fifty-three, in 1630, after the death of Isabella Brandt, he married a girl of sixteen, Helena Fourment: his passion for his young bride gave his art an emotional warmth, inspiring him to paint love scenes and to celebrate the charms of nature which he painted each year at his estate at Steen, near Antwerp. He still continued, however, to work on great decorative schemes, such as the ceiling for the Banqueting Hall in Whitehall. He spent the last five years of his life in retirement at Steen, painting for Philip IV and for his own pleasure.

SEGHERS, Hercules Pieterszoon (b. Haarlem or Amsterdam 1589/90; d. The Hague or Amsterdam before 1638), was a pupil of Gillis van Coninxloo in Amsterdam. In 1612 he became a member of the Painters' Guild of St Luke at Haarlem, but by 1614 he was living in Amsterdam. He worked at Utrecht and The Hague. He was particularly closely concerned with new methods of expression, for which he found etching the most satisfactory medium, and his paintings are comparatively few in number.

TERBRUGGHEN, Hendrik (b. Deventer 1588; d. Utrecht 1629), was a pupil of Abraham Bloemart in Utrecht before going to Italy about 1604. He remained in Italy for ten years, becoming closely associated with the aesthetic ideas of the school of Caravaggio, the *tenebrosi*. In 1614 he was working in Milan, and in the autumn of that year he returned to Utrecht, where he married in 1616. There he developed a personal style which came to owe less and less to Caravaggio as it evolved towards a lighter palette.

VELÁZQUEZ, Diego Rodríguez da Silva (b. Seville 1599; d. Madrid 1660), was of Portuguese origin, descended from a family of *hidalgos* through his father Rodríguez da Silva; he adopted the family name of his mother, who also seems to have been of noble blood. In 1613 he entered the Seville studio of Francisco Pacheco, the painter and theorist of academicism, and married his daughter in 1618, a year after he became an independent master. His early paintings show strongly the influence of Caravaggio's 'naturalism', but he detached himself from this realistic manner after contact with the court. A portrait he painted of Philip IV in 1614 was so successful that at the king's command he remained in Madrid. In 1627 he won the prize in a competition for a historical composition; he was then appointed usher of the chamber to the king and given accommodation in the palace. In 1628 he welcomed Rubens, who had arrived in Madrid on a diplomatic mission, and became friendly with him. There is no doubt that this meeting helped Velázquez to free himself of his first style, especially since Rubens painted several pictures while he was in Madrid. It was certainly Rubens, too, who advised him to go to Italy to see the works of the Renaissance painters and the moderns. While in Italy in 1629–30, Velázquez visited Venice, Bologna, Rome and Naples where he met Ribera. He was back in Madrid in January 1631, and painted the *Surrender of Breda* ('*Las Lanzas*') for a gallery of battles in the Buen Retiro Palace (now in the Prado). He returned to Italy in 1649, to buy pictures and statues for the Crown, and visited Pope Innocent X. To mark their esteem for his genius, the painters of Rome elected Velázquez to the Accademia di San Luca. Despite the king's urgent messages to him to return to Spain, he lingered in Italy until 1651. Back in Madrid, he found awaiting him the challenging task of painting the new Queen Mariana of Austria and the royal children. He benefited increasingly from the friendship of Philip IV, who in 1652 appointed him marshal of the royal household, a post involving heavy responsibilities. In 1659 the king overruled the protests of his nobles and created him a Knight of the Order of Santiago, a high honour.

VERMEER, Jan (b. Delft 1632; d. there 1675), spent his whole life in Delft. Nothing is known of his childhood upbringing. The earliest document we possess for him, after his baptism certificate, is his marriage certificate, dated 5 April 1653. The same year he was admitted to the Painters' Guild of St Luke at Delft. His first dated work is of 1656, though some other paintings are doubtless earlier. He seems to have been esteemed by his colleagues, since he was elected dean of the guild in 1662–3 and again in 1670–1. Nevertheless, he had a difficult life, selling his paintings infrequently and at low prices. He pondered his compositions deeply beforehand and was then slow in completing them: his total output is only in the region of forty paintings. Some plausible imitations of his earlier style were exposed as forgeries in 1945.

Eighteenth century

ASAM, Cosmas Damian (b. Munich 1686; d. Mannheim 1750), completed his apprenticeship in the studio of his father who was a follower of Andrea Pozzo, then studied at Rome. He worked in close association with his brother Egid Quirin, who was a sculptor, stucco-worker and architect, while he devoted himself entirely to painting. They collaborated on the decoration of a number of buildings and churches in Bavaria, the Tirol, Switzerland, Bohemia, Silesia and the Palatinate.

PIAZZETTA, Giambattista (b. Venice 1682; d. there 1754), was the son of a woodcarver, and at first followed his father's craft. The most important factor in his formation as a painter was his discovery at Bologna of the works of Crespi, whose pupil he became; Crespi's influence is apparent in his contrasted treatment of volumes in chiaroscuro, which makes him one of the last of the *tenebrosi*. Back in Venice in 1711, he specialized in easel-paintings rather than decorative schemes. In 1750 he became director of the Venice Accademia di San Luca.

RICCI, Sebastiano (b. Belluno 1659; d. Venice 1734), studied at Venice, but his stay in Emilia instilled in him a certain sense of formal strictness and, above all, allowed him to become acquainted with the work of Correggio; he was also influence by Pietro da Cortona. He worked first in Lombardy and then at Venice; his growing reputation secured him commissions in Tuscany, and in 1712 he went to London with his nephew Marco. Later he travelled in Flanders and Germany before settling in Venice.

SPIEGLER, Franz Josef (b. Wangen 1691; d. Constance 1757), commenced his career as a painter with a series of decorations for the Swabian monastery of Ottobeuren (1725). He received commissions to paint monumental frescoes throughout southern Germany, at Constance, and at the monastery of Zwiefalten (1748–51) which contains his most significant works.

TIEPOLO, Giambattista (b. Venice 1696; d. Madrid 1770), was received into the Fraglia (Guild) in 1717, and in 1719 married the sister of Guardi. Precociously talented, he was by 1729 already the most celebrated painter of his native city. The artist who exercised the greatest influence on his formation was Piazzetta, although he soon broke free from this dark tenebrist model to assume a lighter and looser style. He painted fresco decorations for various palaces and churches in Venice and throughout the Veneto, notably the Palazzo Labia in Venice (1750) and the ballroom of the Villa Pisani at Stra (1761–2). He also worked at Bergamo and Milan. In 1750 the Prince

Bishop of Würzburg invited him to decorate the ceiling of the Kaisersaal and the staircase in the Residenz. In 1762 his fame resulted in an invitation to Spain to decorate the ceilings of the new royal palace, a task he accomplished in four years with the help of his sons and a team of assistants; he died a few years after the completion of this great undertaking.

TROGER, Paul (b. Zell, Vorarlberg, 1698; d. Vienna 1762), received his training in the studio of the painter Alberti at Cavalese in the South Tirol. The grant of a bursary allowed him to spend the years between 1717 and 1722 visiting the art centres of Italy, including Venice whence he brought back a feeling for space and joyous colouring. His first work in Austria was the decoration of the cupola of the Kajetankirche Sankt Maximilian (1727–8). He completed many commissions for the monasteries and palaces of Austria and Hungary. His master work is the ceiling fresco for the monastery of Altenburg, depicting the *Apocalypse* (1733).

Nineteenth century

CÉZANNE, Paul (b. Aix-en-Provence 1839; d. there 1906), was the son of a wealthy banker who had at one time been a hatter. He was educated at Aix, with Emile Zola as a fellow pupil and close friend. In 1862 he arrived in Paris to study art, and met Pissarro, Guillaumin, Monet, Sisley, Bazille and Renoir. In the years 1846 to 1870, the initial romantic phase of his art, he divided his time between Aix and Paris. In 1871 he arrived back in Paris with his companion Hortense Fiquet who gave him a son. His so-called impressionist period then commenced, and in 1872 he and his family went to live near Pissarro at Pontoise, near Auvers-sur-Oise, where he remained until 1874, learning from Pissarro the theories of colour and light which the impressionists were then developing. That year he took part in the first impressionist exhibition, contributing *The House of the hanged man* (*La Maison du pendu*) (1873, Louvre) which marks the transition from his first to his second style. Subsequently, he painted at Pontoise, Aix, L'Estaque (near Marseilles), Auvers, Chantilly, Fontainebleau, on the banks of the Seine and the Marne, and in the studio; he completed many still-lifes. From 1881 onwards his trips away from Aix became less and less frequent. His art grew increasingly Mediterranean in feeling, and in his provincial landscapes he attempted to go beyond the atmospheric preoccupations of the impressionists. The Montagne Sainte-Victoire near Aix became his favourite theme; from about 1895 his landscapes of Sainte-Victoire, the Bibémus quarry, the Château Noir reveal a trend towards an increasingly ardent lyricism of expression. At the same time, he sought to concentrate all his artistic energies on the big compositions of *Bathers*, of which he made three versions between 1895 and 1906, preceded by numerous studies, and which herald the art of the twentieth century.

CONSTABLE, John (b. East Bergholt, Suffolk, 1776; d. London 1837), was the son of a miller. From childhood onwards, the beauty of his native East Anglia continued to stir his imagination. He was admitted to the Royal Academy Schools in 1799, but worked mostly from nature. Recognition of his talent was slow in coming, and he was not elected an academician until 1819, three years after his marriage. About this time his style began to change from a descriptive approach similar to that of the eighteenth-century watercolourists to an increasingly subjective approach. The paintings in this new manner which he exhibited at the Paris Salon of 1824, such as the *Hay-Wain* (National Gallery), had a great influence on the development of the French school. His favourite themes were Salisbury Cathedral, Weymouth Bay, Hampstead Heath and the Suffolk countryside. His daughter bequeathed a large collection of his work to the Victoria and Albert Museum, which explains the relative scarcity of his works outside England.

COROT, Jean-Baptiste-Camille (b. Paris 1796; d. there 1875), avoided academic training as a painter, and between 1825 and 1828 formed himself by painting from nature during a long stay in Italy. Back in Paris in 1829 he began a satisfying career, painting oil sketches (*pochades*) at sites in France and Italy from which he worked up the composed pictures that he sent to the Salons. He made two further journeys to Italy in 1834 and 1843. He owned a country house on the edge of the lake of Ville-d'Avray, and after 1850 his frequent stays there encouraged him to indulge rather too freely in a dreamy, rather fuzzy type of landscape; the immense popularity of the compositions led him to over-produce, sometimes with the collaboration of pupils. Happily, he retained throughout his life, and into old age, the full spontaneity of his talent when working from nature.

COURBET, Gustave (b. Ornans 1819; d. La Tour de Peilz, Switzerland, 1877), was the son of a well-to-do farmer in the Franche-Comté. He received his first drawing lessons at a private school in Besançon. He went to Paris in 1840 to study law, but soon turned to painting. His first landscapes and portraits demonstrate a rather banal romanticism of which he cured himself by means of assiduous studies at the Louvre and in the museums of the Netherlands during a visit there in 1847. He exhibited his first realist paintings at the 1850 Salon, including the *Burial at Ornans* (Louvre) which created a scandal. A stay at Montpellier, in the Midi, led him to abandon finally the dark shadings of romanticism, as is apparent in *Bonjour, Monsieur Courbet* (Montpellier). In 1855, the year of the Great Exhibition in Paris, he opened a private exhibition of forty of his paintings in a shed near the main building; this first of all 'one-man shows' included a painting refused by the French pavilion, the *Painter in his studio* (Louvre), and created a sensation. During the winter of 1858–9 he visited Frankfurt, and he returned to Germany on later occasions, attracted by the pleasures of hunting and by the welcome he received from the artists of that country. In 1870 he joined the National Guard, and took an active part in the revolutionary government of 1871. After the Commune he was declared

responsible for the destruction of the Vendôme column, imprisoned, and condemned to pay the costs of re-erecting the monument. He returned to Ornans, then fled to Switzerland in 1873 to escape arrest, going to live in La Tour de Peilz, near Geneva. In his efforts to pay off the indemnity exacted by the French government he turned out a constant stream of Swiss landscapes, helped by a team of assistants who were more or less successful in following his style.

DAUMIER, Honoré (b. Marseilles 1808; d. Valmondois 1879), was the son of a picture-framer. He went to Paris in 1816, attended several academies of painting, and in 1828 learnt the newly invented process of lithography. As a cartoonist for *La Caricature* and, later, *Le Charivari*, he became noted for his attacks on the July Monarchy, and a caricature of Louis Philippe led to his imprisonment for six months in 1831. In about 1845 he reverted to painting as a virtually self-taught artist, continuing to produce lithographs for a living. He also made a few sculptures, but not nearly as many as have been attributed to him at one time or another. He became friendly with the painters of the Barbizon school: Millet, Théodore Rousseau and Corot. His moment of official glory came when he was awarded the prize at the competition set up in 1848 for an official effigy of *The Republic* (Louvre). He gradually lost his sight, and with only a small State pension to support him he was rescued from dire poverty by Corot who bought him a house at Valmondois, where he died almost blind.

DAVID, Jacques-Louis (b. Paris 1748; d. Brussels 1825), was a kinsman of Boucher, who gave him some instruction. He then studied under Vien who gave him a grounding in the principles of neoclassicism which he consolidated during his stay in Rome between 1775 and 1780. In 1783 he became an academician, and returned to Rome to paint the *Oath of the Horatii* (Louvre) which had been commissioned by the royal administration. This picture had a tremendous success when exhibited in Rome in 1784, a success repeated the following year at the Paris Salon. Under the revolutionary government of the Convention he took an active part in politics, became a deputy in the National Assembly, and voted for the death of Louis XVI. He painted a few pictures with revolutionary themes, including *Le Peletier de Saint-Fargeau dying*, the *Death of Marat*, and the *Little drummer-boy Bara*, and was imprisoned briefly after the fall of Robespierre. Fascinated by the genius of Napoleon, he became an ardent Bonapartist and painted historical compositions such as the *Consecration of the Emperor Napoleon I* and the *Emperor distributing the eagles*. Exiled in 1815 as a regicide after the restoration of the Bourbons, he retired to Brussels. He refused Louis XVIII's offer of a pardon, and remained in Brussels, painting mainly portraits during the last years of his life.

DEGAS, Edgar (b. Paris 1834; d. there 1917), came of a wealthy family, his father being a banker. He studied at the Ecole des Beaux-Arts under a pupil of Ingres, Lamothe, and completed his classical education in 1856 by a voyage to Italy during which he made numerous studies after the masters. His first paintings showed the great influence that Ingres had had on him (the *Misfortunes of the town of Orleans*, 1865, Louvre). By the late 1860s he had begun to develop a personal style incorporating psychological analysis and realistic observation (as in the *Bellelli family*, *c.* 1858–9, Louvre) which he carried further, after 1870, in racecourse scenes, character portraits in offcentre compositions, and paintings of the theatre and ballet. A visit to his brother René de Gas at New Orleans (where his mother's family had settled after the Revolution) produced an interesting and typical example of his new manner in the view of the *Cotton Exchange*, *New Orleans* (1873, Pau, Musée des Beaux-Arts). He soon extended his interest in character studies to scenes of everyday life, in pictures such as the *Washerwomen*, *Women ironing* and *Absinthe* (1876), all in the Louvre. Nudes, dressing and bathing, and ballet dancers provided him with endless subject-matter for studies of manner and movement. From 1884 onwards, failing sight turned him to pastel and then to sculpture, and from 1898 his blindness forced him to abandon painting as a medium.

DELACROIX, Eugène (b. Saint-Maurice nr Paris 1798; d. Paris 1863), was the son of a senior Napoleonic official, who had preceded Talleyrand as foreign minister, and legend has it that his real father was in fact Talleyrand. In 1816 he entered the studio of the neoclassical painter Guérin, but also spent considerable time studying Rubens at the Louvre. His first large painting was *Dante's barque* (1822, Louvre). The *Massacre at Chios* (Louvre) was bought by the State at the 1824 Salon. A visit to England in 1825 allowed him to discover English painting, and on his return to Paris he frequented English artists, including Bonington. The *Death of Sardanapalus* (Louvre), shown at the 1827 Salon, revealed his admiration for Rubens. The 1830 Revolution inspired his *Liberty leading the People* (*Liberty at the barricades*), his masterpiece. A voyage made to Morocco in 1832, in the company of a special ambassador, made a profound impression upon him. Under the July Monarchy he received important commissions for monumental works: the library and Salon du Roi in the Palais Bourbon, the Senate library in the Palais du Luxembourg, and, later, the Salon de la Paix at the Hôtel de Ville (destroyed), a ceiling of the Galerie d'Apollon in the Louvre and, towards the end of his life, the Chapelle des Saints-Anges in the church of Saint-Sulpice. Painter, writer, moralist, art critic, man of the world, Delacroix, who kept a journal for many years, was one of the most representative personalities of his century.

EMPERAIRE, Achille (b. Aix-en-Provence 1829; d. there 1898), was a deformed dwarf who struggled to earn a living as a painter. He paid occasional visits to Paris in his efforts to get his work accepted by the Salon. A boyhood friend of Cézanne, it seems probable that he influenced the latter, especially with his drawings of nudes: Cézanne himself, as is known, was reluctant to ask models to pose for him. Emperaire's drawings are very fine; his paintings, on the other hand, of which few survive, are mediocre.

GAUGUIN, Paul (b. Paris 1848; d. Atuana, Marquesas Islands, 1903), entered the merchant service in 1865, and his sea voyages took him to Rio de Janeiro among other places. He joined a stock-broker's business in 1871, and two years later married a young Danish woman, Mette Sophie Gad. He also became a Sunday painter, and in 1883 gave up his financial career to devote himself entirely to painting. In 1885 his wife left him and returned to Denmark. His visit in 1886 to Pont-Aven, where he met Emile Bernard, marked his estrangement from impressionism, a development confirmed during his 1887 journey to Martinique. Back in Paris in 1888 he resumed contact with the Pont-Aven group, and that same year made a brief and disastrous stay with van Gogh at Arles. Back in Brittany, at Le Pouldu, he painted his first 'synthetist' pictures: *La Belle Angèle* (1889, Louvre), the *Yellow Christ* (1889, Buffalo, Albright Art Gallery), *Vision after the sermon* (*Jacob wrestling with the Angel*) (1888, Edinburgh, National Gallery of Scotland). After putting thirty of his paintings up for public sale, he left for Tahiti in 1891, and there painted pictures on Polynesian themes before returning to France in 1893. After staying once more in Pont-Aven he went back to Tahiti for good in 1895. For the remaining years of his life there he adopted the way of life of the native population. His health ruined by alcohol and syphilis, he made an unsuccessful attempt at suicide by taking poison after painting a huge picture which was intended to be his final testament, *Whence do we come? Where are we? Whither are we going?* (Boston). In 1901 he left Tahiti for Fatu-Iva in the Marquesas, where he came into conflict with the civil and ecclesiastical authorities and died in great misery.

GÉRICAULT, Théodore (b. Rouen 1791; d. Paris 1824), was born of well-to-do parents. He studied first under the painter of hunting and racing scenes Carle Vernet, 1808–10, and then under the neoclassicist Guérin, 1810–11; he completed his artistic education by studying the works of the masters at the Louvre. His first pictures were inspired by his Bonapartist enthusiasms: *Mounted officer of the Imperial Guard* (1812, Louvre), *Wounded cuirassier leaving the scene of battle* (1813, Louvre). During a voyage to Italy in 1816 he was greatly impressed by the works of Michelangelo, and on his return to Paris attempted realistic subjects in Michelangelo's grand style. He executed a colossal picture, inspired by a marine calamity of 1815, the *Raft of the 'Medusa'* (Louvre), which he exhibited at the 1819 Salon and then took to England to show in a travelling exhibition. Visiting London, he became attracted by English painting and made a close study of horses, his enthusiasm finding expression in *The Derby at Epsom* (Louvre). Back in Paris in 1822, he undertook a series of portraits of insane patients at the Salpêtrière, with the encouragement of his friend Dr Georget. His life was cut short by a riding accident which caused him severe injuries and constant pain during his last years.

GOGH, Vincent van (b. Groot-Zundert, Netherlands 1853; d. Auvers-sur-Oise 1890), was the son of a Dutch pastor. After being employed in The Hague, London and Paris by Goupil & Co., the firm of art dealers for which his brother Theo later worked in Paris, he felt the call of religion and became a missionary, but upset the evangelical authorities by his unorthodox behaviour. He began painting after he had been dismissed from his mission in 1881. Returning home to his parents in Etten he met the painter Anton Mauve, who gave him help and advice. At the same time he discovered the art of Japanese prints. During those early years he painted in a dark, heavy style, using as subject-matter the squalor of peasant life (*Potato eaters*, 1885), still-lifes and landscapes. In 1886 he joined Theo in Paris, remaining there until 1888: under the influence of Monticelli and the impressionists he entirely changed his style, evolving towards a light palette and tone division. From February 1888 to May 1889 he was in Arles, where his quarrelling with Gauguin brought on his first attack of insanity. At Arles he developed his personal style of brilliant and violently contrasting colours. From May 1889 to May 1890 he was confined in the mental hospital at Saint-Rémy; then his brother Theo arranged for him to come to Auvers-sur-Oise where he lived under the supervision of Dr Gachet. On 27 July he committed suicide.

GOYA Y LUCIENTES, Francisco José de (b. Fuendetodos nr Saragossa 1746; d. Bordeaux 1828), was apprenticed at fourteen to a local painter, José Luzán, in whose studio he remained for four years. After failing twice to secure admission to the Academia de San Fernando at Madrid, he left for Italy in 1770. The following year he was back in Saragossa, having received a commission to decorate a cupola of the Cathedral. In 1775, in Madrid, he married Josefa, sister of the painter Francisco Bayeu. In 1776 the painter Anton Raphael Mengs commissioned him to produce a series of forty tapestry designs for the royal factory at Santa Barbara, on which he was engaged until 1791. In 1798 he painted frescoes for the chapel of San Antonio de la Florida in Madrid, an important royal commission which gave him the opportunity to display his romantic manner. He remained in Madrid under the French occupation. His wife died in 1812. In 1819 he bought a country house which became known as the Quinta del Sordo (the Deaf Man's House). His position during and after the Napoleonic invasion of Spain was uneasy. When Ferdinand VII was driven out he continued to work for the usurper Joseph Bonaparte; the restoration of Ferdinand brought reaction and persecution, and although Goya was not penalized he was faced with hostility and intrigue at the court. He decided to go into voluntary exile in France, settling in Bordeaux. He visited Madrid in 1826 and again in 1827, the year before his death in Bordeaux.

MANET, Edouard (b. Paris 1832; d. there 1883), was the son of a wealthy magistrate. After a trial voyage to Rio de Janeiro as a naval cadet, he was allowed to study under Thomas Couture from 1850 to 1856, but formed himself as an artist during this period chiefly by spending much time at the Louvre copying the masters. His early work shows the influence of seventeenth-century Spanish painting (for example, *Lola de Valence*, 1861–2, Louvre). After a journey to the Netherlands in 1857 he married

Suzanne Leenhoff. His *Luncheon on the grass* (*Déjeuner sur l'herbe*) (Louvre), exhibited at the Salon des Refusés in 1863, caused a scandal. His *Olympia* (Louvre) was accepted for the 1865 Salon, and created even greater uproar, though Emile Zola came to the picture's defence in *L'Evénement* (1866). During the Franco-Prussian War he served as an officer in the National Guard. After 1870 he abandoned his 'black' painting and adopted the *peinture claire* technique discovered by Monet, while his outlook tended increasingly towards a Zolaesque realism (*Nana*, 1877, Hamburg; *Chez le Père Lathuille*, 1880, Tournai). He always longed for official recognition and refused to take part in the impressionist exhibitions, persisting in sending work to the Salon where it was nearly always accepted but usually greeted with hostile comment.

MONET, Claude (b. Paris 1840; d. Giverny 1926), was brought up in Le Havre, where his family moved when he was five. There he met Boudin who encouraged him to paint landscapes from nature. In 1859 he went to Paris to study, and met Pissarro. His art studies were interrupted by his military service in Algeria, which was cut short by illness. He returned to Paris in 1862 and entered Gleyre's studio, where he met Renoir, Sisley and Bazille: this last encounter was to prove of material importance, since Bazille came from a wealthy family and in the years to come provided regular financial help for his impoverished friend. He painted from nature at Fontainebleau, on the beaches of Normandy, on the banks of the Seine, and in the environs of Paris, but his true aim was to show figures in the reality of the open air (*Women in the garden*, 1868, Louvre). In 1870 he married his companion Camille, then, to escape the war, went to London, where he discovered Turner, and to the Netherlands. From 1872 to 1878 he worked at Argenteuil, on the banks of the Seine, and while there developed his vibrant technique for rendering the movement of light in colour. He tended to concentrate his researches into light variations on a single site (*Argenteuil*; *Les Débâcles*), and soon began to paint series of pictures of a single subject (the *Haystacks*, 1891; the *Poplars*, 1892; *Rouen Cathedral*, 1892–5; the views of *London*, 1900–1, and *Venice*, 1908). Monet carried his researches beyond the sites of Normandy and the Ile-de-France to Holland, Provence and the Italian Riviera. He had already started work before 1900 on the vast luminous poem constituted by his *Water-lilies*, which he painted in the specially constructed water-garden of his house at Giverny. This vast cycle of studies was interrupted in 1922 for some time by temporary blindness caused by a cataract; the very large paintings in the series begun in 1916, which remained in his possession until his death, were bequeathed to the State and are now housed in a special museum (Orangerie, Paris). He died at Giverny at the age of eighty-six.

MONTICELLI, Adolphe (b. Marseilles 1824; d. there 1886), was of Italian descent, his family having emigrated from Piedmont in the eighteenth century. He learned to paint, between 1841 and 1844, at the local municipal art school. After a first visit to Paris in 1846, he moved constantly between the capital and his native town from 1851 to 1862, Diaz and Delacroix being the painters who had the greatest influence on him at that time. He lived in Paris from 1862 to 1870, when he fled from the war back to Marseilles, where he remained for the rest of his life apart from landscape-painting expeditions in Provence. Unfortunately he indulged in a good deal of facile but successful studio painting, which harmed his reputation after his death, more especially since several of his pupils painted fakes of these works.

ROUSSEAU, Henri, known as 'Le Douanier' (b. Laval 1844; d. Paris 1910), spent some years in the army and claimed to have taken part, as a sergeant, in the Franco-Prussian War. After leaving the army, probably in 1871, he came to Paris and obtained a post in the municipal toll department (hence, erroneously, 'le Douanier'). He began painting, about 1880, without any training. He also opened a sort of school of music, painting and elocution, as well as writing poems and plays. He exhibited at the Indépendants (which had no jury system) from 1886 to 1898 and from 1901 to 1910; the symbolists, as well as Gauguin and Pissarro, knew and admired his work, though it was the applause of Alfred Jarry, Apollinaire and Picasso which in his later years made him known.

ROUSSEAU, Théodore (b. Paris 1812; d. Barbizon 1867), spent some time, while young, in the Jura, of which his father was a native, and his imagination was struck by the region's mountains and forests. He was a pupil of his cousin the landscapist Pau de Saint-Martin who took him to the countryside near Compiègne for painting lessons. From the age of sixteen he frequented official studios. In 1830 he made enthusiastic studies of the Auvergne mountains, then undertook an equally fruitful voyage to Normandy. In 1832 he visited Mont-Saint-Michel in company with de Laberge, a nature-loving painter. In 1834 the contemplation of Mont Blanc seen from the Col de la Faucille (Jura) inspired him to paint one of his most romantic pictures, now in Copenhagen. This same voyage also produced the *Cattle going down to the Morvan* (sketch at Amiens Museum), a picture which was refused by the Salon. The juries made such a habit of turning down his pictures that he became known as '*le grand refusé*', and he was able to show his works only when Salons without juries were introduced in 1848. From this time onwards his art evolved towards an objective devotion to nature; he worked increasingly in the forest of Fontainebleau, and finally settled down at its fringe, in the village of Barbizon. He continued travelling, though less frequently, in Vendée, the Landes, Isle-Adam, the Jura and Picardy. He lived a solitary life, often in extreme poverty.

TURNER, Joseph Mallord William (b. London 1775; d. there 1851), was the son of a barber in Maiden Lane. His general education was rudimentary, and his lifelong thirst for culture was that of a self-taught man. He was precociously talented: already selling drawings and watercolours at the age of twelve, he had started working from nature by the time he was sixteen. He studied in the Royal Academy Schools 1789–93. The Academy recognized his genius early; he became an ARA in 1799 and, at the age of twenty-seven, an RA in 1802. He continued to travel widely and continuously in various parts of Britain as well as in Europe, particularly Italy where he was able to study the works of Claude Lorrain, whom he much admired. He lived a solitary existence and was considered something of a misogynist. He bequeathed to the nation some 280 paintings and 19,000 drawings and watercolours, which are now divided among the National and Tate Galleries and the British Museum; this is the reason for the comparative scarcity of his work in foreign collections.

VALENCIENNES, Pierre-Henri de (b. Toulouse 1750; d. Paris 1816), received his basic art training at the Toulouse Académie de Peinture, and began his peripatetic life as a painter in the Midi. He made his first journey to Italy in 1769, and later visited Touraine and the forests near Paris; at dates which it is difficult to establish precisely he also visited England, Spain and Germany. He was in Italy from the end of 1777 to 1780, visiting the Roman countryside, Campania and Sicily; he returned to Paris by way of Umbria, Tuscany, the Marches, Emilia, Lombardy, the lakes, Piedmont, Savoy and Switzerland. He returned to Italy in 1782, and there is no record of his whereabouts from then until the beginning of 1787, when the indefatigable traveller set off for Greece, Egypt, the Middle East, Turkey and the Greek archipelago. He was elected to the Académie Royale de Peinture in 1787. From then on he exhibited composed landscapes worked up from his oil studies and his drawings from nature (several hundred examples of which are now in the Louvre). Appointed a professor of perspective at the Ecole des Beaux-Arts in 1812, he wrote a treatise on landscape-painting, *Eléments de perspective pratique*, whose principles were followed throughout the first half of the nineteenth century.

Twentieth century

BRAQUE, Georges (b. Argenteuil 1882; d. Paris 1963), was the son of a painting and decorating contractor who moved to Le Havre when he was eight years old, and he learned to paint as an apprentice in his father's business. He arrived in Paris in 1900. He first painted landscapes in the fauvist manner, then his art changed radically, under the influence of Cézanne, in 1907 while he was working at L'Estaque. He exhibited at the 1908 Salon, and the conservative art critic Louis Vauxcelles described his pictures there as being made 'with little cubes'. He organized a 'one-man show' the same year. For several years he worked in close association with Picasso. Sent to the front in 1914, he was wounded in 1915, and after a long convalescence began painting again in 1917. Between 1919 and 1930 he passed through an almost 'realist' phase in which his art respected appearances to a greater degree. Subsequently his manner held a balance between the real and the abstract, with a tendency in his last years towards an increasingly summary form.

CHIRICO, Giorgio de (b. Volo, Greece, 1888), studied art at Athens and Munich. Painting in Paris between 1911 and 1915, he produced imaginative compositions incorporating incongruous elements, acknowledged by the surrealists to have provided a primary source of inspiration. Returning to Italy in 1916, he and Carlo Carrà evolved the short-lived *scuola metafisica* the following year. Since the 1920s he has devoted his time to violent attacks on modern art, and his talent to pastiches of romantic classicism and baroque.

DELAUNAY, Robert (b. Paris 1885; d. Montpellier 1941), took to painting about 1905, evolving from a naturalistic art towards cubism in 1910, a progression followed also by his wife Sonia Terk. His cubism soon developed rapidly towards pure abstraction, and in 1912 his series of *Windows* and *Circular forms* were described as 'Orphist' by Apollinaire. He was a true founder of non-figurative art.

DUBUFFET, Jean (b. Le Havre 1901), takes his inspiration from wall 'graffiti' and amateur art, especially that created by psychotics. His *pâtes* are not, strictly speaking, paintings, being composed of tar, glass, sand and pieces of junk which he colours and assembles to produce human shapes.

He studied art for a short time in Paris at the age of seventeen, gave up painting in 1924 to travel and set up a wine business, but has been devoting himself exclusively to art since the early 1940s.

DUCHAMP, Marcel (b. Blainville 1887; d. Neuilly-sur-Seine 1968), brother of the sculptor Raymond Duchamp-Villon and the painter Jacques Villon, was first influenced by Cézanne, but about 1911 changed suddenly to a kind of cubism in which the newly evolved ideas of futurism played an important part (*Nude descending a staircase*, 1912, Philadelphia). He abandoned painting in 1915, the year that he began his first preliminary studies for the 'Large Glass' ('Grand Verre') called *The Bride stripped bare by her bachelors, even*, a construction incorporating designs in oil and lead wire on glass, upon which he worked intermittently until 1923, when he left it unfinished. He was the inventor of Readymades, everyday objects promoted to the dignity of works of art by the fact of the artist's choice of them. He was one of the founders of the dada movement. From 1913, the year he exhibited the *Nude descending a staircase* and three other paintings at the Armory Show in New York, he acquired considerable fame in the United States. After 1938 he lived in New York, though returning regularly to Europe for visits to France and Spain. He became an American citizen in 1954.

ENSOR, James (b. Ostend 1860; d. there 1949), was the son of an English father and a Flemish mother. Apart from his art training at the academy in Brussels he spent his life in Ostend, working quietly in his studio, 'happily confined', in his own words. 'to the solitary realm where the mask rules'. His early works showed the influence of Turner and of certain aspects of impressionism, but about 1880 he developed a very personal manner expressing a macabre imagination.

His masterpiece is the huge *Entry of Christ into Brussels* (1888, Knocke-le-Zoute). This burst of inventive power lasted until about 1900, after which his inspiration faltered and his art became stereotyped. Together with Edvard Munch he may be considered the originator of expressionism.

GORKY, Arshile (b. Hajotz Dzore, Turkish Armenia 1904; d. Sherman, Conn. 1948), lived in the United States from the age of sixteen onwards. After being influenced successively by Cézanne, the cubists and Picasso, he came under the influence of surrealism shortly before the Second World War. His art belongs firmly to the surrealist abstract tradition of Miró, Tanguy and Matta, and he forms the link between European surrealism and American abstract impressionism.

HARTUNG, Hans (b. Leipzig 1904), left Germany in 1935 and went to Paris, where he now lives, a naturalized French citizen. He lost a leg fighting with the Foreign Legion during the Second World War. He began to paint in the abstract manner at the age of eighteen, then studied art in Leipzig, Dresden, and Munich in 1924–8. His first contact with the work of Kandinsky in 1925 encouraged him to continue in his abstract style. His paintings, usually dark on a light background and with numbers instead of titles, are represented in French, Swiss and American collections, as well as the Tate Gallery in London.

JONES, Allen (b. Southampton 1937), an English painter and graphic artist whose work is frequently based on erotic themes. He uses simple, striking colours with all the freedom of the abstract painter. He has taught at the Croydon College of Art and the Chelsea School of Art, and lives in London.

KANDINSKY, Wassily (b. Moscow 1866; d. Neuilly-sur-Seine 1944), decided to become an artist on seeing an impressionist exhibition in Moscow in 1895. In the following year he went to Munich to learn painting, and in 1901 founded the Phalanx group there, and opened a school of painting. After travelling widely inside Germany and abroad, including a visit to France in 1906, he returned to Munich in 1907. He painted his first purely abstract works in 1910, and set out the theory of his art in *Über das Geistige in der Kunst*, 1912, translated in a 1947 English version as *Concerning the Spiritual in Art*. In 1911 he was one of the founders of the *Blaue Reiter* group of expressionists. On the declaration of war he left for Switzerland, and from there went to Russia where he supported the revolutionary movement actively. He returned to Germany in 1921, and taught at the Bauhaus in Weimar from 1922, until it was closed by order of the Nazi government in 1933, when he went to Paris.

KIRCHNER, Ernst Ludwig (b. Aschaffenburg 1880; d. Davos 1938). was the principal founder, in 1905, of the *Die Brücke* group in Dresden, which moved its activities to Berlin in 1911. From 1904 the influence of African and Polynesian sculpture had led him towards a painful and gloomy expressionism. He suffered from tuberculosis, and in 1917 he left Germany

for Switzerland and settled in Davos, painting mountain landscapes. He committed suicide in 1938.

KOONING, Willem de (b. Rotterdam 1904), has lived in the USA since 1926, where he shared a studio with his friend Arshile Gorky for some years. Though his early training was influenced by De Stijl, he is a prominent action painter. He has taught at various American art schools and painted a mural for the New York World's Fair of 1939. His work has been exhibited at several Biennales and his pictures are in a number of American museums including the Museum of Modern Art in New York.

LICHTENSTEIN, Roy (b. New York 1923), a leading representative of American pop art, is also an experimental sculptor, using coloured plastics, brass and enamelled metal. His paintings operate with strong primary colours and with the striking effect produced by the contrast of black and white. They are mostly large, and interpret details taken from advertisements and comic strips. He uses dots of pure colour in imitation of the crude screen process used in printing comic strips.

MANESSIER, Alfred (b. Saint-Ouen, France 1911), is exceptional among abstract painters, in that he sometimes works on religious themes (a series of lithographs on the subject of Easter, 1949; stained-glass windows for churches in Bresseux, Arles and Basle, 1953). He lives in Paris and his pictures are to be found in many European galleries including the Tate, as well as in New York (Guggenheim) and Pittsburgh.

MATHIEU, Georges (b. Paris 1922), a gestural abstract painter, came to prominence after the Second World War as the leading European publicist of 'action painting', which he called *art informel*. A born showman, he once emphasized the importance of the pictorial gesture by painting a canvas in full view of an audience.

MATISSE, Henri (b. Le Cateau 1869; d. Cimiez 1954), was a pupil of Gustave Moreau from 1892 to 1897, and met Rouault, Camoin and Marquet, among others, in his studio. He did a great deal of copying in the Louvre. In 1896 he exhibited a realistic painting, the *Dinner table* (*La desserte*), at the Société Nationale des Beaux-Arts, repeating the same theme in 1908 in a fauvist version. In 1904 he was painting landscapes in the south of France. His first fauvist pictures date from 1905. From 1909 to 1910, however, his art became more refined, as in *The Dance* and *Music* (Moscow), and involved an increasing stylization of nature. In 1908–10 he ran a school which was thronged by foreigners, and began to assume the stature of the leader of a movement. After the First World War he lived for the most part on the Riviera, and during the following decade his painting became more figurative and almost sensual. The commission by the Barnes Foundation (Merion, Pa.) for a large-scale decoration on the theme of *The Dance* (1931–3) brought him back to a more abstract conception. After the Second World War he settled in Nice, and in 1947–51 he worked on a chapel for a Dominican convent at Vence which was decorated after his designs. Crippled and almost blind towards the end of his life, he came to use mostly cut-outs in coloured paper for his compositions.

MICHAUX, Henri (b. Namur 1899), moved to Paris as a young poet and began drawing only in 1926. He was preoccupied, in his writing as in his painting, with the discovery of 'new worlds' of sensation and emotion through purely spontaneous and uncontrolled creativity; calligraphic elements play a large part in his visual work. Between 1955 and 1961, Michaux experimented with mescalin, producing large numbers of pen drawings in a distinctive style in which compact and ordered abstract structures are built up with an obsessive zigzag line.

MONDRIAN, Piet (b. Amersfoort, Netherlands 1872; d. New York 1944), started as a painter of realistic landscapes. After his arrival in Paris in 1911 he came under the influence of the cubists and painted his series of *Trees*. His approach to abstraction altered gradually, and in 1914 the stylization he practised was transformed into a purely geometrical art of determined relations. Returning to Holland he joined with Theo van Doesburg and others in founding the De Stijl group; the journal of the same title, which started appearing in 1917, preached the creation of an art made of pure relations of form and colour and making no demands on appearances. He continued to paint in this manner, which he called neoplasticism, from about 1919 until his death.

MOTHERWELL, Robert (b. Aberdeen, USA 1915), studied philosophy at Harvard before taking up painting. An abstract expressionist, he was a friend of Matta and belonged to the group which also included Pollock, Gorky, De Kooning and Baziotes. Together with William Baziotes and Barnett Newman, he founded an art school in 1948. He has also taught at Hunter College in New York. His fascination with the tragic twentieth-century history of Spain and Ireland, as revealed in many of his paintings, makes him in a sense the most literary of abstract impressionists. He has edited a number of important volumes in the *Documents of Modern Art* series.

MUNCH, Edvard (b. Löten, Norway 1863; d. Ekely nr Oslo 1944), was a pupil of Christian Krogh, and in 1889 visited Paris. From 1892 to 1895 he lived in Berlin, and his exhibition of paintings in the gallery of the Association of Berlin Artists in 1892 created a scandal and led to the break-up of the group. In Paris in 1896 he frequented the symbolist group associated with the journal *Mercure de France*. For the next ten years he travelled widely, in Germany, Italy, Norway and France. In 1908 he had to undergo psychiatric treatment in a clinic, and for the rest of his life he lived in retirement on his estate at Ekely.

NICHOLSON, Ben (b. Denham, England 1894), is the leading British abstract painter and the first winner of the Guggenheim award. In the 1930s, at a time when English art was at its most insular, he was the chief link between England and the Continent. His compositions – sometimes treated plastically as

bas-reliefs – are geometrically inspired, deriving from the severer forms of cubism and from Mondrian; his art is precise, controlled, and chaste in style. His activity over the past ten years has if anything increased, and he is represented in museums all over the world.

OLDENBURG, Claes (b. Stockholm 1929), graduated from Yale University and was a newspaper reporter in Chicago before he took up art. He is chiefly known for his 'food sculptures' made of vinyl plastic, kapok, canvas, rubber and cloth and representing hamburgers, ice-cream sundaes, hot dogs and french fries. In 1960 he founded the 'Ray Gun Theatre', where he staged, in particular with Jim Dine, a series of Happenings many of which have been filmed. He has exhibited in the Judson Gallery and the Martha Jackson Gallery, New York.

PAOLOZZI, Eduardo (b. Edinburgh 1924), was a member of 'The Group', the association of artists which pioneered the term 'pop art'. Using a magic lantern to project huge images of advertisements and everyday objects, he played a major part in the early stages (in 1952) of this exploitation of mass culture. Himself an intellectual, rather literary artist, he has stood a little aloof from the mainstream of pop.

PICASSO, Pablo Ruiz y (b. Malaga 1881) began his painting career in Barcelona, and first went to Paris in 1900. Influenced by Toulouse-Lautrec he painted the disenchanted pictures of his 'blue period' (1901–4), followed by the 'rose period' (1905–6). The study of African sculpture led him to paint a large-scale picture, *Les Demoiselles d'Avignon* (1907), in which the violently broken forms anticipated the cubist formalism which he was to develop methodically, in company with Braque, until 1914. After Braque's departure for the front in that year Picasso wavered between an Ingrist classicism and the monstrously distorted female nudes of the 'antique period'. Between 1920 and 1925 a comparatively relaxed atmosphere permeated a cubism in which the forms are harmoniously and solidly disposed (*Three musicians*, 1921). From 1928 he went through a symbolist period which coincided with the development of surrealism. The horror of the Spanish Civil War inspired him to make dramatic use of cubist dislocation of forms (*Guernica*, 1937). After this he continued to paint 'butchered' figures, alternating these with purely plastic compositions inspired sometimes by the antique: this latter tendency eventually predominated (the 'Antibes period'), and it seemed that the atmosphere of the Riviera brought some relief to his dramatic tension. More recently he has involved himself enthusiastically, at Vallauris, in the design and production of pottery. He joined the Communist Party shortly after the end of the Second World War, and has produced a few more 'committed' paintings (*War and peace*, 1952).

POLLOCK, Jackson (b. Cody, Wyoming 1912; d. New York 1956), arrived in New York in 1929 to study at the Art Students' League. Influenced early in his career by the baroque dynamism of the Mexican mural painters Siqueiros and Orozco, he soon came under the spell of Picasso, and then of the surrealists. He was

subsequently to apply to painting the surrealist technique of automatism. He abandoned the use of brushes, and took to dripping paint direct on to a canvas which was stretched on the floor. Moving over his work without premeditation and without hesitation, he produced the dynamic superimposed networks and swirls of colour which are characteristic of 'action painting'. From about 1950 onwards, he was successful and famous; but there was still much incomprehension of his work, and he remained temperamentally an isolated figure. He died in a car crash at the age of forty-four.

ROSENQUIST, James (b. North Dakota 1933), started off as a billboard painter, working particularly on the vast posters in Times Square, New York. As one of the 'New Super Realists', he still works on immense canvases, enlarging certain parts of the subject and placing them as blown-up fragments across the painting, as in *Flower Garden*, where an athlete's torso is supported by an arm the size of his actual figure. Rosenquist has the same preoccupation with 'infinity' and 'totality' as the abstract expressionists, but, unlike them, he uses representational elements; he paints 'anonymous things in the hope that particular meanings will disappear. . . .'

ROUAULT, Georges (b. Paris 1871; d. there 1958), was the only one of Gustave Moreau's pupils to retain the master's influence for any length of time. In 1904 the example of Cézanne's *Bathers* inspired him to evolve a tragic distortion of form which served to evoke the harsh existence of prostitutes and clowns. He admired the vehement style of the Catholic writer Léon Bloy, and his art assumed a deeply Christian significance which is unique in our modern age. With Matisse he was one of the progenitors of fauvism.

SMITH, Richard (b. Letchworth 1931), trained at the Royal College of Art in London (1954–7) and since 1959 has divided his time between London and New York. Influenced both by American abstract painters and by pop, his paintings reflect a fascination with the forms of commercial packaging, as they appear in advertising art, and a rejection of the limitations of the two-dimensional canvas. He has summed up his work as follows: 'I set myself the task of mingling commercial atmosphere with abstract art.'

SOULAGES, Pierre (b. Rodez, France 1919), a self-taught artist and one of the leading French abstract painters, has been much influenced by the romantics and by van Gogh. He took up abstract painting in 1946, after wartime service in the army. His pictures bear no titles, being distinguished by the date of completion (as in the *23 May 1953* in the Tate Gallery). Soulages has travelled in the USA and Japan, and is well represented in American collections.

TOBEY, Mark (b. Centerville, Wis. 1890), was successively a failed technical draughtsman in Chicago, a fashion illustrator in New York, and an interior decorator, before moving in 1922 to Seattle, Wash., where he developed his own theory of art as a manifestation of inner experience. He was much influenced by

North-west Coast Indian art, and above all by the art of China and Japan. In the course of subsequent travels as a teacher of art he became an adept of Zen, and developed his technique of 'white writing'.

VLAMINCK, Maurice de (b. Paris 1876; d. Rueil-la-Gadelière 1958), was of Flemish extraction (his name means Maurice the Fleming). He professed ardently libertarian views throughout his life, even though, towards the end, both his polemics and his art began to seem slightly traditionalist. He met Derain in 1900 and shared a studio with him. Taking van Gogh as their model, the two artists painted convulsive landscapes in arbitrary colours and showed these feverish compositions at the 1905 Salon des Indépendants and Salon d'Automne. In 1906 the dealer Ambroise Vollard bought his entire output. In 1908 his colouring and treatment became inspired by Cézanne's final manner, and this period lasted until 1919. Thereafter his art became increasingly concerned with imagery.

WARHOL, Andy (b. Pittsburgh, Pa. 1927), is the most publicized member of the American pop art movement. He started as a commercial artist, working mostly on window displays. He specializes in the obsessive repetition of images from mass media (Marilyn Monroe, Jackie Kennedy), and in the theme of packaging (soup cans, Brillo boxes). He uses the silk-screen printing process, not in order to produce his works in quantity, but to achieve the effect of exact mechanical repetition. He is a prolific film-maker, setting out to shock largely through the medium of boredom (as in his six-hour film of a man sleeping), and has staged a number of Happenings. He survived an attempt on his life in 1968.

WESSELMANN, Tom (b. Cincinnati, Ohio 1931), graduated from art school and then came to New York. Like the other pop artists he makes use of images from mass culture sources such as advertisements, billboards, comic strips, films and television. He has produced a sequence of paintings called *The Great American Nude* in which a woman's body, in a series of erotic poses, is reduced to two-dimensionality and sexlessness; this is both an exercise in stylization and a commentary on the dehumanizing effect of 'glamour', as interpreted by the mass media.

Index
Acknowledgments

Index

ACKNOWLEDGMENTS

Thanks are due, in particular, to the following collectors and publishers, who have kindly authorized us to reproduce works from their collections or illustrations from their books: the Dowager Lady Aberconway (*177*); Dr Doris Neuerburg (*225*); the Earl of Pembroke (*130*); Société Guerlain (*209*); Balance House, New York (Masters and Houston, *Psychedelic Art*: *251*); Casa Editrice Ceschina (Suida, *Luca Cambiaso*: *128*); Edizioni del Milione (Ragghianti, *Pittori di Pompei*: *13*); Edizioni Le Tre Venezie (Fiocco, *Il Pordenone*: *95*); Libreria F. Valardi (Borda, *La Pittura Romana*: *5*).

COPYRIGHT NOTE

PHOTOGRAPHIC SOURCES

A. C. L., Brussels *169*, *192*. Alinari *9*, *22*, *26*, *27*, *30*, *44*, *62*, *64*, *75*, *78*, *89*, *94*, *109*, *115*, *116*, *117*, *119*, *122*, *131*, *132*, *134*, *143*, *146*, *147*, *150*, *151*, *152*, *153*, *179*, *180*, *184*. Anderson *8*, *17*, *18*, *20*, *21*, *24*, *25*, *28*, *29*, *43*, *60*, *61*, *65*, *66*, *67*, *71*, *72*, *77*, *80*, *81*, *82*, *83*, *84*, *85*, *98*, *120*, *121*, *123*, *124*, *125*, *133*, *135*, *136*, *137*, *145*, *149*, *182*, *195*. Archives Photographiques, Paris *170*, *194*. Bayerische Staatsgemäldesammlungen, Munich *50*, *139*. Biblioteca Nacional, Madrid (Tomás Mayallón Antón) *172*. Bibliothèque Nationale, Paris *51*. Blauel *109*, *160*. Boudot-Lamotte *118*. British Museum, London *59*. H. Bron *207*. Bruckmann Verlag, Munich (Württ. Landesamt f. Denkmalpflege) *188*. Bulloz, Paris *42*, *54*, *55*, *58*, *86*, *87*, *99*, *111*, *165*, *221*, *225*. Canai *12*, *92*, *97*, *176*, *185*. Domínguez Ramos *53*, *164*. Editions Braun *31*. Ferruzzi *88*. Foto-Hutter *186*. Galeri Bischofberger *250*, *252*, *259*. Galerie Charpentier (J.-P. Leloir) *7*. Giraudon *36*, *38*, *41*, *52*, *57*, *79*, *113*, *114*. Brogi *3*, *19*, *91*, *126*. Graphische Sammlung der Universitäts-Bibliothek Erlangen *102*. The Solomon R. Guggenheim Museum, New York *231*. Gundermann *187*. Hachette *32*, *33*, *35*, *40*, *46*, *49*, *68*, *73*, *74*, *76*, *90*, *93*, *101*, *155*, *157*, *158*, *161*, *167*, *175*, *181*, *183*, *190*, *191*, *193*, *201*, *202*, *204*, *205*, *209*, *210*, *216*, *217*, *218*, *219*, *227*. Fleming *45*, *96*, *130*, *144*, *200*, *206*. Frans Halsmuseum, Haarlem (A. Dingjan) *163*. Graf Harrach'sche Gemäldegalerie, Vienna (Benno Key Belitz) *178*. Institut Français, Athens *15*. Johan Maurits van Nassau Foundation, The Hague (A. Dingjan) *162*. Kunsthaus, Zurich *233*. Kunsthistorisches Museum, Vienna *106*, *110*, *112*, *166*. Laboratoire du Musée du Louvre, Institut Mainini *159*, *168*, *203*, *212*, *215*. Mella (Perotti) *127*. Minneapolis Institute of Arts *236*. Musée des Beaux-Arts, Marseilles (Borel) *148*. National Museum, Stockholm *171*. Musées Nationaux de France *235*. Museo del Prado, Madrid *141*. Museu Nacional de Arte Antiga, Lisbon (A. A. de Abreu Nunes) *56*, *138*. Museum für Kunst und Kulturgeschichte, Dortmund *47*. Museum of Modern Art, New York *223*. Nasjonalgalleriet, Oslo (O. Vaering) *226*. National Gallery, London *37*, *63*, *69*, *70*, *222*. National Museum, Stockholm *171*. Öffentliche Kunstsammlung, Basle: Kunstmuseum *48*, *104*; Kupferstichkabinett *103*, *232*. Österreichische Nationalbibliothek, Vienna *39*. Österreichisches Archäologisches Institut, Vienna *11*. Pinacoteca di Brera, Milan *156*. Publifoto *2*, *6*, *10*, *11*. Pushkin Museum of Fine Art, Moscow *210*. Rijksmuseum, Amsterdam *174*. Rijksmuseum Kröller-Müller, Otterlo *234*. Roger-Viollet *105*. Scala *197*. Sidney Janis Gallery *258*. Skira *5*, *196*. Soprintendenza alle Gallerie, Naples *154*. Soviet Embassy, Paris *16*. Staatliche Graphische Sammlung, Munich *107*. Staatliche Museen, Berlin-Dahlem: Antikenabteilung (Jutta Tietz-Glagow) *14*; Gemäldegalerie (W. Steinkopf) *34*. Städelsches Kunstinstitut, Frankfurt-on-Main *129*, *173*. Szépmuvészti Muzeum, Budapest *108*. Tate Gallery, London *198*, *199*, *245*. Vernacci *140*, *142*. Victoria and Albert Museum, London *213*. Whitney Museum of American Art, New York (Geoffrey Clements) *237*.